Understanding
LEADERSHIP

ENDORSEMENTS

Leadership is not a static concept, especially in a disruptive and connected world. It is complex and multi-dimensional. It needs to be understood and applied at contextual, operational and micro levels. Certainly it is much more than a set of competencies.

More has probably been written and spoken about leadership than almost any other topic throughout history. However, to understand leadership is to understand the concept from multiple perspectives. That is what this very comprehensive book provides. There is no single approach to leadership and the variety of perspectives provided in this book will further enhance our understanding and practice of leadership.

An important book with highly qualified and insightful contributors which will add to the conversations about leadership for a long time to come. An essential read for leaders and those responsible for leadership in their organisations now and in the future.

Terry Meyer, Strategy & Leadership Consultant, Leadership SA

Truly a standout book that packs a real punch in the sea of books on leadership. This extraordinary book has to be the most updated, and most comprehensive and definitive compendium on leaders and leadership, written by an impressive array of prominent and respected experts in the field.

Understanding the "what" and "how" of leadership is something that most organisations continue to grapple with in these volatile, complex, uncertain and ambiguous times. This book offers advice on the toughest challenges leaders are facing in business today.

This is compulsory reading for anyone seeking to understand and distil powerful perspectives on leadership and how to become a better leader.

The book provides robust perspectives on leadership fundamentals ranging from leadership theory, models and frameworks on leadership, leadership principles and philosophy, and, in addition, offers authentic, actionable examples. It is bursting with great tips and advice that are immediately applicable and anchored in research.

An indispensable and essential resource for leaders and aspiring leaders at all levels.

Shirley Zinn, Professor Shirley Zinn, Group HR Director, Woolworths

This book is rooted in the challenges facing leaders today, and offers current and future leaders a perspective to help them lead in a VUCA world. The authors take a unique view of leadership from a "value chain" perspective. They provide executives and those in the leadership development business a framework and insight into both being and building better leaders for tomorrow. I believe this book – a product of frontline leaders – will prove to be a great handbook for those who regard leadership as both an interest and a passion.

Paul Norman, MTN Group: Group Human Resources and Corporate Affairs Officer

I have read dozens of books on leadership but none of them has tackled this complex topic in the way that *Understanding Leadership* has done. This book tackles the real issues of leadership from understanding the foundations of leadership to examining leadership within its unfolding context; to leadership identification, growth and development; to issues of leadership transitions and leadership wellbeing. The insights and models are based on research and on real experiences and I particularly enjoyed the section on leadership articles and stories – real-life leadership experiences as told by the leaders themselves.

This book is that rare mix of a treasure house of up-to-date knowledge about every aspect of leadership and at the same time full of insights and suggestions for practical implementation. It is both thought-provoking and enlightening, and a must-read for anyone trying to understand the complex issues surrounding leadership. This is one of the best books on the topic of leadership I have been privileged to read.

Italia Boninelli, HR Strategist, Executive Coach and Author, (recent past Executive Vice-president: People and Organizational Development, AngloGold Ashanti)

The seminal guide to the kind of transformational leadership required in the 21ˢᵗ century and beyond.

S'ne Mkhize, Senior Vice President, Human Resources – Sasol

What a phenomenal work!

This is the most comprehensive, insightful and well-grounded work on leadership ever published in South Africa.

It unpacks leadership in its many facets and perspectives – from individual to organisational and global leadership.

The authors are thought leaders, scientists and subject-matter experts; they ask the difficult questions and reveal the essence of leadership as an art and science.

This book is a must for everybody in leadership positions – be it the business sector, public sector, religious organisations, education, or community organisations.

An ideal reference work for the consultant or business science practitioner.

Dr Johan de Beer, Human Capital Executive, Africa Division, Imperial Logistics

Understanding Leadership is a feast for scholars, students and practitioners alike who will find a comprehensive reference book on leadership theories, a diversity of the schools of thought that have influenced and continue to shape the evolution of leadership as a fully fledged discipline that is applied to complex and changing contexts. As someone trying to master the leadership discipline and as an aspirant leadership expert myself, I was pleasantly surprised at how much there is still to know and learn about this enthralling subject called leadership.

Dudu Msomi, Chief Executive Officer, Busara Leadership Partners

Given the plethora of books on Leadership, one is tempted to think, "What else can be written about leadership?"

This masterful creation crushes that thought. It is a call to choose to be a different and better leader, to stand up and … lead.

I recommend that current and future leaders, young and old, study this gem and weave the learnings into their approach to leading our most precious asset, people.

Leon Steyn, Group Human Resources Executive, Bidvest

Given dramatic shifts in globalisation, demographics and technology, this book on Leadership is a timely contribution to enable students as well as new and established leaders to gain insights into the skills, attributes and behaviours that will contribute to building a better working world.

Ajen Sita, CEO – Ernst & Young

First published in 2017

ISBN: 978-1-86922-686-2 (Printed)
ISBN: 978-1-86922-687-9 (ePDF)

Published by KR Publishing
P O Box 3954
Randburg
2125
Republic of South Africa

Tel: (011) 706-6009
Fax: (011) 706-1127
E-mail: orders@knowres.co.za
Website: www.kr.co.za

Printed and bound: HartWood Digital Printing, 243 Alexandra Avenue, Halfway House, Midrand
Typesetting, layout and design: Cia Joubert, cia@knowres.co.za
Cover design: Marlene de'Lorme, marlene@knowres.co.za and Cia Joubert, cia@knowres.co.za
Editing: Adrienne Pretorius, pretorii@mweb.co.za
Proofreading: Valda Strauss: valda@global.co.za
Project management: Cia Joubert, cia@knowres.co.za

Understanding
LEADERSHIP

Edited by

Theo H Veldsman and Andrew J Johnson

kr
publishing

2017

ACKNOWLEDGEMENTS

What a pleasure to work with authors who see the unquestionable criticality of leadership, and are passionate about the difference leadership must make in assuring a desirable, sustainable future for all. It was wonderful to have worked with each and every one of our 69 authors over such an extended period of time. Your wisdom, expertise, suggestions and time willingly shared in crafting your invaluable contribution in making *Understanding Leadership* the outstanding and trend-setting Thought Leadership Book it has turned out to be is gratefully acknowledged.

A warm word of thanks is due to:

- All of our Peer Reviewers for your valuable input and time.
- To all our Endorsees for your time given, to offer our book the cachet it deserves.
- Wilhelm Crous, Managing Director of KR, for your constant stretch and guidance; constructive criticism; ongoing encouragement; infectious enthusiasm; and advice and help in working around and through barriers, that made it such a pleasure to work on our book.
- Joann Hill for organising the peer reviews and endorsements.
- Cia Joubert, for your excellent project management of our book that was mission critical in ensuring that the right things happened at the right time and in the right way so that our book became a reality.
- Adrienne Pretorius, our technical editor, for ensuring the technical quality excellence of our book.
- Valda Strauss, for the excellent proofreading of our book after layout.

Last but not least, a warm, appreciative "Thank you" to our families for their understanding, support and sacrifices throughout the painful birth process of the book which took two years from initiation, through conceptualisation and production, to final delivery.

TABLE OF CONTENTS

FOREWORD BY DR JERRY GULE

The practice of leadership is both pervasive and essential in organisations, society and on the world stage. Therefore, any discussion of leadership at any level is vital and advances our knowledge and understanding of this important subject. As the world transforms and becomes more interdependent as a result of advances in globalisation and technology, the role of leadership at all levels becomes even more important. A globalised world demands leaders who understand what is required to lead in a modern way, are interdependent and transparent. The effect of technology to shrink distance between and among peoples located on different continents and to accelerate the generation and spread of information at the speed of light requires new leadership paradigms.

Understanding Leadership is a timely synopsis of the subject of leadership. It offers the reader a variety of views and different windows into what makes for progressive and effective leadership practice. The leadership models, theories, frameworks and processes offered in this essential book provide useful insights and advance our appreciation of not only the complexity but the continued importance of leadership practice in all spheres of life. There is no doubt that leadership has been democratised and can be found in unexpected corners of the society, organisations and the world.

The advent and emergence of social media has proved to be a game changer in how leaders practise their craft. Leaders no longer have a monopoly on information, nor can they successfully suppress information they do not wish to be in the public domain. People or followers now have many avenues to spread information either officially or by using unofficial channels or platforms. The days of a leader's indiscretions staying under wraps for many years are a thing of the past. Advances in information technology and communication have made it possible for information to be available online in an instant. Leaders have to be attuned to these possibilities and to what their followers think of them. They must also be quick to listen attentively and intentionally to what is being said and respond to it before it's too late. A precursor to this is that leaders must have objective self-awareness and be confident that they are able to learn from the feedback they collect from their environment.

Clearly, this book offers a wealth of information to leaders to enable them to learn new leadership tactics and to acquire knowledge emanating from modern psychology in order to become more effective in practising the leadership craft. *Understanding Leadership* offers new insights to this all-important subject and provides practical ways to apply new leadership practices.

This book enhances our understanding of leadership models and frameworks. It also provides new tools that leaders can add to their arsenal in order to be effective. The concept of what is referred to as 'leadership stances' in the book is very interesting and should provide useful insights for leaders when combined with the now well-explored concept of leadership styles. What is brought to the fore in this book is the fact that leaders can have a positive or a negative impact on those they lead, their organisations, society and the globalised world through their actions. This book therefore highlights the importance of leading with prudence and personal self-awareness so that a leader does not negatively impact those they lead or their organisations.

There is an increasing understanding that a leader's psychological make-up or brain has a significant impact on how they lead or practise leadership. Neuroscience has become an important field in understanding how and what differentiates effective from dysfunctional leadership. According to this book, it is vital that leaders have an appreciation of how their brains work. It is also abundantly clear that in order to truly Understand Leadership a multi-disciplinary approach is required. This book makes it clear that the practice of leadership has to be re-set on an ongoing basis as the general environment changes.

There are many tips and lessons that can be gleaned from this book, the overarching lesson being that leadership is not static and nor can it be successful if it is unresponsive. This is a worthy contribution to our understanding of leadership.

Dr Jerry Gule, Interim Chief Executive Officer, Institute of People Management, South Africa.

ABOUT THE EDITORS

Prof Theo H Veldsman

Theo, who is regarded as a thought leader in South Africa with respect to people management and the psychology of work, has demonstrated his ability to proactively identify emerging people and leadership needs and arrive at fit-for-purpose, innovative solutions that are theoretically and practically sound.

Theo holds a PhD in Industrial Psychology and is a registered Industrial Psychologist and Research Psychologist and accredited HRM Practitioner. He prefers to call himself a Work Psychologist. He has extensive research and development, as well as consulting experience gained over the past 35 years in strategy formulation and implementation; strategic organisational change; organisational (re)design; team building; leadership/management and strategic people/talent management. He consults with many leading South African companies as well as organisations overseas, in the roles of advisor, expert and coach/mentor.

In addition to being the author of nearly 200 technical/consulting reports/articles, he has done numerous management and professional presentations and attended seminars at a national and international level. He is the author of two books, and has contributed nine book chapters.

Up to the end of 2016, when he retired, he was Professor and Head of the Department of Industrial Psychology and People Management, Faculty of Management, University of Johannesburg. Since the beginning of 2017 he is a Visiting Professor at the sam eDepartment. He has led the profession of Psychology and Industrial Psychology nationally as president on several occasions. He has been awarded fellowship status by the Society of Industrial and Organisational Psychology of South Africa (SIOPSA), and is the 2012 recipient of a Life-Long Achievement Award from the South African Board for People Practices (SABPP).

Dr Andrew J Johnson

Andrew is the Chief Learning Officer at Eskom's Academy of Learning. An Industrial Psychologist by profession, he holds an MSc in Occupational Psychology (Nottingham) and a PhD in Industrial Psychology from the University of Johannesburg (UJ). He has also completed formal philosophical, theological and exegetical studies at Sts. Peter & John Vianney Seminaries and St Joseph's Scholasticate.

A seasoned HR executive, his special interests are HR strategy consulting, leadership development, talent and succession management, organisational transformation, and change management. His career in Organisational Effectiveness in the private sector has seen him working for Edcon, MTN, Avmin, JSE and Liberty in senior positions, and he has consulted to other state-owned entities, private companies, and African and BRICS (Brazil, Russia, India, China and South Africa) utilities.

He held non-executive roles in FASSET, the NEF, the COJ Property Company, Transparency SA, NSFAS, & King II; currently he serves on the Advisory Committee of the Industrial Psychology Department of UJ (where he is an occasional lecturer), and the HR (Staffing) Committee of the University of KwaZulu-Natal (UKZN). Andrew is involved in the Society for Industrial & Organisational Psychology of South Africa (SIOPSA) (president in 2011/12), and the Global Forum on Executive Development and Business Driven Action Learning. He is the winner of the prestigious IPM HR Director of the Year (2014), and the recipient of the SABPP Lifetime Achievement Award (2014) and of SIOPSA's Honorary Life Membership (2012).

He is in high demand as a speaker, coach and mentor. At his core he is a deeply passionate student of human behaviour in the context of work, and how this can create a better self, team, organisation and society.

ABOUT THE CONTRIBUTORS

Freddie Crous

Freddie is Professor of Industrial Psychology at the University of Johannesburg. He is an aesthetician at heart and therefore prefers to approach life in general and work in particular from an appreciative stance.

Ingra DuBuisson-Narsai

Ingra is a registered Industrial and Organisational (I/O) Psychologist in private practice, specialising in the field of applied organisational neuroscience. She is co-founder and Director of NeuroCapital Consulting, which consults to some of South Africa's most admired companies.

With 16 years of executive-level experience in corporate South Africa, including as Group HR Director (Famous Brands Ltd), HR executive (Aegis Insurance/RMBH Group), and HR Director (Usko/Bytes Technology), Ingra's special skills lie in being a catalyst for change and creating break-through organisational behaviour solutions, using neuroscience-based diagnostics. She is currently pursuing a PhD in consulting psychology, focusing on the behavioural anchors of neuroscience-based leadership in formal organisations.

Part of the adjunct faculty of Wits Business School, she is also a founding member of the International Neuro Practitioners Guild. See ingra@neurocapital.co

Jim Ferrell

Jim is co-founder of the Arbinger Institute and founding and managing partner of Arbinger Training and Consulting. He has authored several bestselling books, including Arbinger's international bestsellers, *Leadership and self-deception* and *The anatomy of peace*, as well as the forthcoming book, *The outward mindset*, to be published in June 2016. His publications have sold multiple millions of copies and have been translated into more than 30 languages. Jim, who has degrees in Economics and Philosophy, is a graduate of Yale Law School. He is a sought-after speaker, teacher and advisor to leaders of corporations, governments, communities and organisations of all kinds around the world.

Paul Fouché

Paul is a registered Counselling Psychologist who obtained a BSoc Sc, BSoc Sc (Hons) (Psychology), and MSoc Sc (Counselling Psychology) at the University of the Free State (UFS). Thereafter he moved to the University of Port Elizabeth (UPE), where he obtained a DPhil (Psychology). For his doctoral research, he completed a psychobiography on Field-Marshal Jan Christiaan Smuts. Paul is currently employed in the Department of Psychology at UFS where he coordinates departmental research projects. He was previously employed at Vista University (Welkom Campus) and UPE. His research focus is on psychobiographical projects, particularly in the fields of health psychology, psychological wellness and spirituality. During 2015 he was guest editor of a special issue of the *Journal of Psychology in Africa* that focused on psychobiographical studies. He is a former member of the editorial board of *Acta Academica* (2008–2012). E-mail: fouchejp@ufs.ac.za

Pieter Koortzen

Pieter, who holds a DCom from the University of South Africa (Unisa), is a counselling and Industrial and Organisational (I/O) Psychologist who is registered with the Health Professions Council of South Africa. As a consultant he specialises in training and development, interpersonal and leadership development, executive coaching, the facilitation of learning and growth for individuals and teams, group relations from a systems psychodynamic stance, trauma debriefing, post-trauma counselling, and organisational wellness and employee assistance programmes. In his private practice he has been rendering consulting and development services to various South African organisations for the past 20 years.

His work experience includes 13 years as a professor in I/O Psychology at Unisa and as visiting faculty member at Alliant International University, San Diego. From October 2006 to June 2009 he was a senior consultant at Resolve Encounter Consulting, where he managed the assessment centre and coordinated large-scale assessment projects, acted as an executive coach for organisations, conducted leadership and team development interventions and presented training programmes. His consulting experience includes spending time at JvR Consulting Psychologists, where he managed a team of consultants delivering team development, coaching, assessment, leadership and organisational development services. Currently, he is an Organisational Development Consultant at Investec Bank, where he consults to leaders and teams on teaming, coaching, leadership development, diversity and conflict. He is continuing his academic interests as a Visiting Professor in the Department of I/O Psychology and People Management at the University of Johannesburg (UJ). His role entails teaching professional leadership, individual and group facilitation and executive coaching. He also supervises Master's and doctoral research.

Ian Lawson

Ian holds a BJourn (Law) from Rhodes University and a Higher Diploma in Personnel Management from Wits Business School (WBS). An independent consultant for over 20 years, his current focus is on providing decision makers with greater insight into, and influence over, their decisions.

Ian's work is based on cognitive science, developmental psychology and systems science. It offers decision makers the technology and skills to better think through decisions by cognitively modelling options, avoiding self-deception, and improving their everyday skills for making accurate predictions. He has consulted to a wide range of organisations in South Africa.

Mark Perry

Lt-Col Mark Perry is a Clinical Psychologist and Staff Officer: Psychology at the Area Military Health Unit Eastern Cape in Port Elizabeth. Mark obtained a BA, BA (Hons) (Psychology) and an MA (Clinical Psychology) at the University of Port Elizabeth. Thereafter he transferred to the University of the Free State, where he obtained a PhD in Psychology. For his doctoral research, he completed a psychobiography on the life of Olive Schreiner. Earlier in his career, Mark worked as private psychological practitioner and he was also employed by the Department of Correctional Services. E-mail: markperry561@gmail.com

Cobus Pienaar

Cobus graduated from the University of the Free State (UFS) in 1994 and completed his postgraduate studies in 2005, obtaining all his degrees with distinction. He is registered as an Organisational Psychologist with the Health Professions Council of South Africa, and has been appointed senior psychologist and organisational development consultant for a number of organisations.

From 2002–2015, he was senior lecturer in Industrial Psychology at UFS, chairing the department from 2007–2010. He still conducts research on topics related to leadership, careers and dysfunctional leadership and organisations, and has published in peer-reviewed academic journals such as the *South African Journal of Education, Acta Academica, South African Journal of Psychology, Tydskrif vir Geesteswetenskappe, South African Journal of Business Management, Southern African Business Review* and *South African Journal of Industrial Psychology*. In addition, he has read scientific papers at various international conferences such as Advances in Management, the International Congress on Leadership in Post-School Education, the IPED Conference, the International Conference in Contemporary Business, and the 6th European Conference on Leadership, Management and Governance. He is often approached to review academic articles for scientific peer-reviewed journals.

Since 2008, Cobus has represented the Arbinger Institute in South Africa as Managing Director. The institute is a world-renowned management consulting and training firm and scholarly consortium that specialises in changing mindsets. Cobus leads the delivery of Arbinger's programmes and consulting services in this country, and is often consulted by companies in the private and public sectors, focusing on the development of leaders, teams and organisations.

Rosetta Pillay

Rose began her career after completing an honours in accounting. She has worked at a state-owned company since graduating and has spent eight years in the financial environment. During this time, she completed a Cost Engineering qualification, along with an MCom in leadership.

Rose is currently the custodian of the Business-Driven Action Learning programme at the Eskom Leadership Institute. She has four years' work experience in the executive development space, where she predominantly focuses on embedding action learning methodology into leadership developmental solutions. She recently graduated with a PhD in action learning and is now packaging the systemic model for action learning, for practical uptake by end-users.

Her business interests and passions include holistic approaches to problem-solving, mindfulness/reflective practices to elevate thinking, talent nurturing and creating opportunities for return on investment (ROI) through leadership development.

Dan Radecki

Dan is Chief Scientific Officer at the Academy of Brain-based Leadership (ABL), which offers a scientifically validated, brain-based approach for future-oriented leaders and organisations interested in optimising their performance, relationships and health. He also serves as Senior Director of Research and Development at Allergan Inc., where he is a global leader for drug development programmes.

Dan holds a bachelor's in Psychology, a Master's in Biopsychology and a PhD in Neuroscience. Working as a leader in the corporate world affords him a unique perspective on how our knowledge of brain functioning can aid leaders in maximising their results, as well as those of their teams. With this unique perspective from roles in both the leadership and neuroscientific world, in 2009

Dan created the content for the educational arm of the NeuroLeadership Institute and served as the lead professor and advisor for the MSc programme in the Neuroscience of Leadership – the first university-accredited programme ever to incorporate cutting-edge neuroscience research into an optimal model of leadership. In the following five years, Dan taught over 400 leaders in 40 countries on the neuroscientific underpinnings of effective leadership.

He has been published in the *Harvard Business Review*, and has lectured internationally on the neuroscience of resilience, bias, creativity, leadership wisdom, the aging brain, the biology of collaboration and the impact of stress on the brain.

Chené Swart

Chené Swart is the author of *Re-authoring the world: The narrative lens and practices for organisations, communities and individuals*. Her international training, coaching and consulting practice applies the re-authoring approach in co-constructing alternative narratives that guide personal, communal and organisational agency, new mindsets through different ways of doing and being, and transformed lives. Chené works with individuals, businesses and civil society organisations across the world. She trains newcomers to re-author ideas and conversations from various disciplines on the pre- and postgraduate levels, as well as diploma and MBA levels. Chené teaches re-authoring leadership practices as part of the postgraduate Diploma in Leadership at the University of Stellenbosch Business School. She is also part of the faculty for Duke Corporate Education and a guest lecturer at the Kaospilot School for innovative thought leaders and entrepreneurs in Denmark. For the last couple of years, a vibrant community of practice from various places in the world has joined her in apprenticeship journeys to learn together how to practise and apply these ideas in their work with individuals, leaders, organisations and communities.

Chené is a contributing author on Coaching from a Dialogic OD paradigm in the ground-breaking 2015 organisational handbook *Dialogic organization development and change: Theory and practice* edited by Gervase Bushe and Bob Marshak. An adapted version of her chapter was published in *The OD Practitioner* vol. 48, no. 2, 2016.

Roelf van Niekerk

Roelf is a registered Clinical and Industrial Psychologist as well as a Chartered Human Resource Practitioner. He obtained a BA in Theology, a BA (Hons) (Psychology) and an MA (Industrial Psychology) from the University of Stellenbosch; an MA (Clinical Psychology) and DPhil (Psychology) from the University of Port Elizabeth, and an MEd (General Education Theory and Practice) from Rhodes University. He is currently the Head of the Department of Industrial and Organisational Psychology at the Nelson Mandela Metropolitan University, having previously been employed at the universities of Port Elizabeth, the Free State, Fort Hare and Rhodes.

His research focus is on psychobiographical research projects, particularly in the fields of personality, career and leadership development. He teaches a range of modules including psychological assessment, career management, organisational development, personality psychology, psychotherapy and psychopathology. E-mail: roelf.vanniekerk@nmmu.ac.za

Gerrit Walters

Gerrit predominantly spent his career as an HR professional/Industrial Psychologist in various roles at a state-owned company. In 2011 he joined the Eskom Leadership Institute as Senior Manager: Executive Development. In his current role, he is responsible for the delivery of leadership solutions with a key emphasis on action science, action learning, reflective practices, integral coaching and new leadership conversations. Gerrit holds a Master's in Industrial and Organisational Psychology as well as an MBA. He is working towards completing his PhD, which centres on leadership sustainability.

Gerrit's business interests and passions include the integration of leaders, leadership and leadership culture; and behavioural change and sustainability.

SECTION 1
SETTING THE SCENE

Chapter 1

ORIENTATION

Theo H Veldsman and Andrew J Johnson

On many fronts, and in many ways, our insight into and the exercise of leadership is under severe scrutiny because of a radically changing and significantly different world; reinventing organisations; and working persons with significantly different, or significantly shifting, needs, expectations and aspirations. Without doubt, leadership is in the overheating crucible of a reframed/reframing world that is in the throes of fundamental and radical transformation.

The current fierce debate about leadership and leadership excellence (or lack thereof) may be one of the most important issues of our present time, alongside issues such as demographic shifts, the distribution of economic prosperity, food and water security, world peace, global warming, and sustainability. It could even be argued that these issues in and of themselves are but symptomatic of poor leadership; or, at worst, of the inability and/or a lack in the commitment to lead.

The clarion call is clear and unequivocal. At this critical juncture in our history, the search is on for better *and* different leadership. Leaders and leadership have to reinvent themselves if they wish to be successful in the unfolding world of tomorrow. Old recipes and conventional ways of leading will no longer suffice. They may even be detrimental and destructive. It can be argued that those nations, societies, communities and organisations that are able to demonstrate leadership excellence consistently will dominate and inherit the future, in particular in the case of emerging countries in Africa. Our very future is predicated on the quality of our current and future leadership who will either make us architects or victims of the future.

Without any doubt leadership is *the* critical strategic capability of nations, societies, communities and organisations, making them sustainably future-fit. The primary trigger for *Understanding Leadership* is therefore to be found in the snowballing crisis around leadership, and the consequential imperative for better and different leadership.

The Strategic Leadership Value Chain Perspective: A Meta-framework From Which to View Leadership

Leadership is a critical organisational capability and intervention. To the best of our knowledge no overall, systemic, integrated and holistic perspective is available in the literature viewing leadership from a Strategic Leadership Value Chain perspective. Such a perspective would provide a meta-framework from which to look at leadership systemically and holistically as an organisational intervention. Such a perspective would assist one not only in bringing order to the overwhelming, exploding leadership literature, but also serve as an overall, integrative map for organisations in engaging with leadership. At best numerous, piecemeal treatises are available dealing with specialised leadership intervention topics, e.g. leadership assessment, leadership development, or leadership well-being but no overarching meta-framework exists.

Figure 1.1 provides our take on the make-up of the Strategic Leadership Value Chain in terms of which leadership as a mission-critical, strategic organisational capability and intervention can be viewed.

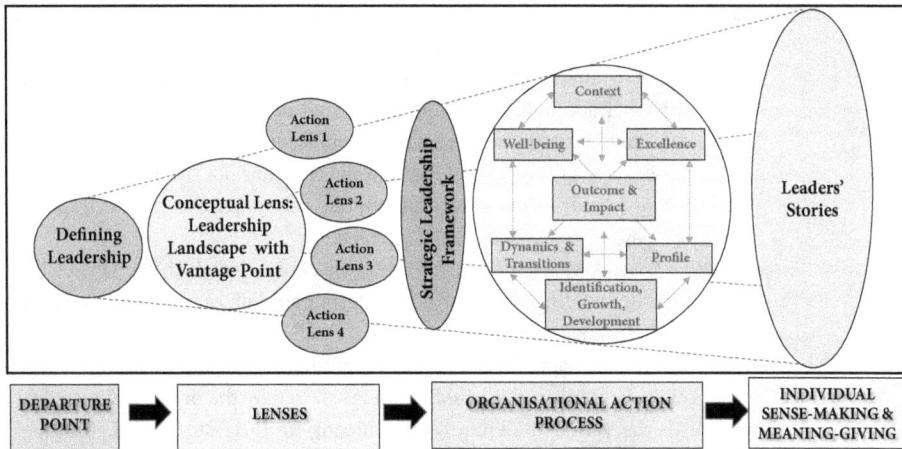

Figure 1.1 A Strategic Leadership Value Chain Perspective on leadership as an organisational capability and intervention

The make-up of the Strategic Leadership Value Chain

With reference to Figure 1.1, the Strategic Leadership Value Chain is composed of the following elements:

- *Departure point: Defining leadership*

  In crafting an organisation-specific leadership thinking framework, the organisation as a starting point must formulate explicitly and intentionally what they understand "leadership" as a phenomenon to be conceptually, in order to correctly demarcate the territory called "leadership". An incorrect definition of leadership can delineate the phenomenon either too narrowly, consequently excluding essential elements of leadership; or too broadly, resulting in the inclusion of unrelated elements ("noise") in its definition.

- *Lenses*

  Having demarcated the territory called "leadership" by defining it, the organisation must next construct and/or select the lenses it will use to map, make sense of, and give meaning to the demarcated leadership territory. The lenses represent the "toolbox" the organisation will use in engaging with the leadership territory. Three types of lenses can be discerned:

  o   *Conceptual lens:* This represents the organisation's meta-view – its "Google map" – of what building blocks (= "towns with their suburbs") with their interdependencies (= "roads") make up the demarcated leadership territory. We call this meta-conceptual view the "Leadership Landscape".

The value of the Leadership Landscape as meta-conceptual view of the leadership territory is three-fold:

3

- *to simplify*, organise and integrate at a meta-level the complexity of the field of leadership with its ever-expanding and overwhelming literature;
- *to provide* a common meta-language for an all-inclusive, coherent leadership dialogue about leadership, for example in teaching, or in an organisation; and
- *to structure* an organisation's conversation about leadership, enabling it to arrive at a customised Strategic Leadership Framework (see below) for the organisation that will direct and guide its thinking, decisions and actions regarding leadership as a strategic organisational capability and intervention.

o ***Interpretative Lens:*** A Vantage Point next must be chosen by which the Leadership Landscape with its building blocks will be interpreted. For example, Appreciative Inquiry or Critical Management Theory.

o ***Action Lenses:*** Having mapped the leadership territory, and having chosen a Vantage Point, the Action Lenses serve as enabling tools selected by the organisation to deal and work with the various building blocks making up the Leadership Landscape. Action tools represent various disciplines and theoretical/practical approaches that can be used to engage with the leadership territory in order to make sense of it. Examples of such action tools are neuroscience, action science, psychodynamics, narratives, and psychobiographical profiling.

- *Strategic leadership framework*

In proceeding along the Strategic Leadership Value Chain (see Figure 1.1), the organisation next has to make choices regarding its specific position on each of the building blocks making up the Leadership Landscape as Conceptual Lens, based on how it strategically wants to position leadership in its organisation.

For example with respect to some of the building blocks of the Leadership Landscape, the choices are:

o Its chosen *Leadership Stance* regarding leadership for the organisation: Does leadership need to be task- and/or people-centric? Must leadership be present and/or future focused?

o Its desired *Leadership Style(s)*: Tell, Consultative, Co-determination and/or Self-Governance?

o Its repertoire of expected *Leadership Roles*: Resources, Coach, Guide, Networker?

o *Leadership Talent Management*: its make-up; strategic talent timeframe; and talent pools.

The Strategic Leadership Framework therefore forms the reference point and basis regarding all the organisation's decisions and actions with respect to leadership. Its sits as a bridge between the organisation's Leadership Thinking Framework on the one hand, being part of the Thinking Framework itself. And, on the other hand, the Framework directs and guides how "things" must happen in the organisation with respect to leadership.

- *Organisational action processes*

The organisational action process refers to the frontline decisions and actions the organisation has to take on a daily basis regarding leadership. This process is made up of an integrated, reciprocally interdependent, set of organisational actions, embedded in an organisational change navigation process (represented in Figure 1.1 by the circle in which these actions are contained).

The actions are as follows:

o   ***Action 1:*** Understanding the unfolding *Leadership Context* with its leadership challenges, demands and requirements;

o   ***Action 2:*** Formulating a context-relevant *Leadership Excellence* model;

o   ***Action 3:*** Generating a future-fit *Leadership Brand and Profile*;

o   ***Action 4:*** *Identifying, Growing and Developing* the organisation's leadership talent;

o   ***Action 5:*** Managing the ongoing, everyday *Leadership Dynamics and Transitions* in the organisation;

o   ***Action 6:*** Ensuring and enhancing *Leadership Well-being* (and countering leadership mal-being); and

o   ***Action 7:*** Monitoring and tracking *Leadership Outcomes and Impact*

- ***Individual sense-making and meaning-giving: Leadership stories***

In the final instance, leaders have to be prolific, enticing storytellers. Through the stories they construct and share, leaders make sense of and give meaning to their leadership experiences, for themselves and others. Hopefully and ideally speaking, leadership experiences are transformed into information; information into knowledge; and knowledge into wisdom. In turn, the distilled wisdom can be applied to ground, enhance and enrich in a recursive fashion the preceding Strategic Leadership Value Chain elements as elucidated above.

This book – *Understanding Leadership* – forms part of a five-book series covering the respective elements of the Strategic Leadership Value Chain. The accompanying box gives a list of the books in the series, and what portion of the Strategic Value Chain they address.

Book	Portion of Strategic Leadership Value Chain Addressed (Refer back to Figure 1.1)
Book 1: Understanding Leadership (This book)	Departure Point: Defining Leadership Lenses: Conceptual, Interpretive, Action Strategic Leadership Framework
Book 2: Leadership in Context	Organisational Action Process • *Action 1: Understanding the unfolding Leadership Context with its leadership challenges, demands and requirements*
Book 3: Leadership Excellence	Organisational Action Process • *Action 2: Formulating a context relevant, Leadership Excellence Model* • *Action 3: Generating a future-fit, Leadership Brand and Profile* • *Action 7: Monitoring and tracking Leadership Outcomes and Impact*
Book 4: Building Leadership Talent	Organisational Action Process • *Action 4: Identifying, growing and developing the organisation's leadership talent*

Book	Portion of Strategic Leadership Value Chain Addressed (Refer back to Figure 1.1)
Book 5: Leadership Dynamics and Well Being	Organisational Action Process • *Action 5: Managing the ongoing, everyday Leadership Dynamics and Transitions in the organisation* • *Action 6: Ensuring and enhancing leadership well-being (and countering leadership mal-being)*
Leadership Stories	Throughout the above five books stories by prominent SA leaders are given to illustrate how they have made sense of and given meaning to leadership

Purpose and Structure of *Understanding Leadership*

Understanding Leadership deals with the Thinking Framework of the Strategic Leadership Value Chain. The aim of this element of the Value Chain is to provide the organisation with an overall way of thinking about leadership, specific to the organisation concerned. The location of the Thinking Framework within the Value Chain, and its make-up, is indicated by the arrows and the circle in Figure 1.2.

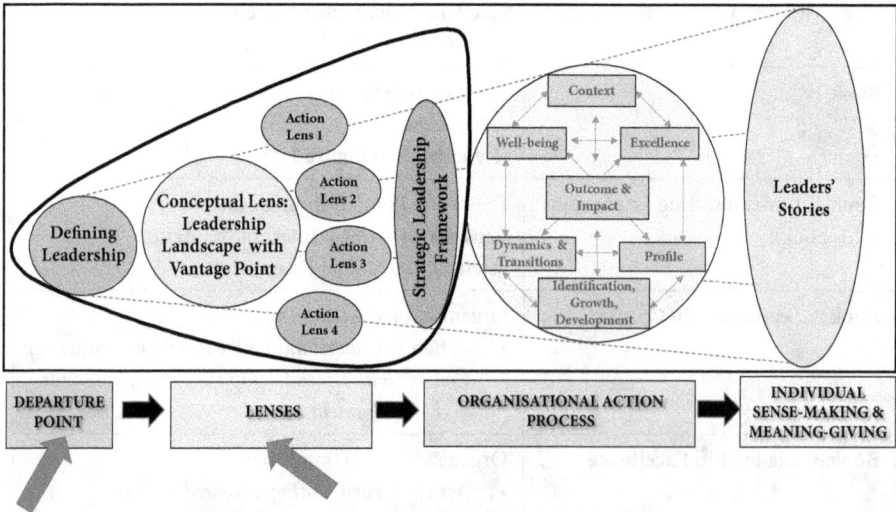

Figure 1.2 Strategic Leadership Value Chain: Thinking Framework

The elements of the Thinking Framework (see Figure 1.2) discussed in *Understanding Leadership* are:

- Defining Leadership
- Conceptual Lens – Leadership Landscape
- A Vantage Point – Appreciative Inquiry
- Action Lenses

Action tools can be organised into four application domains relative to the four relationships in which leadership stands: Myself, Others, Organisation, and World, depicted in Figure 1.3. This classification would assist in deciding when what action tool is needed. The list of included Action Tools does not claim to be exhaustive and cover all available tools. It serves more to provide illustrations of some of the more important, and in some cases interesting, available Action Tools to apply to the Leadership Landscape.

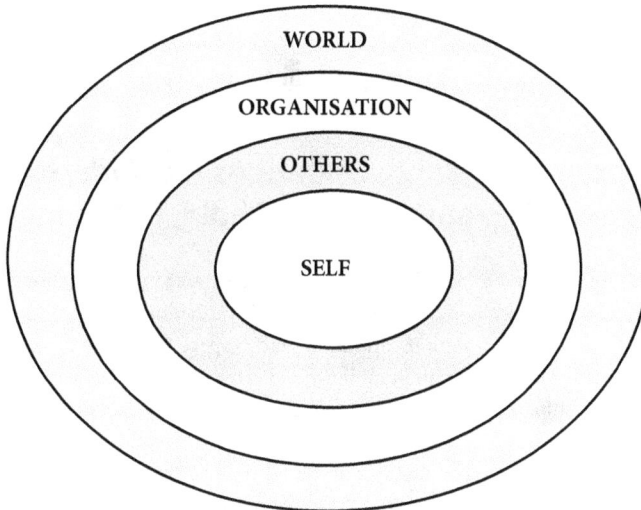

Figure 1.3 The relationships in which leadership stands as a way of classifying Action Tools

LEADERSHIP RELATIONSHIP	ACTION TOOL	CHAPTER
Section 2: Conceptual Lens	Leadership Landscape (including Definition of Leadership; Strategic Leadership Framework)	2
Section 3: Interpretive Lens	Appreciative Inquiry	3
Section 4: Action Lenses		
Self	Neuroscience	4
	Action science	5
	Psychobiographical Profiling	6
Others	Kegan's Competing Commitments	7
	Arbinger's Changing Mindset	8
	Leadership Psychodynamics	9
	Narratives	10
Organisation/World	Action Learning	11

Leadership stories (Section 5: Chapter 12)

In this section prominent leaders express their personal views on leadership from the front line where it is happening for them, illustrating many of the topics discussed in *Understanding Leadership*.

The future of leadership (Section 6: Chapter 13)

In this chapter we would like to gaze into the crystal ball by answering the question: Is there is a need for better and different leadership going into the future? If yes, what would it look like with the conditions attached to such future-fit leadership?

Our intention with and aspirations for *Understanding Leadership* – ambitious and bold, but humble

Our intention with and aspiration for *Understanding Leadership* is for it to be a thought-leadership book on leadership at the front line in two ways. *Firstly*, by providing cutting edge, present-into-the-future, and future-into-the-present, thinking with respect to leadership lenses, leveraged from the best currently available insights and informed views about the expected probable future to be faced by leadership. *Secondly*, by providing actionable knowledge and theory-informed practice about leadership lenses where it matters at the organisational front line.

We realise we may be overly ambitious and bold both in our intention and aspiration by making the total Strategic Leadership Value Chain the focal point of *Understanding Leadership*. Also, in covering in the comprehensive menu of topics what we believe are the most critical topics related to each element of the chain, while applying the Pareto principle of the 20% telling 80% of the story. Simultaneously, however, we are fortuitously humbled by the depth, richness and diversity of the overwhelming, exploding body of knowledge regarding leadership. In no way can we claim, or wish to claim, that at a topic level a high degree of seamless conceptual and practical integration within an element or across the total Strategic Leadership Value Chain exists. That would be arrogant.

The Intended Audience of *Understanding Leadership*

In the first place, *Understanding Leadership* intends to assist executives and leadership specialists within organisations, whether public or private, to direct, guide and build – confidently and with well-grounded insight – leadership as a mission critical organisational capability and intervention in their organisations, using a Strategic Leadership Value Chain perspective. In this way we hope that they will be able to ensure a future-fit organisation and leadership who are able and willing to be architects of the future they so ardently desire.

In the second place, *Understanding Leadership* aims to assist academics and their students in the teaching and studying of leadership as a critically important subject. In the third place, the topics covered in *Understanding Leadership* may also provide creative triggers to future leadership research.

The Intended Use of *Understanding Leadership*

The intended use of *Understanding Leadership* is to serve as a handy daily "desktop" reference book on leadership lenses to our intended audience:

- for ongoing referral as and when ways of understanding leadership matters arise in an organisation, and
- where input from a thought leadership source is desired and necessary on available leadership lenses.

Thus *Understanding Leadership* is not intended to "Rest in Peace" on the bookshelf but to be a "Working Manual" by being an ever-present companion for continuous, daily consulting, referral and advice. Also, in a similar fashion, to assist as a reference for teaching on and research into leadership.

The Expected Value-add of *Understanding Leadership*

We hope *Understanding Leadership* will provide you as the reader with four overriding insights (or Lessons-to-be-Learnt):

- Accepting the criticality of a carefully considered and debated *Leadership Thinking Framework* as a point of reference and a frame to direct and guide dialogue about leadership wherever the topic of leadership comes under discussion: in teaching, research or in organisations.
- Understanding with respect to a *Leadership Conceptual Lens*, the typical make-up of the Leadership Landscape, and the range of available choices to be considered with respect to the respective building blocks making up the Landscape.
- Recognising the need to make well-considered, wise choices with respect to a *Leadership Vantage Point* and *fit-for-purpose Leadership Action Tools* from the vast array available in order to engage insightfully and effectively with the Leadership Landscape.
- Operationalising all of the above into an organisation specific *Strategic Leadership Framework* to act as a reference point and basis for all of the organisation's leadership related decisions and actions.

We wish you a stimulating, enriching and capacitating
journey through *Understanding Leadership*

SECTION 2

CONCEPTUAL LENS:
LEADERSHIP LANDSCAPE

Chapter 2

THE LEADERSHIP LANDSCAPE AS META-FRAMEWORK
Theo H Veldsman

Our thinking about and understanding of every phenomenon, one of which is leadership, is framed in terms of a world view, explicitly expressed or implicitly adopted.[1] A world view sets the way in which a phenomenon is conceived, constituted, developed, validated, and utilised. A world view regarding a phenomenon 'liberates' one by opening up a range of potential perspectives regarding the phenomenon. Concurrently, however, a world view 'imprisons' one by creating blind spots and/or by setting constraints with regard to the very same phenomenon.

In order to make proper sense of and engage in an informed manner with the phenomenon of 'leadership', an organisation needs to interrogate its world view with regard to leadership – its leadership meta-framework – which it uses to direct and guide its thinking and action regarding leadership. Its meta-framework will provide the organisation with a high level conceptual frame of reference to look at and deliberate about leadership in an integrated, systemic and holistic manner. Metaphorically, a leadership meta-framework provides the organisation with a Google map of the territory called 'leadership'.

At present, the exponentially ever-expanding and bewilderingly vast body of literature on leadership is populated by siloed leadership constructs, models and theories dealing in isolation with a single or only a few building blocks of leadership, for example, personal traits, leadership styles, leadership processes, or leadership competencies.[2] As a result, apart from having a Google map of the leadership territory, a further dire need exists for a conceptual compass – metaphorically, a leadership meta-framework as a GPS – to allow one at a meta-level to systematise, organise and integrate the leadership literature.

All in all, a leadership meta-framework would allow the organisation to see the 'big picture' with regard to leadership; it would guide and direct the leadership conversation in the organisation; and would not get overwhelmed and swamped by detail. In this way richer, truer perspectives of and narratives about leadership can emerge in the organisation. Such a framework would also form the foundation of and enable an organisation to craft its own, individualised Strategic Leadership Framework.

The chapter's purpose is to present a leadership meta-framework, called the 'Leadership Landscape'. The chapter proceeds by following the typical way in which a leadership meta-framework would come about:

- *Firstly,* defining 'leadership' as a phenomenon in order to demarcate the territory called 'leadership'
- *Secondly,* elucidating the principles informing the leadership meta-framework, based on a certain view of reality (in other words, an ontology)
- *Thirdly,* presenting a leadership meta-framework, made up of a set of interconnected leadership building blocks, called the Leadership Framework
- *Finally,* discussing in greater detail the respective building blocks making up the proposed Leadership Landscape.

Departure Point for a Leadership Meta-Framework: A Sound Definition of Leadership in order to Demarcate the Territory Correctly

The first step in crafting a leadership meta-framework is to define conceptually the phenomenon of 'leadership' in order to demarcate correctly the territory referred to as 'leadership'. An incorrect definition of leadership can either delineate the phenomenon too narrowly, consequently excluding essential elements of leadership, or it can do so too broadly, resulting in the inclusion of unrelated elements ('noise') in the definition thereof. Of course, a major assumption of any definition of the phenomenon called 'leadership' is that the phenomenon truly exists, and is not a mere figment of our imagination. This assumption will be accepted as valid in what follows. However, it is true – as will be argued below – that although the phenomenon 'leadership' exists, a person may choose or not choose to be a leader. In this sense a team, organisation, community or society can be leaderless if no-one demonstrates a will to aspire to leadership. A leaderless choice, however, does not imply that the phenomenon as a phenomenon does not exist.

At least in the academic literature, literally thousands of definitions of leadership have been proposed.[3] For the purpose of this chapter, and by implication for *Understanding Leadership*, the to-be-proposed definition of leadership in the accompanying box attempts to capture the essence of the phenomenon and account for essential thrusts of the major schools of thought regarding leadership. The definition also endeavours to take into account trends within the emerging, new world order.

Leadership can be defined as acts of persuasive influence exercised by a collectivity of individuals (= shared leadership) engaging a set of stakeholders (= mobilised followers) in enabling and empowering ways with regard to a joint course of action intended to bring about a shared, desirable, future-referenced outcome (= dream) with a desired effect (= legacy) within a specific context, past, present and future referenced.

What does the above definition of leadership imply in our search for better and different leadership in the emerging, new world order?

- *Firstly, the exercise of leadership is a choice.*

A person needs to decide consciously and deliberately to act as a leader.[4] A will to aspire to leadership needs to exist. (The level of leadership excellence is not now under consideration.) Leadership does not automatically come with a formal post or title, although it may be seen to be inherent therein. A person may decide, or be expected, to take up a post/role in a 'leaderless', technocratic and bureaucratic manner. No will to aspire to leadership may exist. At present there appears at multiple levels a disturbing worldwide decline in the will to aspire to leadership. In contrast, a person outside a formal post/role may decide to demonstrate leadership in response to a need for leadership.

- *Secondly, increasingly leadership is the shared responsibility of a set of persons in an organisation.*

This set of persons is known as the leadership community. (For the purpose of this chapter the term 'organisation' must be seen as a proxy for nation, society, community.) The challenges and demands within the context are typified by increasing complexity, uncertainty, change and ambiguity which require shared (or distributive) leadership.[5] The community needs to exercise leadership in a collective, mutually supportive and aligned manner if the organisation is to be successful and sustainable in the emerging context. This shared responsibility for leadership within the leadership community may continuously shift over time and location in terms of reconfigured leadership accountabilities and responsibilities. This is in contrast to the conventional view to defining leadership in terms of THE leader located in a formally designated position where this sole leader is seen as the saviour of the organisation. Hence the shift from using the term 'leader' to that of 'leadership'.

- *Thirdly, stakeholders are the dominant focus of leadership's acts of influence.*

This is true of leadership in its endeavour to convert stakeholders into passionate followers.[6] This is in contrast to the conventional view of defining leadership only in terms of immediate subordinates to be turned into followers. Why? Because in the first instance the organisational terrain is conceived, constituted, moulded together, sustained, and frequently destroyed by the psycho-social dynamics and psycho-social contract pervading the set of stakeholders populating this terrain, its action community. Also, in the current world, many more stakeholders believe they have an interest in the pursuits, decisions and actions of leaders because these impact on the stakeholders' futures as well. Nowadays leadership needs to build relationship (or social) capital with a wide and diverse set of stakeholders to identify and realise a desired future. It is a relative shift from 'power-over': the ability to command to 'power-to': the ability to affect institutionalised change. Leadership is increasingly in the merciless public eye, especially since the growing pressure to adopt a triple bottom line approach to organisational initiatives, performance and success, as well as the advent of the social media. Hence buy-in and ownership by many more stakeholders have become mission critical to masterful leadership.

- *Fourthly, judge leadership by both outcomes and the effect of the outcomes.*

Leadership is judged not only by the outcomes achieved – the dream realised – but also by the effect of the outcomes achieved. The effect pertains to the **legacy,** whether positive and/or negative, which the realised dream will leave behind. Is it lasting and worthy; and will it leave the world a better place?

- *Fifthly, identify the context of leadership.*

Leadership is always embedded in a **specific context** with its associated leadership challenges, demands and requirements. The ongoing fit and appropriate engagement with leadership with the context – current and emerging – have become mission critical.[7]

- *Finally, leadership is about the past, present and future.*

Leadership has to be seen in an **integrated past, present and future timeframe**, instead of predominantly only in the present. A here-and-now-only perspective not only results in a short-term time perspective, but also negates the continuity between the past, present and future. Leadership is about history making, and how leadership makes that history in enacting time as contained in the past, present and future.[8]

Principles Informing the Proposed Leadership Meta-Framework Based on a Chaos/Complexity World View

Having demarcated the territory called 'leadership', the next step in the crafting of a leadership framework is to elucidate the principles informing the leadership meta-framework, based on a certain view of reality (that is, an ontology). Metaphorically, we need to specify the 'laws' according to which the territory – in this case the territory of 'leadership' – as well as the map and GPS used with regard to the territory function.

It is suggested that the proposed leadership meta-framework – referred to below as the 'Leadership Landscape' – must be based on a complexity/chaos view of reality.[9] At present, this world view appears to supply the most powerful insight into the true nature and dynamics of reality. Simply put, according to this world view, reality must be seen as an interconnected whole of reciprocally influencing, interacting variables, where everything affects everything else. This interconnected whole is characterised by the ongoing resolution of dynamic, opposing tensions manifesting themselves in the ongoing emergence of non-predictable, self-organising and self-destructing patterns. The patterns converge over time into virtuous or vicious cycles. Pattern dynamics is the manifestation of a limited number of underlying organising rules as the interconnected whole moves through successive states of chaos (that is, absence of a pattern) and order (that is, presence of a pattern).

Based on a chaos/complexity world view as elucidated above, the to-be-proposed leadership meta-framework – called the Leadership Landscape – rests on at least the following principles:

- The exercise of the will to leadership by the leadership community is composed of a distinct set of building blocks that form a **systemic and holistic whole:** a Landscape. Because of the **interconnectivity** of the building blocks, a change in one or more building blocks ripples across the whole, interconnected Landscape and affects all the other building blocks to a greater or lesser extent.
- The building blocks with their constituent elements stand in **dynamic tension** in respect of each other because of opposing requirements which create dilemmas and paradoxes. A dynamic fusion of 'and' and not an 'either–or' has to occur between them.
- Given the resolution of the respective dynamic tensions, **a pattern of leadership** emerges over time in the Landscape as the outcome of the building blocks' enactment by the organisation's leadership.
- A pattern forms of either a **virtuous ('good')** or a **vicious ('bad') leadership cycle** (or dynamic) within the Leadership Landscape, which directly affects the dynamics within the organisation, its performance, success and image.
- An individual leader or leadership is fully **immersed** in the Leadership Landscape with its associated leadership dynamics. None of them can in any way set themselves apart from or above the Landscape.
- Changing a pattern with its commensurate leadership cycle, be it virtuous or vicious, is **a large-scale, systemic, organisational change process** involving the whole leadership community of an organisation as embedded in a certain context, and encompassing past, present and future.

Towards a Leadership Meta-framework: The Proposed Leadership Landscape

A conceptual definition of leadership demarcates the territory called 'leadership', the first step in the journey towards a leadership meta-framework. The next step is to craft a leadership meta-framework that will act as a Google map of and GPS for the territory, showing the 'towns' with their relative locations and connections to each other.

To recap, the value of a meta-framework is threefold: to simplify, organise and integrate at a meta-level the complexity of the field of leadership with its ever-expanding and overwhelming literature; to provide a common meta-language for an all-inclusive, coherent leadership dialogue about leadership in the organisation; and to structure an organisation's conversation about leadership, enabling it to arrive at a customised Strategic Leadership Framework that will direct and guide the organisation's thinking and actions regarding its leadership.

A proposed Leadership Landscape with its building blocks as the Google map and GPS for the territory called 'leadership' is depicted in Figure 2.1. A building block represents a meta-theme or meta-concept informing and framing the territory called 'leadership'[10] (metaphorically speaking, a 'town' in the territory). It is important, firstly, to retain a meta-perspective, that is, a big-picture perspective in constructing the leadership meta-framework; and, secondly, to decide what to extract as meta-perspective building blocks – the towns – and their relative location to each other. This highlights the value of using the metaphor of constructing a map of the territory called 'leadership'.

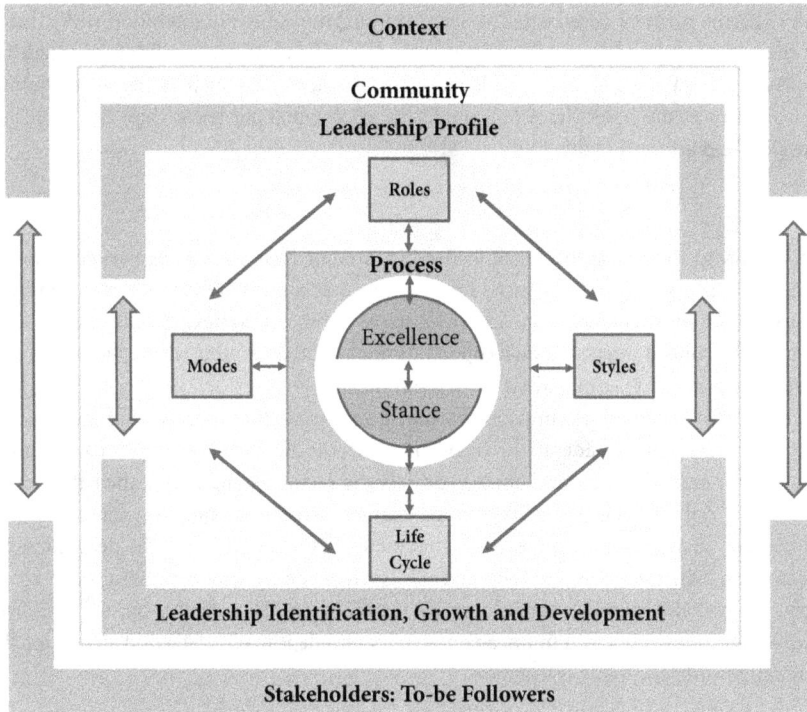

Figure 2.1: The Leadership Landscape

A short trip through the proposed Leadership Landscape is taken here as an orientation exercise. A detailed exposition follows in the next section. Important to note during the orientation is the relative location of the building blocks ('towns') to each other, which implies certain interdependencies. According to Figure 2.1, Leadership Context and Stakeholders – the prospective Followers – form the outer context of the Landscape. They set the scene, so to speak, for the other building blocks.

At the centre of the Leadership Landscape, acting as its fulcrum, are Leadership Stance and Excellence. This centre is encircled by Leadership Process: the acts making up leadership. Four 'levers' serve as enablers in respect of the execution of the leadership process: Roles, Styles, Modes, and Life Cycle.

In turn, all of the abovementioned building blocks are encircled by the building blocks Leadership Profile and Leadership Identification, Growth and Development. All of the above are embedded in Leadership Community. Altogether, these building blocks (except for Leadership Context and Stakeholders) form the inner context of the Landscape.

Exploring the Leadership Landscape as Map for and Compass to the Leadership Territory

Using as a guide the order of the above short orientation trip though the Leadership Landscape depicted in Figure 2.1, the nature and make-up of the respective Landscape building blocks (or towns in the Leadership Landscape) is elucidated next. During the journey of exploring the Leadership Landscape, it should quickly become clear that each building block contains a range of choices regarding what form leadership could take in an organisation. Metaphorically, how should a specific town be constructed to serve the purposes of the organisation well? Through these choices an organisation will be crafting an organisation-specific Strategic Leadership Framework. The value of having a leadership meta-framework – such as the to-be-discussed Leadership Landscape – to direct and guide the choice-making leadership discourse in an organisation is reinforced in this way.

Context

Context refers to the setting in which leadership is embedded with its associated leadership challenges, demands and requirements.[11] It forms the outer context of the Leadership Landscape. The organisation must demarcate its operating arena within the context; decide how it sees the make-up of the context impacting on its operating arena; and determine what engagement mode must be used to make sense of and act upon the context.

In terms of make-up, an organisation must decide on the 'breadth' and 'depth' of the context it will take into consideration. The former refers to the range of contextual dimensions to consider, for example, the world at large, or only my sector (or industry). The latter pertains to considering only the 'superficial' contextual characteristics – the tangible, concrete features of the context, such as, for example, the infrastructure of a country – or the deep contextual characteristics – the intangible, invisible features, such as the cultural orientations of a specific country. The engagement mode entails donning the set of glasses leadership has to put on when looking at the context. At a minimum, an engagement mode is made of a world view-, decision-making framework, and value orientation.

Stakeholders: The 'to-be' followers

Unlocking of value and wealth creation by the organisation is ultimately about meeting the diverse needs/interests of multiple stakeholders in a balanced, fair and equitable manner, the outer context of the Leadership Landscape. Leadership has to turn stakeholders into followers sharing in the future-directed dream and legacy of the leadership. Without followers, there can be no leadership.[12] A stakeholder can be described as anyone (an individual or individuals, groups, institutions) that can affect and/or are affected by the direction and actions of the organisation, intended or real, and consequentially having an impact on its reputation.

An organisation therefore has to have an intense discourse regarding who their stakeholders are; what interests, needs and stakes they have; what type of followers they need to be turned into; what type and amount of relationship (or social capital) must be built with them;[13] and consequently the type of relationship leadership must form and maintain with them.

Leadership stance

The importance of having a sound conceptual definition of leadership as a departure point to correctly demarcate the territory called 'leadership' was stressed above. This definition represents a generic, theoretical view of the phenomenon. Within the Leadership Landscape, this definition has to be operationalised (or customised) in order to make it of direct practical value and relevance to the organisation, its leadership and its people. This operationalised definition can be called the leadership stance of the organisation and its leadership. Put differently, the stance forms the vantage point of the landscape relative to context and stakeholders (see Figure 2.1).

Because the stance provides the organisational specifications of what leadership is all about in the organisation, it infuses and colours all the other building blocks making up the inner context of the Leadership Landscape (except leadership context and stakeholders, the outer context, which set the scene for the stance). Systemic congruence must exist between the choices made with respect to the stance, and consequently the other inner context building blocks, in order to increase the likelihood of bringing about a virtuous leadership cycle within the landscape.

What typical elements – that is, operationalised specifications – make up the leadership stance? And what continua exist with regard to these elements?[14] Figure 2.2 depicts these elements and continua.

Figure 2.2: The elements and continua making up the Leadership Stance

According to Figure 2.2 six elements make up the leadership stance, for example, basis of influence, or the time perspective, among others. Each element has a continuum. In the case of basis of influence, the range is from Personal/Reputational to Positional influence. The choice with regard to a continuum can either be a single pole or a relative mixture of the two poles of the continuum. Important to note is that the choice offered on one extreme of a continuum, for example, personal/reputational influence, does not eliminate the other pole (= positional influence) of the continuum. The 'lesser' pole will still be active, but only within the dominant choice's frame of reference. Using these elements with their commensurate continua, an organisation and its leadership can craft its current and desired leadership stances.

Three basic leadership stances are contained in Figure 2.2, as illustrated in Figure 2.3: Transactional, Transformational and Transcendental.[15]

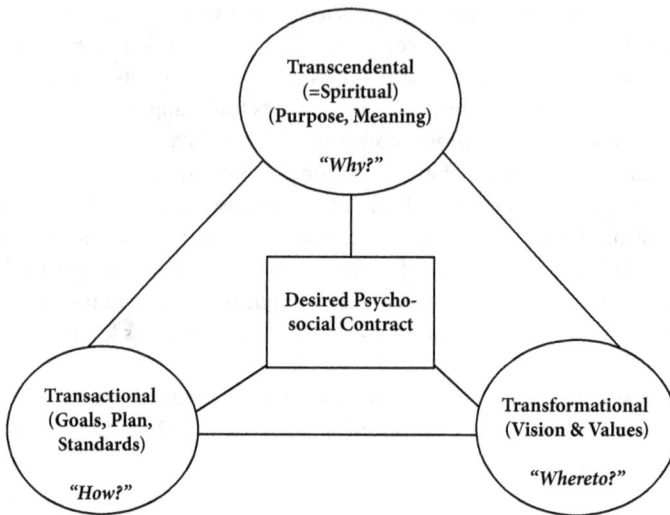

Figure 2.3: Basic Leadership Stance

Table 2.1 lists the choices which make up the basic stances based on Figure 2.2. To simplify the three stances, the transactional stance is about operational execution; the transformational stance represents the inspiring dream; and the transcendental stance encompasses the worthy, lasting legacy.

Table 2.1: Choices making up Basic Leadership Stances

Transactional leadership stance	Transformational leadership stance	Transcendental leadership stance
Goals, Plans, Standards	Vision, Values	Meaning/Purpose
Task	Task/People	People
Present	Present/Future	Future
Positional Influence	Personal/Reputational Influence	Personal Influence
The Existing	The New	The New
Single	Distributed	Distributed

All three of the basic leadership stances are required by an organisation. It is not a case of 'either–or' but of 'and'. What is needed for an appropriate leadership stance, therefore, is the right weighting (or permutation) of the three basic stances as shown in Figure 2.3. This differential weighting is a function of at least the following factors: the organisation's context and stakeholders; what it wants to be and achieve; its strategic intent; who and what the organisation is, and what it stands for: its ideology; where it is in its life cycle (for example, start-up; dynamic growth); and the psychosocial contact it desires to have with its stakeholders (see below). Within an organisation, its chosen basic leadership stance may also be weighted differently, given the organisational level implicated. Lower levels may have a greater weighting of a transactional stance; higher levels, a greater weighting of a transcendental stance.

As mentioned above, the weighting of the three basic leadership stances is influenced by the psychosocial contract which the organisation and its leadership wish to establish with its stakeholders as prospective followers. Therefore, the placement of the contract is in the middle of the triangle of the basic leadership stances, as depicted in Figure 2.3. The psychosocial contract refers to the two-way, reciprocal sets of expectations the two parties have of each other in terms of contributions and expected benefits. Four types of contact can be distinguished:

- *Coercive:* Do as you are told or leave.
- *Bartering:* Equitable rewards are exchanged for the achievement of contracted effort and performance.
- *Partnering:* Co-responsibility by everyone is required for success, and consequentially the co-sharing of rewards.
- *Identification:* This represents the internalisation of what the organisation stands for and wishes to achieve, and acting correspondingly.

Typically, the overall psychosocial contract of an organisation is a mixture of the above four types of contracts, but one type of contact is usually dominant, with one or more of the others secondary. Generally speaking, as one moves from a coercive to an identification psychosocial contract, the mix of basic leadership stances shifts from a dominant transactional stance to a dominant transcendental stance weighting in the leadership stance mix.

Leadership excellence

Leadership Stance and leadership excellence both sit at the centre of the Leadership Landscape, acting as its fulcrum (see Figure 2.1), but their contributions differ. The Leadership Stance forms the vantage point of the Leadership Landscape by being the point where it all begins by specifying the leadership desired and required by the organisation. In contrast, leadership excellence is, so to speak, where it all ends. It specifies the resultant desired outcome of the dynamic interaction between all of the landscape building blocks. In turn, as an outcome it feeds systemically back on the interaction reflective of the current leadership pattern in the landscape, whether virtuous or vicious.

Leadership excellence therefore specifies the critical dimensions that make up the desired leadership end state to be attained. Put differently: it specifies what the right leadership (that is, effectiveness) in the right way at the right time (that is, efficiency) should be. This could include excellence dimensions such as being a thriving, sustainable, well-governed organisation; the effective execution of the leadership process; leadership talent growth and development; and stakeholder legitimacy/credibility. An organisation and its leadership together with its people must debate and reach agreement on what leadership excellence with its commensurate dimensions entails in their organisation.

Leadership process

The leadership process encircles leadership stance and leadership excellence, the last-named forming the base of it (see Figure 2.1). It encompasses the end-to-end, interdependent work flow of leadership actions, such as envisioning, empowering and enabling, and encouraging at the heart. This process is the conduit through which leadership exercises its acts of persuasive influence. An organisation needs to have an intense dialogue regarding the essential acts making up its leadership process. In other words, it must be clear as to what its leadership process must look like.

An example of such a leadership process is given in Figure 2.4. The actions depicted in Figure 2.4 form a systemic, holistic, interdependent whole. The actions making up the leadership process need to happen simultaneously in real time, all the time, in a congruent fashion. In this respect, leadership is like a juggler, juggling a set of balls (that is the actions) simultaneously in real time.

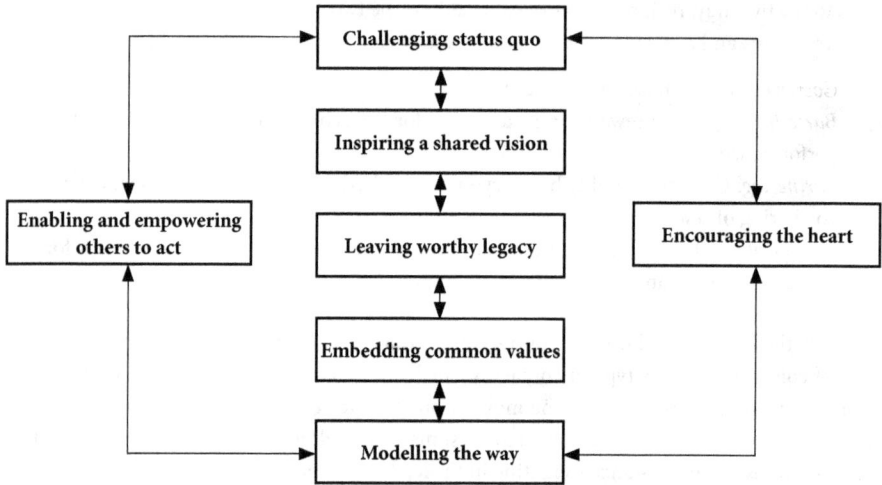

Figure 2.4: The Leadership Process

Leadership roles

In terms of the Leadership Landscape (see Figure 2.1), the leadership role is one of the four influence levers enabling the execution of the leadership process. The others, still to be discussed, are leadership modes, styles and life cycle. A lever is therefore a way of executing the leadership process. Acts of influence exerted by means of the four levers require a power base from which to leverage one's influence as leadership.[16] Using a certain power base, leadership has to fulfil certain roles through which they act out the leadership process.[17] A role refers to the functions fulfilled or parts played by leadership in getting the work done through the leadership process.

Figure 2.5 depicts the different sources of power leadership has, after giving it a certain power base; and also depicts a typical portfolio of leadership roles.

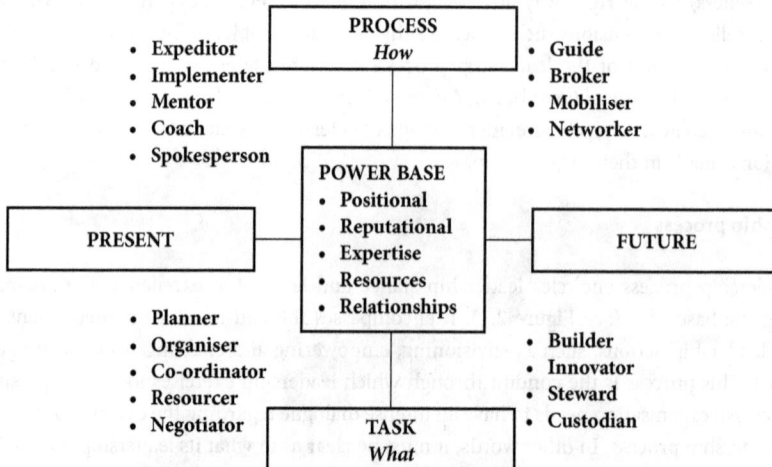

Figure 2.5: Power base and Roles of leadership

As can be seen from Figure 2.5, a leader has at least five sources of power, making up a leader's power base:

- **Positional:** The job a leader holds with its accompanying formal authority and accountability
- **Reputational:** The name I have made for myself and the image I have as a leader
- **Expertise:** My knowledge, skills, expertise and experience as a leader
- **Resources:** Which resources and how much I control as a leader
- **Relationships:** People whom I know as a leader, and what their status and power are.

Generally speaking, the more sources of power leadership has, and the stronger each source, the stronger the leadership's power base, and hence its ability to act persuasively as leadership. The choice and mixture of power sources, and consequently a legitimate power base, is heavily influenced by the desired leadership stance of the organisation. For example, a stance stressing personal/reputational influence will override using one's position as a source of power. Given its chosen leadership stance, an organisation has to deliberate what would be acceptable sources of power to be used as a legitimate power base to leverage the leadership process. In general, the trend globally is away from a position as a dominant source of power, towards other sources, in particular, reputation and expertise.

According to Figure 2.5, the leadership roles as a lever are either process or task; present or future related, defining four leadership quadrants. *Each* of the quadrants has to be populated with the needed, specific leadership roles, like a sports team that requires certain roles. Thus an organisation must specify the portfolio of critical leadership roles it needs which its leadership must fulfil.

Frequently, leaders, in fulfilling these roles as leaders are active in only one or a limited number of quadrants, for example, present/task (the roles of planner/organiser, or resourcer) or task/future (the roles of builder, or innovator). Consequently, the effective execution of the leadership process is severely compromised, because only a limited number of roles out of the necessary portfolio of leadership roles are performed.

All of the organisationally required leadership roles need to be fulfilled at the appropriate times. A leader therefore has to understand at which of the required roles he/she is naturally strong and/or weak. In weaker roles, a leader has to team up with other leaders who are naturally strong in those roles. In the end, the full repertoire of necessary leadership roles, leveraged from an appropriate power base, must be fulfilled by the organisation's leadership.

Leadership modes

Leadership mode is the second of the four influence levers that enables the execution of the leadership process. It refers to what approach leadership uses to exercise influence in mobilising and moving followers collectively towards a shared, desired end state. Followers are mobilised and moved in response to the answer that leadership gives to the question: "Why must I/we buy into the journey you want to take us into the future?"

Figure 2.6 depicts four leadership modes that leadership can deploy, and also again the sources of power base he/she can use to exert this leverage (as already discussed).[18]

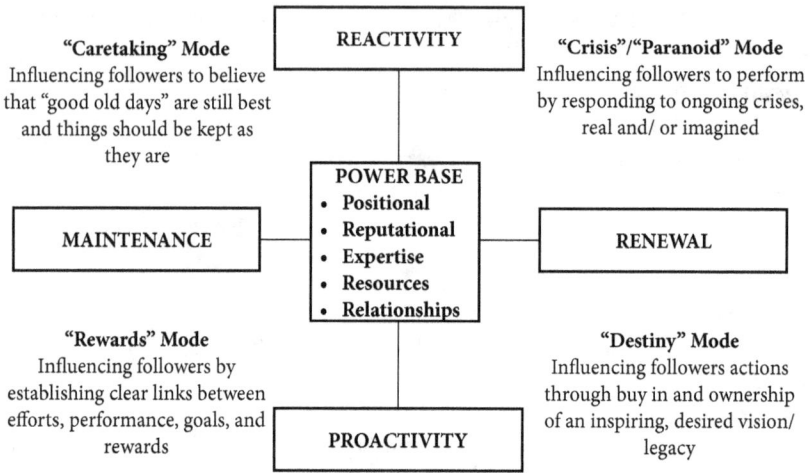

Figure 2.6: Leadership Modes

The overall leadership mode adopted by leadership is a differential weighting of the four modes shown in Figure 2.6. The key is to find the right mix of modes that will be able to influence different followers in the organisation concerned. Overall the emerging trend is towards a higher weighting of a destiny mode – dream and legacy, especially the latter when the backdrop of sustainability is considered – in combination with a rewards mode.

Leadership styles

Leadership style is the third influence lever leadership needs to apply in respect of the leadership process. It relates to the degree of empowerment (or freedom) given by leadership to followers to take action within their respective responsibility areas. As discussed above, every leader uses a mix of leadership modes to energise and move followers. This is in contrast to leadership style, where a leader typically would adopt a dominant style, which would then be exercised through a mix of chosen leadership modes.

Figure 2.7 depicts the range of leadership styles as a function of the ratio of leader autonomy to follower autonomy, and the factors determining that ratio.[19]

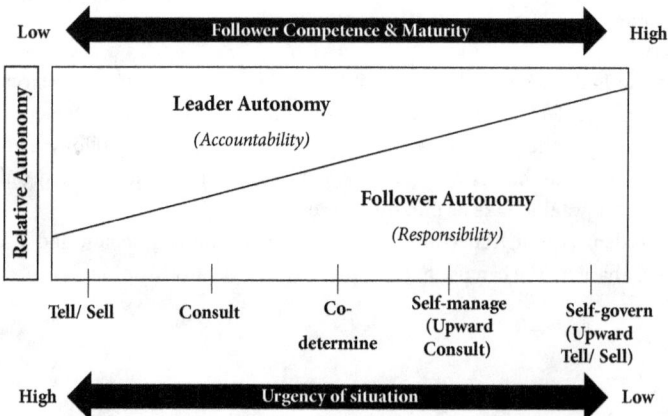

Figure 2.7: Leadership Styles

The possible Leadership Styles given in Figure 2.7 can be described as follows:

- **Tell:** The accountable leader makes the decisions and instructs those who are responsible to do the work (0% autonomy to followers).
- **Consult:** The accountable leader asks for input from the responsible parties, considers their input, makes the decision, and instructs them (25% autonomy to followers).
- **Co-determine:** The accountable leader and responsible parties jointly debate the intended action and make the decision together (equal autonomy between the leader and followers: 50%–50% autonomy).
- **Self-manage:** (Upward consultation): The responsible party (or parties) consults upwards with the accountable leader, makes the decision, and informs the accountable leader accordingly (75% autonomy to followers).
- **Self-govern:** (Upward telling/selling): The responsible party (or parties) takes the decision, and informs the accountable leader (100% autonomy to followers).

The selected power base and chosen leadership style have to resonate, which means that they should be mutually reinforcing. For example, using position as a source of power would not resonate well with a self-governing style. Furthermore, the accountable leader's level of trust in his/her responsible followers to deliver increases significantly as one moves from tell to self-govern (see Figure 2.7). The leader ultimately remains accountable, regardless of the level of autonomy given to his/her followers.

Again, an organisation has to decide what its overriding leadership style is going to be. The emerging trend in people-centric organisations is towards giving followers greater autonomy by moving from co-determine towards self-govern.

Leadership life cycle

Compared to the three previous influence levers which leadership applies to the leadership process, the leadership life cycle as a lever has a different nature. Leadership roles, modes and styles are choice-based and time-independent. They are a function of landscape alignment demands and requirements within the parameters set by the organisation's chosen leadership stance.

In contrast, the leadership life cycle pertains to the time-based, sequential stages through which leadership's relationship with followers moves in order to become established: entry, unfolding, blooming, plateauing, demise, and oblivion.[20] Every move by a leader – promotion, transfer, new employment – places him/her in a new relationship that has to be established *de novo*. Therefore, a next Leadership Life Cycle is triggered with respect to new stakeholders who have to be turned into followers through the establishment of a sound relationship. During a leader's career, she/he will move through many of these life cycles.

In the application of leadership life cycle as an influence lever, there are no choices to be made regarding the life cycle itself with its associated stages. The relationship stages are givens through which a new relationship has to progress in order to become established. Movement through the stages, however, may be shorter or longer but they all have to be transitioned. Sometimes a relationship may even get stuck at a certain stage and never evolve further. The leader also leverages a certain power base, for example, his/her reputation and expertise, to enable and even expedite movement through life cycle stages.

The critical choice for an organisation regarding the life cycle as lever is how frequently leadership moves will be initiated, and how many moves will be affected at any given point in time. Too many moves at the same time, and the organisation could go into 'relationship shock', suffering from too many leaders being in new relationships at the same time. Too few moves, too infrequently, and relationships may grow stale, with few challenges and growth opportunities to leadership.

Leadership profile

This building block is all about the complexity of the picture to be used by the organisation when looking at the leader as a person.[21]

Firstly, consideration has to be given to what dimensions are to be applied by the organisation in looking at the leader as a person. Two dimensions can be distinguished:

- A 'horizontal' dimension pertaining to a person's *domains of being/becoming*, such as physical, physiological/biological, psycho-social, socio-cultural, spiritual.
- A 'vertical' dimension across each of the domains of being/becoming, made up of 'hard' and/ or 'soft', deep or shallow *capabilities*, such as abilities, competencies, wisdom, experience.

At issue here is how comprehensive and complex in terms of the vertical and horizontal dimensions the picture must be that the organisation will use when looking at the leader as a person. For example, recent times have seen the emergence of the neuroscience of leadership, stressing the importance of the brain's programming in bringing about effective leadership; or there may be the acknowledgement of the spiritual dimension, given people's search for life meaning and purpose; or hard (for example, expertise) and soft (for example, personal attributes), as well as deep (mindsets, frames of reference) and shallow capabilities (experience) may be considered.

Secondly, to what extent must the above dimensions be contextualised by the organisation in terms of:

i.   The leader's *life history* as a person: how his/her life has unfolded up to this point in time, and even how it may unfold in the future, and
ii.   The range of exposure to different *locations in place and time* by the leader as his/her life has unfolded up to this point in time.

To illustrate: childhood experiences give rise to the establishment of certain motivational patterns. For example, a leader coming from deprived, poor circumstances may be strongly driven by greed; or a child may have learnt how to handle authority in a certain way. It has been found that leaders growing up in or being exposed to multicultural locations during their early life appear to be more cross-culturally sensitive and have higher cultural intelligence. They are therefore more effective leaders in global, multicultural organisations. Alternatively, a leader growing up in a certain location, for example, a developed versus an emerging country, and at a certain time would have been inculcated with a certain mindset and sociocultural life orientation.

Therefore, under consideration from an organisational perspective with respect to this building block is how the organisation must profile its current and future leaders when it looks at them as persons. Generally speaking, the trend is towards viewing leaders more comprehensively as complex, multi-dimensional, integrated beings, with a certain life and locational history.

Leadership identification, growth and development

This building block embraces the "what" and "how" of leadership talent management in the organisation. The intention of the leadership identification, growth and development process is to have the right leaders in the right numbers at the right time in the right place, able, willing, wanting, and being allowed to perform, thereby giving the organisation a sustainable competitive edge in our chosen markets. The challenge for the organisation is how to bring about this state of affairs in the organisation.[22]

Talent-driven organisations endeavour to gain a competitive edge through their talent by adopting a long-term, holistic and systemic view of their talent, in this case leadership, leveraged from an integrated process of how to think and deal with their talent from an overall organisational perspective. In other words, they adopt a strategic talent posture. As a concrete expression of this posture, they craft a strategic talent plan which is closely aligned time-wise to and in direct support of their organisational strategy. Without such a strategic talent posture, talent management in the organisation will be fragmented, reactive and driven by short-term, operational talent needs.[23]

Leadership community

Given that leadership is distributed and shared throughout the organisation, the leadership of an organisation can be regarded as a community of practice. A community of practice is a relational network of persons in an organisation who occupy a similar role with regard to its expected behaviours, which is, in this case, the role of leadership.[24]

As the inner context of the Leadership Context, a Leadership Community has its own unique ideology, brand, beliefs, value set, and code of practice. Associated with the Leadership Community is also a certain leadership culture and climate: the interpersonal, team, and organisation-wide shared ways of seeing, interpreting and acting upon the world, as well as the dynamics between and amongst the organisation's leadership that in turn sets the tone for the organisational culture and climate.

An organisation must consider what type of Leadership Community it wishes to establish and nurture in its organisation. The criticality of this discourse lies in the fact that all of the above discussed building blocks (except Context and Stakeholders) are embedded in the Leadership Community as the inner context of the Leadership Landscape. The nature of and dynamics within the Leadership Community will directly affect these building blocks and impart them with a certain flavour and colour.

Conclusion

The chapter's purpose was to present a leadership meta-framework, called the 'Leadership Landscape'. The intent was to demonstrate the critical three-fold value of a leadership meta-framework: at a meta-level to simplify, organise and integrate the complexity of the field of leadership with its ever-expanding and overwhelming literature; to provide a common meta-language for an all-inclusive, coherent leadership dialogue about leadership in the organisation; and to structure an organisation's conversation about leadership, enabling it to arrive at a customised Strategic Leadership Framework that will direct and guide the organisation's thinking and actions regarding its leadership.

The chapter proceeded by following the typical way in which a leadership meta-framework would come about: *firstly*, by defining 'leadership' as a phenomenon to demarcate the territory called 'leadership'. *Secondly*, by elucidating the principles informing the leadership meta-framework, based on a certain view of reality. *Thirdly*, by presenting a leadership meta-framework, called the Leadership Framework. *Finally*, by discussing the respective building blocks making up the proposed Leadership Landscape.

Having crafted a Leadership Landscape, an organisation can now formulate its Strategic Leadership Framework. The Framework would consist of the choices the organisation makes regarding its position on each of the building blocks making up the Landscape.

Endnotes

1   Typical equivalent terms for "world view" are a mental model; a foundational framework; a set of lenses; paradigms; schemata; or archetypes (*cf. Hamel, 2007, p. 13 et seq.*).

2   Reference to such confusion is made, for example, by Dihn, Lord, Gardener, Meuser, Liden & Hu, 2014.

3   For a collection of over 1 000 leadership definitions, and construct with an attempt to provide an integrative definition of leadership, see Winston and Patterson, 2005. See also Hackman, 2010.

4   Fairhurst, 2009; Mirvis & Gunning, 2006.

5   For example, *cf. Avolio, Walumbwa & Weber, 2009; Bennis, 2007; Pearce, 2004; Veldsman, 2013.*

6   For discussions of followers, see, for example: Avolio et al., 2009; Barling, Christie & Hoption, 2011; Barling, 2014; Bennis, 2007; Obolensky, 2010; Kellerman, 2012; Schneider, 2002; Winston & Patterson, 2005.

7   For discussions of context, see, for example: Clawson, 2009, p. 45 *et seq.; Dihn et al., 2014; Obolensky, 2010.*

8   Osborn, Hunt & Jauch, 2002; Porter & McLaughlin, 2006.

9   *cf. Avolio et al., 2009; Goldstein, 2008; Hazy, Goldstein & Lichtenstein, 2007; Kurtz & Snowden, 2003; Marion, 2008; Obolensky, 2010; Schneider & Somers, 2006; Stacey, Griffin & Shaw, 2000; Stacey, 2015; Wheatley, 2010.*

10   The building blocks were extracted by a 'conceptual factor analysis' of the 'table of content pages' of the literature endeavouring to cover the leadership territory in its totality in order to identify recurring meta-themes and meta-concepts in the field. Some of the sources consulted were: Achua & Lussier, 2013; Avolio et al., 2009; Barling et al., 2011; Barling, 2014; Biech, 2010; Dihn et al., 2014; Gardner, Lowe, Moss, Mahoney & Cogliser, 2010; Gardner, Cogliser, Davis & Dickens, 2011; Haslam, Reicher & Platow, 2011; Nahavandi, A., 2009; Nohria & Khurana, 2010; Northouse, 2007; Storey, 2011; Western, 2013. In a similar vein, see Fuhs (2008)'s quadrivial analysis of eight leadership books to arrive at a vision of integral leadership.

11   See endnote 7.

12   See endnote 6.

13   Acquaah, Amoako-Gyampah & Nyathi, 2014; Schneider, 2002.

14   The proposed operationalised specifications of the Leadership Stance were extracted from sources such as Achua & Lussier, 2013; Avolio et al., 2009; Barling et al., 2011; Barling, 2014; Biech, 2010; Dihn et al., 2014; Gardner et al., 2010; Gardner et al., 2011; Haslam et al., 2011; Nahavandi, A., 2009; Nohria & Khurana, 2010; Northouse, 2007; Storey, 2011; Western, 2013; Winston & Patterson, 2005.

15   Cf. Achua & Lussier, 2013, p. 301 *et seq.); Luthans, Luthans & Luthans, 2015, p. 377 et seq.; p. 390 et seq.); Parolini, Patterson & Winston, 2009.*

16   For discussions of power, see, for example: Achua & Lussier, 2013, p. 139 *et seq.; Dihn et al., 2014.*

17   For discussions of leadership roles, see, for example: Achua & Lussier, 2013, p. 13 *et seq.); Appelbaum & Pease (undated); Kets De Vries, Vrignaud, Agrawal & Florent-Treacy, 2010; Luthans et al., 2015.*

18   *cf. Schreiber & Carley (2007); Luthans et al., 2015, p. 405 et seq.*

19   Ibid.

20   *cf. Charan, Drotter & Noel, 2001; Porter & McLaughlin (2006); Ward, 2003.*

21   For example of a comprehensive competency model, see Veldsman, 2010.

22   For discussions of Leadership Identification, Growth and Development, see, for example: Barling, Christie & Hoption, 2011; Biech, 2010; Nohria & Khurana, 2010.

23   *cf. Van der Merwe & Verwey (2016); Veldsman, 2011.*

24   Van der Merwe & Verwey (2016); Veldsman, 2013.

References

Achua, CF & Lussier, RN. 2013. *Effective leadership.* 5th ed. Mason, OH: South-Western, Cengage Learning.

Acquaah, M, Amoako-Gyampah, K & Nyathi, NQ. 2014. *Measuring and valuing social capital. A systematic review.* Network for Business Sustainability, South Africa. [Online]. Available: http//:nbs.net/ knowledge. [Accessed 15 June 2016].

Appelbaum, L & Pease, M. s.a. *What senior leaders do: The nine roles of strategic leadership.* White paper (MKTCPWP08-0303). Development Dimensions International (DDI).

Avolio, BJ, Walumbwa, FO & Weber, TJ. 2009. 'Leadership: Current theories, research and future directions'. *Annual Review of Psychology*, 60:421–449.

Barling, J, Christie, A & Hoption, C. 2011. 'Leadership'. In S Zedeck (ed.) *APA handbook of industrial and organisational psychology. Vol 1: Building and developing the organisation*. Washington, DC: American Psychological Association. 183–240.

Barling, J. 2014. *The science of leadership*. Oxford, UK: Oxford University Press.

Bennis, W. 2007. 'The challenges of leadership in the modern world'. Introduction to the special issue. *American Psychologist*, 62(1):2–5.

Biech, E (ed). 2010. *The ASTD leadership handbook*. Alexandria, VA: ASTD Press.

Charan, R, Drotter, S & Noel, J. 2001. *The leadership pipeline*. San Francisco, CA: Jossey-Bass.

Clawson, JG. 2009. *Level three leadership*. Upper Saddle River, NJ: Pearson Prentice-Hall.

Dihn, JE, Lord, RG, Gardener, WL, Meuser, JD, Liden, RC & Hu, J. 2014. 'Leadership theory and research in the new millennium: Current theoretical trends and changing perspectives'. *The Leadership Quarterly*, 25:36–62.

Fairhurst, GT. 2009. 'Considering context in discursive leadership research', *Human Relations*, 62(11): 1607-1633.

Fuhs, C. 2008. 'Towards a vision of integral leadership. A quadrivial analysis of eight leadership books'. *Journal of Integral Theory and Practice*, 3(1):139–162, Spring.

Gardner, WL, Lowe, KB, Moss, TW, Mahoney, KT & Cogliser, CC. 2010. 'Scholarly leadership of the study of leadership: A review of *The Leadership Quarterly*'s second decade, 2000–2009'. *The Leadership Quarterly*, 21:922–958.

Gardner, WL, Cogliser, CC, Davis, KM & Dickens, MP. 2011. 'Authentic leadership: A review of the literature and research agenda'. *The Leadership Quarterly*, 22:1120–1145.

Goldstein, J. 2008. 'Conceptual foundations of complexity science. Development and main constructs'. In M Uhl-Bien & R Marion (eds). *Complexity leadership*. Charlotte, NC: Information Age Publishing. 17–47.

Guest, DE. 1998. 'Is the psychological contract worth taking seriously?' *Journal of Organisational Behaviour*, 19:669–664.

Guest, DE. 2004. 'The psychology of the employment relationship: An analysis based on the psychological contract. *Applied Psychology: An International Review*, 53(4):541–555.

Hackman, JR. 2010. 'What is this thing called leadership?' In N Nohria & R Khurana (eds). *Handbook of leadership theory and practice*. Boston, MA: Harvard University Press. 107–116.

Hamel, G. 2007. *The future of management*. Boston, MA: Harvard Business Management.

Haslam, SA, Reicher, SD & Platow, MJ. 2011. *The new psychology of leadership*. Hove, UK: Psychology Press.

Hazy, JK, Goldstein, JA & Lichtenstein, BB. (eds). 2007. *Complex systems leadership theory. New perspectives from complexity science on social and organisational effectiveness*. Mansfield, MA: ISCE Publishing.

Kellerman, B. 2012. *The end of leadership*. New York, NY: Harper Business.

Kets De Vries, MFR, Vrignaud, P, Agrawal, A & Florent-Treacy, E. 2010. 'Development and application of the leadership archetype questionnaire'. *The International Journal of Human Resource Management*, 21(15): 2848–2863.

Kouzes, J & Posner, B. 2012. *The leadership challenge*. San Francisco, CA: Jossey-Bass.

Kurtz, C & Snowden, DJ. 2003. The new dynamics of strategy: Sense-making in a complex and complicated world. *IBM Systems Journal*, 42:462–483.

Luthans, F, Luthans, BC & Luthans, KW. 2015. *Organisational behaviour. An evidence-based approach*. 13th ed. Charlotte, NC: Information Age Publishing.

Marion, R. 2008. 'Complexity theory for organisations and organisational leadership'. In M Uhl-Bien & R Marion (eds). *Complexity leadership*. Charlotte, NC: Information Age Publishing. 1–15.

Nahavandi, A. 2009. *The art and science of leadership*. Upper Saddle River, NJ: Pearson/Prentice Hall.

Nohria, N & Khurana, R. 2010. *Handbook of leadership theory and practice*, Boston, MA: Harvard Business Press.

Northouse, PG. 2007. *Leadership. Theory and practice*. 4th ed. Thousand Oaks, CA: Sage.

Obolensky, N. 2010. *Complex adaptive leadership*. Farnham, UK: Gower.

Osborn, R, Hunt, JG & Jauch, LR. 2002. Toward a contextual theory of leadership, *The Leadership Quarterly* 13, pp. 797–837.

Parolini, J, Patterson, K & Winston, B. 2009. 'Distinguishing between transformational and servant leadership'. *Leadership and Organisation Development Journal*, 30(3):274–291.

Pearce, CL. 2004. 'The future of leadership: Combining vertical and shared leadership to transform knowledge work'. *Academy of Management Executive*, 18(1):47–57.

Porter, LW, & McLaughlin, GB. (2006). Leadership and the organizational context: Like the weather? *Leadership Quarterly*, 17, 559-576.

Rousseau, DM. 1989. 'Psychological contacts in organisations'. *Employee Responsibilities and Rights Journal*, 2(2):121–139.

Schneider, M. 2002. 'A stakeholder model of organisational leadership'. *Organisation Science*, 13(2):209–220.

Schneider, M & Somers, M. 2006. 'Organisations as complex adaptive systems: Implications of complexity theory for leadership research'. *The Leadership Quarterly*, 17:351–365.

Schreiber, C. and Carley, K.M. (2006). Leadership style as an enabler of organizational complex functioning, *Emergence: Complexity and Organization*, ISSN 1521- 7000, 8(4): 61-76.

Stacey, RD, Griffin, D & Shaw, P. 2000. *Complexity and management. Fad or radical challenge to systems thinking?* London, UK: Routledge.

Stacey, R. 2015. Understanding organisations as complex responsive processes of relating. In GR Bushe & RJ Marshak (eds). *Dialogic organisation development. The theory and practice of transformational change.* Oakland, CA: Berrett-Koehler. 151–176.

Storey, J (ed.) 2011. *Leadership in organisations. Current trends and issues.* 2nd ed. London, UK: Routledge.

van der Merwe, L & Verwey, A. 2016. *Building the corporate leadership community.* Randburg: KR Publishing.

Veldsman, TH. 2010. 'An organisation–person fit competency model appropriate to a newly emerging world of work'. *Human Capital Review*, June.

Veldsman, TH. 2011. 'Crafting and implementing strategic talent management in pursuit of sustainable talent excellence'. In I Boninelli & T Meyer (eds). *Human Capital Trends.* Johannesburg, Knowres Publishing. 359–390.

Veldsman, TH. 2013. *Leadership culture and climate – Enhancing or destroying leadership excellence within the leadership community? Towards a typology of different leadership cultures and climates infusing leadership communities with their consequential effect on the leadership building blocks and excellence.* Paper presented at 16th Congress of 2013 European Association Work and Organisational Psychology, 22–25 May, Münster, Germany.

Ward, A. 2003. *The leadership lifecycle. Matching leaders to evolving organisations,* Houndmills, UK: Palgrave Macmiillan.

Western, S. 2013. *Leadership. A critical text.* Los Angeles, CA: Sage.

Wheatley, MJ. 2010. *Leadership and the new science: Discovering order in a chaotic world.* 3rd ed. San Francisco, CA: Berrett-Koehler.

Winston, B & Patterson, K. 2005. *An integrative definition of leadership.* Working Paper, School of Leadership Studies, Regent University (UK).

SECTION 3

INTERPRETIVE LENS: APPRECIATIVE INQUIRY

Chapter 3

APPRECIATIVE LEADERSHIP

Freddie Crous

It could be argued that all leadership is appreciative leadership. It is the capacity to see the best in the world around us, in our colleagues, and in the groups we are trying to lead ... It's the capacity to see with an appreciative eye the true and the good, the better and the possible.

– David Cooperrider, who introduced appreciation
to the field of organisational behaviour

Leadership is one of the most studied concepts and also one of the most frequently searched-for topics on the Internet. However, the impact of the multi-billion dollar leadership development industry is questioned. Those in leadership positions are often ill-fitted for the job. Because of their positional/hierarchical power, leaders tend to exercise control by means of authority, which tends to inhibit human potential. An alternative way to lead is by means of origination – not to dictate from top down, but rather by facilitating others to 'rise' – to open up, to flourish. A particular 'originative' approach to leadership is appreciative leadership, which has its roots in the positive organisation development and change action research method of appreciative inquiry.

The purpose of this paper is to argue the case for an appreciative inquiry lens in viewing leadership. I proceed by, firstly, sketching a depreciative view of leadership; then move onto the too frequent situation of appreciating the wrong candidate for leading; then pose a reminder about a lonely voice from the past who propagated the case for: 'down with depreciative organising; up with appreciative organising': Douglas McGregor; then deal with the origins of appreciative inquiry; next discuss how to move from a deficit-based organisational problem-solving to an affirmative approach; profile the appreciable leader; and end off by answering the question whether a leader can be too appreciative.

A Depreciative View of Leadership

"The dirty little secret about leadership development is that it doesn't work," I overheard somebody at a leadership conference last year. This remark made me uneasy and got stuck in my head. As an academic in the field of Industrial and Organisational Psychology who sometimes facilitates leadership development in the private and public sectors, I could not shrug it off. It also primed me to spot the title of Jeffrey Pfeffer's newest book[1] first among more than a 100 titles on the business bookshelf at my favourite book store.

Pfeffer, well-known professor of organisational behaviour at the Stanford Graduate School of Business, is deeply cynical about leadership development and its impact. He laments that in spite of "many fabulously fantastic people with exceptional credentials and ethics working mightily to improve organisational workplaces and leaders' careers",[2] most of what the leadership industry offers is BS. It is an industry driven by money, rather than evidence-based, useful knowledge. Notwithstanding being a billion-dollar industry, its impact seems to be dismal. Workplaces are mostly toxic and stressful, with far too many dissatisfied, disengaged, alienated employees, and too many leaders and aspiring leaders losing their jobs.

To emphasise his pessimism, he quotes Barbara Kellerman of Harvard's Kennedy School and founder of the Centre for Public Leadership, who wrote that the leadership industry "has failed over its roughly forty year history to in any major, meaningful measureable way improve the human condition" and that "the rise of leadership as an object for our collective fascination has coincided precisely with the decline of leadership in our collective imagination".[3] Pfeffer concludes that organisational leaders often are toxic, and mostly in it for themselves. Even beneficent leaders should not be trusted because economic impermanence makes them unreliable. For the same reason, businesses do not promise much more these days and tend to break implicit contracts with their employees. He leaves the reader with the following guiding principle for personal career management: "Take care of yourself and assiduously look out for your own…"

Appreciating the Wrong Candidate for Leading

One of the most popular books on leadership is *Good to Great* by Jim Collins.[4] A former colleague of Pfeffer at Stanford University, Collins and his research team's surprising discovery was that the defining characteristic of great organisational leaders is personal humility, but blended with professional will. It seems that leaders of this kind have an extremely strong calling orientation.[5] Collins explains that these leaders channel their ego needs away from themselves into a larger goal of building a great organisation. They are incredibly ambitious. But not for themselves, always for the institution. Collins defines this kind of leader as being one who wants to *build* a level 5 leader.

Disturbingly, Collins found that level 5 leaders are almost always deselected for leadership positions in favour of egocentric people who want to *get* – be it power, money, status, adulation. And what's more – the person with narcissistic[i] [6] tendencies. He wrote: "… boards of directors frequently operate under the false belief that they need to hire a larger-than-life, egocentric leader to make an organization great … Level 5 leaders rarely appear at the top of our institutions".[7] Pfeffer confirms that research findings are overwhelmingly clear that the likelihood of a narcissist being selected for a leadership position is far greater than that of a modest person. The irony is that, according to Collins's findings, no sustainable, good-to-great transformations are possible without the qualities of a level 5 leader.

Evidence from extensive research findings by Pfeffer explains why narcissists obtain and hold on to leadership positions: it is the overlap between narcissistic characteristics and prototypical attributes associated with effective leaders, two of which are related to the psychological states of confidence and self-esteem. The two others are related to positional hierarchical power, namely authority and power.

The emerging science of embodied cognition, also referred to as conceptual metaphor theory, may help to make sense of this phenomenon.[8] In essence, it means that the mind is shaped and primed by the body. To be more specific, concepts are shaped by our bodies and brains, especially by our sensorimotor system.[9] As our bodies perceive and move in space, engaging with its environment, they are provided with certain primitive image schemas, one of which is vertical orientation. We humans have internalised the physical bodily experience of verticality in order to make sense psychologically to the extent that we have become spatially orientated to positioning everything that we regard to be good at the top (*up*) and everything that we perceive to be bad (negative) at the bottom (*down*).

The term *up* may therefore be regarded as the root metaphor for everything positive.

---

i   Narcissism should not be confused with charisma. Narcissistic leaders may project themselves as charismatic leaders. However, they eventually show themselves to be destructive and depreciative of others, because their motive for gathering power is for personal aggrandisement and they use their social skills and exceptional persuasive abilities for domineering and making their followers submissive. On the other hand, constructive charismatic leaders are directed to serving, empowering and transforming their followers.

Leadership is *up*, but so is power, and so are the positive states of confidence and self-esteem.[10] Many would (wrongly so) regard humility to be a weakness (*down*), while it is in fact a strength (*up*).[11] It seems that having conflated leadership, hierarchical power, authority, confidence and self-esteem with the larger-than-life image of the narcissist has cost many an organisational stakeholder dearly.

A Lonely Voice from the Past: 'Down with Depreciative Organising. Up with Appreciative Organising'

For the elevation of the state of the leadership industry, Pfeffer advocates for more science, in particular more social science. In addition, he emphasises that those who want to change the world should focus and act more on what is known (= the descriptive), and less on what we hope for (= the normative).[12]

This is exactly what another prominent academic did many decades ago. In 1960, the MIT professor, Douglas McGregor, published a thorough, descriptive, yet critical study (from a social science perspective) on the state of management and leadership practised in business. McGregor condemned the way businesses were organised way back then. Interestingly, he pointed out that verticality was (and mostly still is) at the core of business organising:[13]

"If there is a single assumption which pervades conventional organisational theory, it is that authority is the central, indispensable means of managerial control. This is the basic principle of organisation in the textbook theory of management. The very structure of the organisation is a hierarchy of authoritative relationships. The terms *up* and *down* within the structure refer to a *scale of authority*. Most of the other principles of organisation [...] are directly derived from this one" (emphasis in the original).[14]

Leaders and managers (positioned at the top of the organisation, having power and authority) tend to construct a particular theory of human nature. McGregor coined this as Theory X which, according to him, consists of a number of remarkably pervasive and implicit (that is, non-conscious) assumptions which the manager holds as quoted below, and given in the accompanying box.

> 1. *"The average human being has an inherent dislike of work and will avoid it if he can.*
> 2. *Because of this human characteristic of dislike of work, most people must be coerced, controlled, directed, threatened with punishment to get them to put forth adequate effort toward the achievement of organizational objectives.*
> 3. *The average human being prefers to be directed, wishes to avoid responsibility, has relatively little ambition, wants security above all."* [15]

In essence, Theory X suggests that by metaphorically looking *down* on those at the lower levels in the organisational hierarchy, managers/leaders are bound to form a depreciative view of their "subordinates". This may still be the case even today, regardless of the fact that almost every manager/leader would contest such a claim. However, considering the nature of human resource strategies, policies and practices, Theory X appears to be still the theory in use. McGregor pointed out that aligned to Theory X is a 'carrot-and-stick' theory of motivation for the management of performance, undermining workers' intrinsic motivation.

How did this state of division between organisation leadership and members develop? More or less 6 000 years ago, when societies numbered around 1 000 people, it was possible for a single individual – with a dominant personality, or the physical power to take control – to position himself at the top. He ruled by controlling power through a rank-based structure. Since then we have maintained a hierarchical society in general, as manifests in hierarchical organisations.[16] This top-down development is in sharp contrast to the way in which systems in the world tend to develop: they emerge from the bottom up; or put differently, they unfold from the inside out,[17] allowing for the possibility to flourish.

Based on social science knowledge from 60 years ago, McGregor suggested an appreciative alternative to Theory X, with its depreciative assumptions about human nature and behaviour. Named Theory Y, it consists of the appreciative assumptions, quoted below in the accompanying box.

4.	*The expenditure of physical and mental effort in work is as natural as play or rest.* The average human being does not inherently dislike work. Depending upon controllable conditions, work may be a source of satisfaction (and will be voluntarily performed) or a source of punishment (and will be avoided if possible).
5.	*External control and the threat of punishment are not the only means for bringing about effort towards organizational objectives. Man will exercise self-direction and self-control in the service of objectives to which he is committed.*
6.	*Commitment to objectives is a function of the rewards associated with their achievement.* The most significant of such rewards, for example, the satisfaction of ego and self-actualisation needs, can be direct products of effort directed towards organisational objectives.
7.	*The average human being learns, under proper conditions, not only to accept but to seek responsibility.* Avoidance of responsibility, lack of ambition, and emphasis on security are generally consequences of experience, not inherent human characteristics.
8.	*The capacity to exercise a relatively high degree of imagination, ingenuity, and creativity in the solution of organizational problems is widely, not narrowly, distributed in the population.*
9.	*Under conditions of modern industrial life, the intellectual potentialities of the average human being are only partially utilized.*"[18]

According to McGregor, whereas the central principle of organisation which derives from Theory X is that if direction and control exist through the exercise of authority, the central principle deriving from Theory Y is that of integration: "… [t]he creation of conditions such that the members of the organisation can achieve their own goals *best* by directing their efforts towards the success of the enterprise".[19] This requires all organisation members to commit to working together for the success of the enterprise, so that all may share in the fruits of its achievements. Authority – which McGregor admits to be sometimes appropriate – is, of course, an inappropriate means for obtaining this kind of commitment.

McGregor was a voice in the wilderness. It took many years for another academic to invite leaders and managers to approach organising appreciatively.

The Origins of Appreciative Inquiry

The typical, intuitive approach that organisational leaders and managers take to bring about change is to identify what they think is the central *problem* prohibiting change. What mostly follows is that the professional help of an organisational behaviour consultant/psychologist is contracted to conduct action research in order to diagnose the causes of the problem and to identify interventions appropriate for targeting these.

In a quest to better their services, the board of the Cleveland Clinic – despite being one of the best public hospitals in the world – suggested that the following question should drive their organisational change project: What is wrong with the human side of the Cleveland Clinic?

David Cooperrider, a young doctoral student in organisational behaviour at Case Western Reserve University's School of Management in Cleveland, Ohio, was afforded the opportunity of conducting the required action research in this hospital. He had great expectations for his project, but these were soon to be dampened. In his experience, problem diagnosis and feedback were energy depleting. The more people were made aware of their problems, the more discouraged and dispirited they became.

This approach had a particularly negative impact relationally: higher levels of problem awareness gave way to higher levels of blaming and defensive behaviours.[20] Cooperrider discovered that the unintended consequences of problem-focused action research is that, by amplifying the problem, the people affected by it tend to become overwhelmed by it, or they resist efforts to change the problem. Moreover, informed by the work of the world's thought leader on social constructionism, Kenneth Gergen, he came to the realisation that as people focus on what is wrong with their organisations – weaknesses and deficiencies – they create vocabularies of deficits, which may reinforce the negatives which they had hoped to eliminate.

Despondent, Cooperrider was on the verge of giving up a career in organisation development and change. However, while busy with his action research, he had begun reading the autobiography of Albert Schweitzer (1969), the Nobel Laureate. He was captivated by Albert's notion of a reverence for all life. David questioned whether he was giving life to the organisation by constantly interrogating what was wrong with the staff and management working at the hospital. While gathering data, he observed something which gave him hope: high levels of co-operation, innovation and egalitarian governance.[21] Despite being eager to work with the identified organisational strengths, Cooperrider could not do so since these did not address the problem-focused question of his research.

In a conversation with his doctoral supervisor, Prof Suresh Srivastva, Cooperrider expressed his frustration with action research as limiting because of its problem-orientated view of the world. In his view it incapacitates both researchers and practitioners in constructing novel theory suited to engendering the inspirational commitment and passionate dialogue required for fundamental organisational change.

With the support of his supervisor and the hospital's chairman, Cooperrider made the decision to move away from a problem-solving approach towards "what gives life" to the system. His final report to the hospital board highlighted generative themes, extracted from what he had discovered, namely "moments of success, experiences of high points, stories of innovation, hope, courage and 'positive change'".[22] This transformation of the traditional action research model had an immediate and dramatic effect on the participants. Relationships and co-operation improved, and measurable performance reached an all-time high.

In a footnote to his feedback report to the board of directors, Cooperrider referred to the approach he had taken as an "appreciative inquiry". Its assumption is clear:

"Every organisation has something that works right – things that give it life when it is most alive, effective, successful, and connected in healthy ways to its stakeholders and communities. Appreciative Inquiry begins by identifying what is positive and connecting to it in ways that heighten energy, vision, and action for change.[23] To appreciate, quite simply, means to value and to recognise that which has value – it is a way of knowing and valuing the best in life. [...] It is a way of being and maintaining a positive stance along the path of life's journey. And not incidentally, to appreciate is to increase in value too. Appreciative Inquiry is simultaneously a life-centric form of study and a constructive mode of practice."[24]

Moving from a Deficit-Based Organisational Problem-Solving Approach to an Affirmative Approach

Appreciative inquiry therefore moves from a deficit-based organisational problem-solving approach to an affirmative approach embracing and committing to the organisation as it is. From an appreciative stance, organisations are not viewed as machines that need to be fixed. They need continuous reaffirmation.

For the application of appreciative inquiry, this constructive, highly participative action research process is started by choosing an *affirmative topic* (this may begin with a problem which is then reframed into the positive). Related to the topic, for the *discovery phase*, unconditional positive questions are crafted, which, by means of interviews in pairs and group discussions, culminate in the identification of the organisation's positive core. This provides for the participants to continue to the *dream phase*, moving them to envision a positive future for themselves and their organisation. In order to make their dream a reality, an *architecture for action* is developed in the design phase which is to be delivered. The delivery phase is also referred to as the *destiny phase*: inviting the participants to make appreciative inquiry their destiny, providing for an upward cycle of continuous positive change.

Because of its dialogic nature – in contrast to the diagnostic nature of the traditional action research method – appreciative inquiry, apart from being used for organisation development and change purposes, is applied for a myriad change agendas. But it is by means of appreciative leadership that positive change in organisations is sustained.[25]

The appreciative leader, however, does not approach organisation members from a position of authority. Whitney suggests appreciative leadership is "a relationally grounded, dialogically expressed form of leadership … that focuses on bringing out the best of people, organisations and communities, through conscious acts of discovery, dream and design".[26] In a later work she and her co-authors[27] define appreciative leadership as "the relational capacity to mobilize creative potential and turn it into positive power – to set in motion positive ripples of confidence, energy, enthusiasm, and performance – to make a positive difference in the world".

Based on their research into appreciative leadership and their extensive application of the appreciative method in the domain of leadership, they identified five areas of relational practice, which they refer to as the five core strategies of appreciative leadership. These core strategies are identified and discussed below.[28]

Inquiry: Ask positively powerful questions

This lets people know that the leader values them and their contributions. Appreciative leadership is therefore inquiry based. Recognising that people and groups move in the direction of what they study, appreciative leadership puts forth [constructive] questions more often than prescriptions.

Illumination: Bring out the best of people

This helps people understand how they can contribute. Appreciative leadership therefore sees people and the world as they are – for better and for worse; and it chooses to live and work in the energetically positive, to bring out the best.

Inclusion: Engage with people to co-author the future

This gives people a sense of belonging. By being inclusive, engaging, and inviting, appreciative leadership extends its relational reach in order to ensure that everyone whose future it is has a voice in creating the future. It fosters enquiry and dialogue across divides and among improbable pairs.

Inspiration: Awaken the creative spirit

This provides people with a sense of direction. By being inspiring and life-affirming, appreciative leadership unleashes the creative spirit and gives hope for the future. In so doing, it mobilises people's hearts, minds and hands towards visions of a better world.

Integrity: Make choices for the good of the whole

This lets people know that they are expected to give their best for the greater good, and that they can trust others to do the same. By being integral and holistic, appreciative leadership holds forth integrity. It lives, works, and serves in support of human well-being, life-affirming organisations, and a sustainable world.

Appreciative leadership has 'originative' consequences in that it opens up possibilities for flourishing. Whitney and her co-authors suggest that by being a practising appreciative leader, you will *cultivate your character* by realising your inherent positive core. You will be able to *liberate others' creative potential*. By holding all people in positive regard you will coach and facilitate others in such a way that you bring out the best in them. Through strengths-based inquiry, dialogue, and communication you will liberate the creativity of others. The practising appreciative leader *fosters engagement and collaboration across divided lines* towards creating a shared future. As a practising appreciative leader you *design innovative social structures* which are life-giving – influencing optimal performance and experience – and ultimately you facilitate positive change.

As these authors conclude: Everything that appreciative leadership does *focuses on positive change*: from personal development to coaching to large-scale transformation. They are adamant that appreciative leaders make a positive difference by using appreciative inquiry.[ii]

The Appreciable Leader

Schnall indicates that because of the experience of verticality, the mind is pulled up to higher values. People use the vertical dimension to distinguish between virtue and vice.[29] The example she uses is of an *upstanding* person (a metaphor for being ethical) as opposed to the *lowlife* of society. Some charismatic leaders embody positivity to the extent that they have a positive *physical* effect on others. Lord and Brown[30] quote the former leading member of President Bill Clinton's presidential campaign and later senior advisor in his administration, George Stephanopoulos's (1999) recollection of his earliest encounter with Clinton: "*But I was moved more by more than what he stood for or how much he knew. It was how I felt around him* ..." Some years later Clinton (2006), in turn, wrote about the positive effect (embedded in the dimension of verticality) which President Mandela had on him and others: "Every time Nelson Mandela walks into a room we

---

ii For information about appreciative inquiry visit the Appreciative Inquiry Commons web site hosted by Case Western Reserve University, where David Cooperrrider is a professor in the Weatherhead School of Management.

all feel a little bigger, we all want to stand up, we all want to cheer, because we want to be him on our best day."[31]

Leaders of this kind may be referred to as originative leaders. They affect others on a visceral level, making them want to rise up: to feel elevated in their presence, wanting to emulate what these leaders do, moving them to be generative. In line with Barbara Fredrickson's (2003)[32] work on positive emotions, one may argue that such leaders broaden and build others' thinking and action repertoires. This kind of effect is not brought about by authority. Lord and Brown[33] suggest that it is through followers' positive relational experiences of leaders that leader-impact is determined.

Can a Leader be too Appreciative?

I recently reported the following in the *Appreciative Inquiry Practitioner*.[34] In a 2014 literature study, a former Master's student of mine, Charlotte Crisp, found that many organisations which strive towards high employee engagement do so by encouraging those in leadership positions to employ appreciative behaviours alongside their task-orientated leadership behaviours. As such, the regression line between appreciative leadership and employee engagement should be linear, suggesting that as appreciative leadership increases, so will employee engagement.

Then we stumbled upon the work of Kaplan and Kaiser,[35] which suggests that an individual (for example, a manager or leader) may demonstrate too little optimal, or too much, appreciation – each of which may have a unique effect on the organisation's employees. Moreover, the authors postulate that too much of a good thing – such as being too appreciative – can actually be detrimental to both the individual and the organisation. My colleague Deon de Bruin and I subsequently challenged Charlotte to test Kaplan and Kaiser's suggestion that the relationship between appreciative leadership and work engagement is curvilinear, meaning that too much or too little appreciative leadership is negatively related to work engagement, while optimal appreciative leadership is positively related to work engagement.

She took up the challenge and developed the Appreciative Leadership Questionnaire with the aim of measuring five strategies of appreciative leadership: inquiry, illumination, inspiration, inclusion and integrity.[36] Each strategy was measured using two items. The scale therefore consisted of a total of ten items. Each item presented the participants with a scenario. The questionnaire required the participants to select one of three responses (in each case) that best described how their leader would most likely react in a given situation.

The three possible responses were structured to represent a team leader/floor manager who is respectively unappreciative, optimally appreciative, or overly appreciative. An example of an item from this questionnaire is:

"I feel overwhelmed, because I believe that I do not have the skills required to successfully complete my work tasks. I approach my team leader to explain this. My boss is most likely to ..."

The participants were required to choose one of the following responses:

"(a) highlight my weaknesses or skill deficiencies; (b) highlight my strengths, and align them with compatible and attainable target outcomes; or (c) overemphasise my strengths."

For the measurement of work engagement the UWES-9 was used.[37] This is a shortened version of the Utrecht Work Engagement Scale (UWES) developed by Schaufeli and Bakker.[38] The scale, which has sound metric properties, measures work engagement in terms of three factors: vigour, dedication and absorption. Charlotte conducted her research at a call centre in Gauteng province in South Africa. Her sample (*n* = 171) consisted of call centre agents and their team leaders.

The results of Charlotte's study do not support Kaplan and Kaiser's claim that the relationship between appreciative leadership and work engagement is not curvilinear, but linear: as appreciative leadership increases, so does work engagement. Furthermore, the results show that there are, indeed, only two significant categories of appreciative leadership, namely under-appreciation and over-appreciation. Charlotte's study implies that there cannot be too much appreciative leadership if the aim is to increase work engagement. Moreover, as far as her findings are concerned, there appears to be no optimal level of appreciative leadership.

Conclusion

I would like to end this chapter with another dirty little secret. Employees do not particularly appreciate organisational leaders, because they do not feel appreciated by their leaders. I have discovered this from having had access to a number of organisations' annual organisational culture surveys. The irony is that managers and leaders know this very well from the feedback they get. They react by shrugging it off, feel incapacitated, or simply do not have the energy and time to face up to this reality. Appreciative leadership is an invitation to change this sad situation.

Endnotes

1	Pfeffer, 2015.
2	See endnote 1.
3	See endnote 1, p. 5.
4	Collins, 2001.
5	Wrzesniewski, 2012.
6	Zaccaro, 2004.
7	See endnote 5, pp. 36 & 37.
8	Landau & Robinson, 2014.
9	Lakoff & Johnson, 1999.
10	See endnote 9.
11	Peterson & Seligman, 2004.
12	See endnote 1.
13	McGregor, 1960.
14	See endnote 13, p. 18.
15	See endnote 13, pp. 33–34.
16	Nielsen, 2004.
17	Ridley, 2015.
18	See endnote 13, pp. 47–49.
19	See endnote 13, p. 49.
20	Ludema, Whitney, Mohr & Griffen, 2003.
21	Watkins & Mohr, 2001.
22	Ludema et al., 2003, p. 6.
23	Cooperrider, Whitney & Stavros, 2008, p. xv.
24	Cooperrider & Avital, 2004, p. xii.
25	Mantel & Ludema, 2004.
26	Whitney, D. 2008, p. 338.
27	Whitney, Trosten-Bloom & Rader, 2010, p. 3.
28	See endnote 26, pp. 23–24, 205.
29	Schnall, 2014.
30	Lord & Brown, 2004.
31	Perkin, 2006, p. 1.
32	Fredrickson, 2003.
33	Lord & Brown, 2004.
34	Crous, 2016.
35	Kaplan & Kaiser, 2009, 2013.
36	Whitney, Trosten-Bloom & Rader, 2010.
37	Schaufeli, Bakker & Salanova, 2006.
38	Schaufeli & Bakker, 2004.

References

Collins, J. 2001. *Good to great*. New York, NY: Harper Business.

Cooperrider, DL & Avital, M. 2004. 'Introduction: Advances in appreciative inquiry – constructive discourses and human organization'. *Advances in Appreciative Inquiry*. Vol. 1. Oxford, UK: Elsevier.

Cooperrrider, DL, Whitney, D & Stavros, JM. 2008. *Appreciative inquiry handbook for leaders of change*. 2nd ed. San Francisco, CA: Berrett-Koehler.

Crous, F. 2016. Can a leader be too appreciative? *AI Practitioner: International Journal of Appreciative Inquiry*, 18(1).

Fredrickson, BL. 2003. 'Positive emotions and upwards spirals in organizations'. In KS Cameron, JE Dutton & RE Quinn (eds). *Positive organizational scholarship: Foundations of a new discipline*. San Francisco, CA: Berrett-Koehler.

Lakoff, G & Johnson, M. 1999. *Philosophy in the flesh: The embodied mind and its challenge to western thought*. New York, NY: Basic Books.

Landau, MJ, Robinson, MD & Meier, BP. 2014. 'Introduction'. In MJ Landau, MD Robinson & BP Meier (eds). The *power of metaphor: Examining its influence on social life.* Washington, DC: American Psychological Association.

Lord, GL & Brown, DJ. 2004. *Leadership processes and follower self-identity.* Mahwah, NJ: Lawrence Erlbaum.

Ludema, JD, Whitney, D, Mohr, BJ & Griffin, TJ. 2003. *The appreciative inquiry summit: A practitioner's guide for leading large group change.* San Francisco, CA: Berrett-Koehler.

Mantel, MJ. & Ludema, JD. 2004. 'Sustaining positive change: Inviting conversational convergence through appreciative leadership and organisation design'. *Advances in Appreciative Inquiry.* Vol. 1.

McGregor, D. 1960. *The human side of enterprise.* New York, NY: McGraw-Hill.

Nielsen, JS. 2004. *The myth of leadership: Creating leaderless organizations.* Mountain View, CA: Davies Black.

Parkin, K (ed). 2006. *Mandela: The authorized portrait.* Johannesburg, RSA: Wild Dog Press.

Peterson, C & Seligman, MEP. 2004. *Character strengths and virtues: A handbook and classification.* Oxford, UK: Oxford University Press.

Pfeffer, J. 2015. *Leadership BS: Fixing workplaces and careers one truth at a time.* New York, NY: Harper Business.

Ridley, M. 2015. *The evolution of everything: How new ideas emerge.* London, UK: Fourth Estate.

Schaufeli, WB., Bakker, AB., & Salanova, M. 2006. The measurement of work engagement with a short questionnaire. A cross-national study. Educational and Psychological Measurement, 66, 701–716. doi:10.1177/0013164405282471.

Schaufeli, WB., Bakker, AB., & Salanova, M. 2006. The measurement of work engagement with a short questionnaire. A cross-national study. Educational and Psychological Measurement, 66, 701–716. doi: 10.1177/0013164405282471.

Schaufeli, WB., Bakker, AB., & Salanova, M. 2006. The measurement of work engagement with a short questionnaire. A cross-national study. Educational and Psychological Measurement, 66, 701–716. doi: 10.1177/0013164405282471.

Schaufeli, WB. & Bakker, AB. 2004. Job demands, job resources, and their relationship with burnout and engagement: A multi-sample study. *Journal of Organizational Behavior,* 25, 293315.

Schaufeli, WB., Bakker, AB. & Salanova, M. 2006. The measurement of work engagement with a short questionnaire: A cross-national study. *Educational and Psychological Measurement,* 66, 701716.

Schnall, S. 2014. 'Are there basic metaphors?' In MJ Landau, MD Robinson & BP Meier (eds). *The power of metaphor: Examining its influence in social life.* Washington, DC: American Psychological Association.

Whitney, D. 2008. 'Designing organizations as if life matters: Principles of appreciative organizing'. *Designing information and organizations with a positive lens. Vol 2: Advances in appreciative inquiry.* 329–363. doi:10.1016/s1475-9152(07)00216-5.

Whitney, D, Trosten-Bloom, A & Rader, K. 2010. *Appreciative leadership: Focus on what works to drive winning performance and build a thriving organization.* Toronto: McGraw Hill Professional. 3.

Wrzesniewski, A. 2012. 'Callings'. In KS Cameron & GM Spreitzer. *The Oxford handbook of positive scholarship.* Oxford, UK: Oxford University Press.

Zaccaro, SJ. 2004. 'Leadership'. In C Peterson and MEP Seligman. *Character strengths and virtues: A handbook and classification.* Oxford, UK: Oxford University Press.

SECTION 4

ACTION LENSES

Chapter 4

NEUROSCIENCE IN LEADERSHIP

Ingra du Buisson-Narsal with Dan Radecki

"We must recollect that all of our provisional ideas in psychology will presumably one day be based on an organic substructure." – Sigmund Freud

As technology continues to evolve, neuroscience is able to become more precise in its quest to understand the biology behind human behaviour. The field of leadership development has been reinvigorated with the potential applications coming out of the field of neuroscience. The fact that leadership has a broad definition (for example, parent, teacher, coach, among others) makes the brain-based leadership space a discipline of great public interest and numerous possible applications, because we are all, to some extent, leaders.

This chapter will introduce some of the key principles which underlie 'how' the brain sees our world and 'why' it reacts the way it does in governing our behaviours, decisions and reactions. Since we all have a brain, this information is universally relevant and can help us understand how to better manage the limitations inherent in a brain that hasn't evolved at the rapid pace at which our society has evolved. Importantly, we will also focus on the practical applications derived from this information, such as, what tangible actions can I take in order to lead in a truly 'brain-friendly' manner?

Following are the topics that will be discussed in in this chapter. They will serve as a reference to the basic information one will need to embark on the journey of cultivating neurally-aware leadership:

- Neuroscience as a lens into leadership: Superfluous or substantive?
- Brain basics – information processing in the brain
- Neuroscience thinking frameworks applicable to leadership
- Five neuroscience insights that are changing our leadership world
- Neurally-aware leadership
- Brain-centric leadership behaviours
- Brain diagnostics.

A glossary of technical terms is also supplied at the end of the chapter.

Neuroscience as a Lens into Leadership: Superfluous or Substantive?

Neuroscience pertains to the science that investigates the relationship between mental processes and the pattern of electrical activity in the neural networks of the brain. Contemporary neuroscience is beginning to provide a scientific platform to support various organisational processes such as leadership, learning, coaching, communication, and change management.[1]

The emerging fields of Integrated Organisational Neuroscience, Social Cognitive Affective Neuroscience, and Organisational Cognitive Neuroscience all aim to apply neuroscientific methods in order to examine and understand human behaviour within the applied settings of organisations: the individual, the group, and organisational or inter-organisational levels. There is also an increasing interest in leadership research in turning to more fundamental characteristics, specifically neurobiologically based factors, as likely determinants of leadership behaviours and qualities.[2]

The brain has gone mainstream, and the field of neuroscience is becoming a compelling option for understanding leadership behaviour. However, an oversimplification of neuroscience-based research can render the study of anything 'neuro-' as a short-lived movement.[3] In a research report entitled 'Superfluous Neuroscience Information Makes Explanations of Psychological Phenomena More Appealing', it was found that when neuroscience-based information that offered no auxiliary insight was added to the end of descriptions such as 'face recognition' and 'emotional states', students rated the statements more highly.[4]

Although methodological limitations exist, and given that a unifying theory of the brain still seems a long way off,[5] the implications of neuroscience phenomena for leadership behaviours are nevertheless noteworthy. A neuroscientific lens can explain to a limited extent the underpinning biology behind leadership behaviour which can result in leaders being more open to developing new skills, because the metaphor of the brain is a more acceptable and 'safe' language for most leaders. Identifying and refining the behavioural anchors of a brain-centric approach to leadership will contribute to bridging the 'knowing' versus 'doing' gap in this new field.

Brain Basics

We are at the beginning of understanding the architecture and connectivity of our brains. In this brief section, we look at the basic structure and processes that enable communication in the brain.

Information processing in the brain

The brain constitutes just 2% of body mass but taps into 20% of the body's energy resource through cognitive demands that draw more oxygenated blood into the brain, as neurons (electrically active nerve cells) need fuel to fire. To conserve energy consumption, the brain has developed ways to process information, such as the capacity to store learned skills in deep subconscious structures of the brain, where they can be automatically retrieved when needed. The exceptionally low energy cost of this highly refined process enables the rest of the brain to optimise the use of oxygen and glucose in order to acquire fresh knowledge and solve complex problems creatively.

The brain comprises of approximately 100 billion neurons. These neurons make up the basic building blocks of the brain and are also known as grey matter. The brain also contains billions of nerve fibres called axons and dendrites, which are identified as white matter. The neurons are connected by trillions of connections called *synapses*. The synapses are minuscule spaces between sending and receiving neurons, called synaptic clefts. Brain functioning is the result of neurons firing and triggering (or activating) each other by using an electrochemical process, all the while constantly monitoring and modifying these connections to maintain optimal processing.

An electrochemical symphony: what brain waves can tell us

From moment to moment during the day our electrical brain wave patterns fluctuate between beta, alpha and theta wavebands without our conscious control. Each of these dominant states has associated neurochemicals, which we experience as bodily sensations and emotions.

EEG readings provide a measure of brain activity which produce electrical fields that have a quantifiable number of cycles per second or frequencies. There are 5 common categories of brainwaves, and each is identified by the number of up/down wave cycles measured per second. Different brainwave frequencies trigger different neurotransmitters.

Figure 4.1 gives an overview of the the effects when each of these 5 types is the most active in the brain.

Delta	0 – 3Hz	Delta is the slowest brainwave type, and is dominant during deep, restorative sleep. High levels of delta during sleep show a deeper, more stable sleep state.
Theta	3 – 8Hz	Light sleep or extreme relaxation. Experienced meditators demonstrate higher theta power during their peak practice, in very tranquil states with almost no "mental chatter".
Alpha	8 – 12Hz	Relaxed wakefulness. Mental states dominated by alpha are commonly described as calm and pleasant- sometimes accompanied by a "floating" feeling.
Beta	12 – 27Hz	Wide awake. Higher beta power is linked to emotional stability, increased energy levels, and focused states of extended concentration.
Gamma	27 or more Hz	Gamma is associated with the formation of ideas, memory processing and learning. Humans and apes are the only living creatures that produce gamma waves.

Figure 4.1: Categories of Brainwaves
Source: (Smyk, 2003)

A practical example of this electrochemical interplay is when a leader battles to concentrate. Problems with concentration can indicate a dopamine deficiency. Dopamine production can be stimulated by calming and relaxing the mind. The moment you experience a hyper-focused state, there are accompanying feelings of agitation and irritation, because dopamine has now been converted into adrenaline. This process cannot be reversed. You need to be aware that adrenaline causes memory to deteriorate. The best way to deal with this type of situation is to take a break and do some relaxing, such as diaphragmatic breathing, for at least five minutes. That will help achieve the calm, integrated state of focus needed for problem-solving.

When the brainwave frequency distribution is harmoniously balanced, one is calm, focused and 'in the zone'. This refers to a parasympathetic state in the central nervous system and optimal physical, intellectual, emotional, and spiritual functioning – 'flow state' or 'peak performance'. Instead of unnecessary and continuous adrenaline production, the body automatically starts producing the chemical substances which help one to experience physical well-being, energy, happiness, contentment, and joy.

You cannot control the waves, but you can learn to surf

The brain receives information via electrical impulses regarding the body's chemical balance, temperature, oxygen use, and so on. This mass of raw data activates chemical whirlwinds and streams of electrical discharges. These sparks run up and down the spidery webs of nerve cells. When an impulse arrive at the brain, the cortex organises the raw data, creating even more complex patterns or electrochemical impulses in order to make the data meaningful. The cortex does not inform us as to how this continuous data processing happens in its grey matter. We can get a glimpse of it through the kind of EEG information used in neuro-feedback training. Through this knowledge, leaders can learn to change their experience of 'reality' by consciously controlling the nature of the electrical activity in the brain. Just being aware of somatic markers such as breathing rate and consciously regulating the rate through slower breathing can automatically quieten down the mind.

Thinking Frameworks for Neuroscience-Based Leadership

Various thinking frameworks and models exist to explain brain functioning. We focus on those that can be applied to the manifestations of the brain in the workplace and their application to leadership behaviour, namely the triune brain model, large-scale network models, and the integrative neuroscience model.

The triune brain model

Neuroscientist Paul MacLean proposed a model of the development of the vertebrate forebrain – the *triune brain* as shown in Figure 4.2.[6] The triune brain model offers a broad theory of brain evolution, or more precisely, how the collection of neurons forms various structures and regions. MacLean called the evolutionary layers the reptilian, the paleomammalian and the neomammalian brains which parallel the structures of the brain stem, limbic system, and neocortex, with each layer having increasingly complex functionality. According to the triune model lower order, more primitive processes tend to override more advanced cognitive processes.[7] This is because, as mentioned earlier, the brain strives to conserve energy and reverts to established patterns and habits engrained in those 'older' regions.

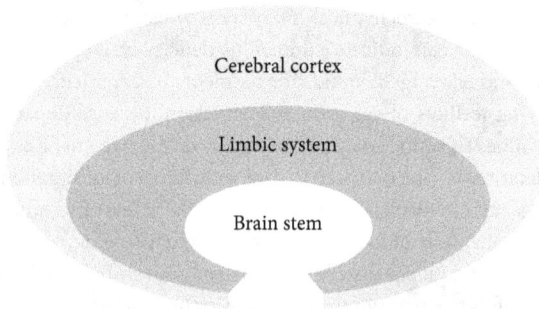

Figure 4.2: Three-layer model of the brain

Source: MacLean, 1990[8]

Though it is easy to see the three layers of the brain, from brain stem, to limbic system, to the cerebral cortex, as separate functional areas processing living functions, emotional processing and higher functions, these meta-regions are all linked together and process information in parallel and with the help of each other.

Implications of the triune brain model for leadership behaviour

The triune brain model implies that the three regions (brain stem, limbic system and cerebral cortex) are highly interconnected. The prefrontal cortex (PFC) is involved in regulating the limbic system. Figure 4.3 depicts a functional model of the limbic system. If there are enduring stressful events (for example, a working relationship filled with conflict, or bullying by a superior) the capacity of the prefrontal cortex to down-regulate the limbic system is diminished. There is chronic activation in the amygdala in response to the ongoing negative stimuli. In addition, the amygdala will adapt to this chronic activation by becoming stronger, thereby perpetuating a vicious cycle leading to an increased stress response and diminished capacity for PFC regulation.

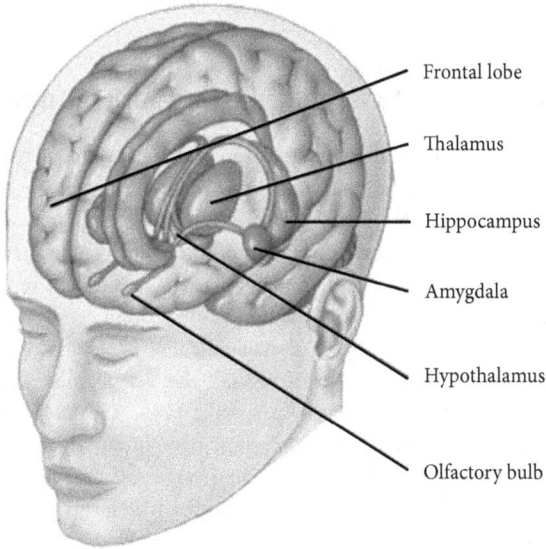

Figure 4.3: The brain's limbic system

This can create over-activation of the stress response, which then results in the production of stress hormones, which in turn leads to a reduction in the form and function of the brain's memory centre, also known as the *hippocampus*. The hippocampus belongs to the limbic system and plays a key role in the consolidation of information from short-term memory to long-term memory. Neuronal volume loss in the hippocampus manifests in the following ways: short-term memory diminishes, emotional volatility kicks in, and problem-solving ability diminishes. With diminished hippocampal capacity, the PFC's capability to reappraise negative stimuli and find solutions successfully is weakened.

As a result, cognitive control over emotions for down-regulation of the limbic system is compromised, and to avoid further violations of fundamental physiological needs, the avoidance-motivational schemas will be activated.[9]

An example of this principle at work may be observed when a perfectionist leader is under a chronically high cognitive load. When another stressor is added, the PFC, which is already activated but has a limited blood supply and, therefore, limited energy, cannot immediately send a message to the limbic system to down-regulate. Much of the blood is already in the limbic system because of the earlier stress and not available for the PFC. This stops blood going to the thinking part of the brain, and the leader struggles to think clearly. The leader therefore falls back on autopilot tendencies or thinking biases.

If the negative 'unsafe' environment persists, the only other option will ultimately be avoidance or 'freezing', which could mean that an affected leader engages only in safe initiatives with limited impact on both organisational growth and team engagement. Sometimes over-arousal occurs, and aggressive behaviour may be the consequence.[10]

To sum up, the theoretical approach of MacLean indicated that human brain development happens in line with these three complexes. Although the triune brain hypothesis of MacLean has now been replaced with more sophisticated models,[11][12][13][14] it provided a foundational knowledge in that it showed that there is a sequence to brain development. This sequence of brain development has a significant effect on neural firing and information flow in the brain as well giving insight into the manifestation of pathogenetic conditions such as narcissism, schizophrenia, and other mental disorders.[15][16]

From functional models to large-scale network models of the brain

We now know that psychological functions do not map directly onto spatially localised brain structures in a one-on-one fashion. Rather, numerous brain areas work together in a spatially distributed way to execute a mental function also known as a large-scale brain network.[17]A large-scale brain network is defined as 'a collection of interconnected brain areas that interact to perform circumscribed functions'.[18] Certain networks act as controllers or task switchers that co-ordinate, direct and synchronise the participation of other brain networks.

On the other hand, other brain networks enable the flow of sensory or motor information and participate in the conscious execution of tasks.[19] The default mode network (DMN) is what the brain does when it is not engaged in specific tasks. The DMN – shown below in Figure 4.4 – comprises an integrated system for autobiographical, self-monitoring, and social cognitive functions. This is also called the mentalising system of the brain. The DMN is also responsible for REST (rapid episodic spontaneous thinking), which forms part of mind wandering.

The Salience Network – indicated in Figure 4.4 in yellow – is a controller or network switcher. The controller decides which information is most important and which should receive priority in the queue of brain signals waiting to be sent, based on the task at hand. The central executive network – shown in Figure 4.4 in red – is engaged in higher order cognitive and attentional control. This is also called the analysing system.

When these networks are in synchrony, optimum brain performance is the result. When synchrony is poor, efficient and normal cognition and motor behaviour are compromised.

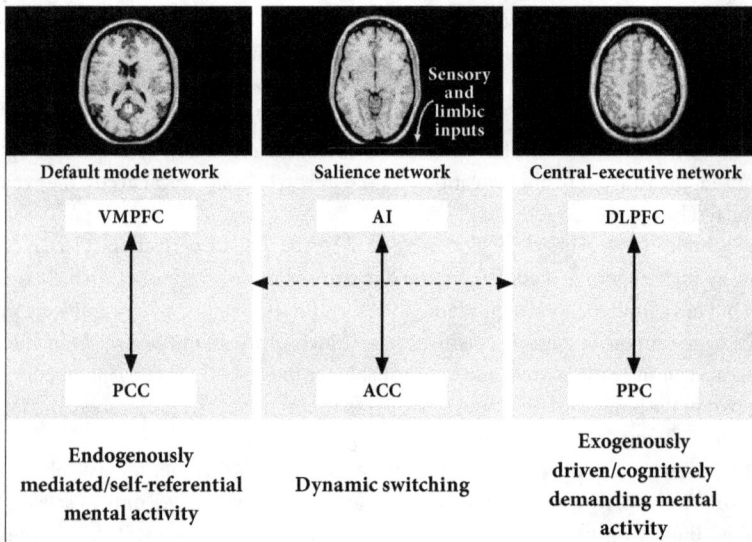

Figure 4.4: Large-scale networks of the brain
Source: Bressler & Menon, 2010[20]

An integrative organisational neuroscience model

The integrative neuroscience approach brings together crucial organising principles across scales of brain function. This has resulted in the INTEGRATE or 124 model, which outlines the brain's core motivations and key functional modes.[21] The 124 model is a framework for explaining brain performance:

- The brain's **one** core organising principle is safety first. Thus the brain wires itself to survive rather than to thrive.[22]
- The brain has **two** modes of processing: conscious, which is rational, verbal, and detail orientated; and non-conscious, which is intuitive and based on awareness of and response to external cues.
- The brain's **four** key underlying processes are emotions (responses to threat or reward signals), thinking (focusing, memorising, and planning), feelings (physiological changes in heart rate, breathing, and perspiration), and successful self-regulation of these functions. All these highly interconnected brain circuits are underpinned by the exquisite timing of electrochemical activity. These include the release of noradrenaline for the fight–flight response, dopamine for reward cues, serotonin for enhancing one's mood, and oxytocin for bonding.[23]

In order to manage information and sensory demands, the human brain operates by using parallel distributed processors, which means that many operations are going on simultaneously, gathering together into larger networks at a later stage in processing.[24] A core principle is a motivation to 'Minimize Danger and Maximize Reward'. This motivation helps a leader to deal with immediate threats, but also drives the search for rewards over longer timescales – from nourishment, through social connectivity, to purpose in life. The core 'Minimize Danger – Maximize Reward' principle continually organises the fundamental brain processes of emotion, thinking, feeling, and selfregulation.

The INTEGRATE or 124 Model – as illustrated in Figure 4.5 – highlights the timing of the brain's key processes. Many emotional reactions, for instance, occur non-consciously within a fifth of a second, without conscious awareness.

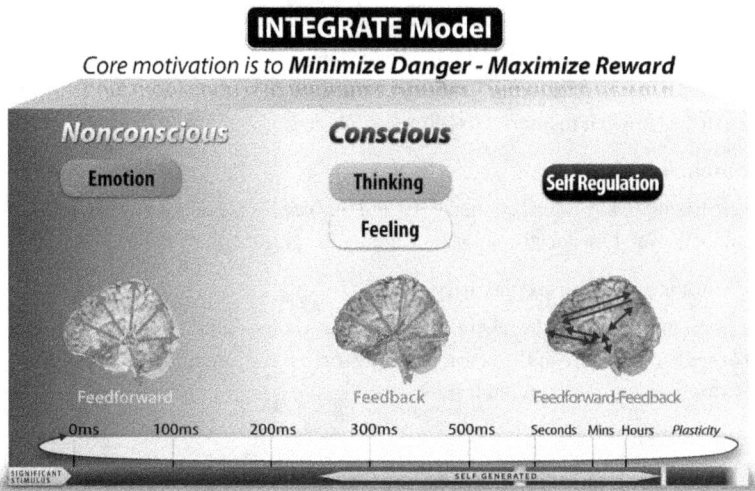

Figure 4.5: The Integrate Model or 124 Model
Source: Gordon, 2009[25]

The emotion-feeling-thinking and self-regulation processes that are unique to each person are shaped by both genetic disposition and life experiences. Genes (= nature) are not destiny, but rather 'disposition'. Bonding and conditioning experiences (= nurture) can have a lasting effect from childhood and shape the human brain's ongoing personal experiences. Neural plasticity enables transformative brain change via the right insights and training, which translates into new behaviours.[26]

The consequences of the 124 model for leadership behaviour is that the crucial threshold for leadership behavioural change is non-conscious, concrete processing, as this mode of processing is automatic and emotionally evocative. Brain effectiveness is primarily determined by how well leaders can train and align their non-conscious and conscious modes of processing.

What should we do with this knowledge of neuroscientific models in the world of leadership?

The fundamental principle is for leaders to create a safe environment for all individuals within the organisation. Leaders need to view others' responses in light of what is happening in their own brain and need to be aware that the most powerful behavioural patterns are subconscious. Ultimately leaders need to allow their central executive network to stay in control through cultivating enriched environments at a neuron, network, and organisational level.

Five Neuroscience Insights that are Changing our Leadership World

There is a mass of information on neuroscience and leadership in the market. To get a clear idea of the brain and how it functions in the context of leadership, we focus on five key insights.

1. **The brain is 'wired to survive', not thrive**

   Our brains distinguish the threat and reward content of every single experience we encounter, mostly subconsciously, and we behave in accordance with the brain's assessment.

2. **The brain uses two modes of processing: the subconscious and the conscious**

   Reflexive and reflective modes of memory systems which give 'feedforward' and feedback in relation to emotional 'action tendencies' are used for processing. The reflexive mode is expressed as implicit memories or 'autopilot' tendencies.

3. **The brain is social first**

   We are hardwired for social connectivity, and this need is as rudimentary as food and water for our survival. Our social cognition is therefore ancient and by design.

4. **The brain is plastic: neuroplasticity**

   The brain has the ability to rewire itself based on where we focus attention. Genes dictate the overall architecture of the brain, but the structure is dynamic, continuing to regenerate cells and changes throughout our lives.

5. **The brain is an open system**

   The brain is a neural network that does not exist in isolation. It is in close symbiosis with its environment. When the environment is compromised, the neural system becomes compromised as it wires itself to survive and disrupts effective neural proliferation.

"Down-regulating distress and facilitating enriched environments enhances neural proliferation." – Eric Kandel

Neurally-aware Leadership

What does the above imply for leadership? The core reality of today's leadership is that it is virtual, global, and is increasingly becoming massively complex. These rigours of 21st-century leadership demands have led to a growing body of research in psychology, sociology and neuroscience that highlights the importance of 'decision fatigue': attempts to make several decisions at once diminish the ability to make wise decisions at all.[27] These indeterminate challenges require the capacity to process a lot of data very deeply, be creative, and at the same time try to think in terms of people.

The inverted U-curve of performance (or the optimal arousal curve) explains the relationship between cognitive demands, arousal or stress, and levels of performance, as illustrated in Figure 4.6. Optimal performance is achieved at the peak of the curve. This mid-point is characterised by a mentally stimulating state. Below the midpoint, performance declines as a result of insufficient arousal. Above the midpoint, arousal builds to levels that induce stress and anxiety caused by the task being perceived as beyond the capability of the individual.

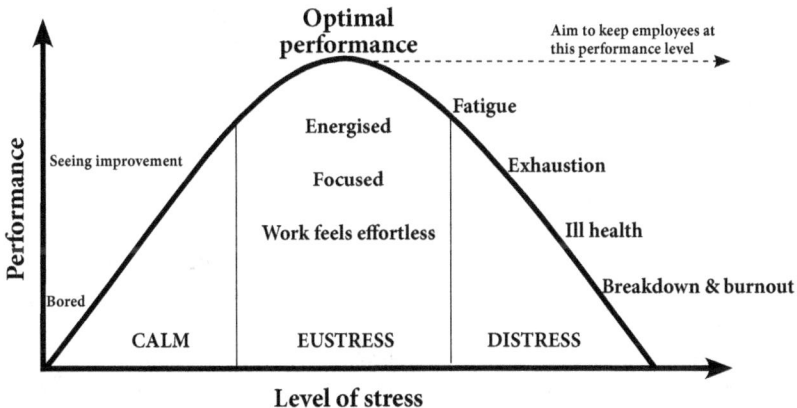

Figure 4.6: The inverted U-curve of performance

Some leaders thrive amidst these challenges; they experience being at the top of the arousal curve or in a state of 'flow'.[28] Others become frazzled or choke under the perceived pressure, which leads to performance decrements – also known as power stress.[29] In a state of high stress, the brain invokes the limbic system, driven by adrenaline and cortisol, and prepares us for fight, flight, or freeze responses.

'Allostatic load' is the expression used to describe the wear-and-tear effects of prolonged stress on the body. High allostatic load leads to high blood pressure, impaired immune function, loss of brain function in the memory circuits of the brain, and growth of the fear circuitry in the brain. However, allostatic load can be contained, and a state of 'flow' can be induced through neurally-aware leadership principles and behaviours.

Neuroplasticity, the discovery that the brain can 'rewire' itself throughout life, offers a real opportunity for leaders and organisations to develop and grow new ways of thinking and acting. By becoming neurally aware through learning how the brain works, what affects the reward and action systems in the brain, and the way that stress and other distractions, distortions and misunderstandings lead to sub-optimal performance, leaders and organisations can effectively change how they lead and perform.

Brain-Centric Leadership Behaviours

"Organic matter, especially nervous tissue, seems endowed with a very extraordinary degree of plasticity." – William James

'Neurally-aware leaders' or 'brain-centric leaders' understand the key principles of the brain and therefore manage their zone of optimal performance through specific behaviours relating to emotional regulation, adequate sleep, moderate stress, positive mood, setting clear and realistic goals and expectations, directing their own attention by practising mindfulness and building relatedness and 'in-group' behaviours up, down and across the organisational landscape. The term 'neurally-aware leaders' will be used in this section to refer to leaders who exemplify the knowledge of the key brain principles and who actively cultivate specific neurobiological proficiencies.[30]

Although the relationship between brain functioning and human behaviour is complex, there are neuroscientifically founded leadership behaviours that can be applied by leaders up, down, and across the organisational landscape. We cover seven behaviours at the heart of neurally-aware leadership.

Neurally-aware leaders down-regulate distress: 'Learning to ride the T-Rex'

Being constantly goal focused by using the analysing system switches off the brain circuits for thinking in terms of people – the mentalising system – which ironically are exactly the circuits that leaders need to have activated for leadership of self and others.[31] This prolonged cognitive load leads to elevated stress and limbic system activation – the amygdala and hippocampus with spiked cortisol release – which reduces working memory, increases pessimism, reduces insight, and reduces verbal fluency.[32][33]

The problem occurs partly because of the interaction among three experiences: (i) chronic elevated stress negatively impacts on sleep and positive affect; (ii) poor sleep makes stress and positive affect worse; and (iii) negative affect tends to make sleep and stress worse.[34] When individuals have high levels of all three experiences, the interaction can result in overly high-stress experiences with substantial cognitive impairment, impacting on basic perception as well as judgement and decision-making.[35]

- *'Neurally-aware leaders' understand the interrelatedness of sleep, stress and mood and manage their sleep/wake cycles.*
- *'Neurally-aware leaders' are cognisant of the innate negativity bias in the brain and deliberately focus on deploying positivity in all interpersonal interactions.*
- *'Neurally-aware leaders' down-regulate distress by building perceived control into their lives through exercise, nutrition and sleep hygiene.*

Neurally-aware leaders deploy cognitive emotional reappraisal: 'Name it to tame it'

Strategies that are used to regulate emotions and significantly impact on social functioning include *expressive suppression* and *cognitive reappraisal*.[36] Suppression has been found to reduce memory and increase the stress felt by the individual, as well as those around them, so this is not ideal. The key strategies, once an emotion has been felt, are to label the emotion, or to make a cognitive change by reappraising it in order to modulate the response. Reappraisal has a stronger emotional braking effect on the brain, so it reduces impulsivity and improves the leader's cognitive abilities and allows the leader to respond more appropriately. Frequent use of reappraisal has the long-term effect of generating an enhanced control of emotion and interpersonal functioning.

- *'Neurally-aware leaders' train their brains to pick up on positive cues: being aware of and being able to override manually an over-aroused sympathetic nervous system.*
- *'Neurally-aware leaders' regulate their experience emotionally through controlled rhythmic breathing, silencing the mind, labelling, and reappraisal – also called self-directed neuroplasticity.*

Neurally-aware leaders facillitate enriched environments: 'The leader becomes the organisation'

The brain's *mirror neuron system* or *resonance circuitry* underpins the construct of emotional contagion. Mirror neurons fire both when we are a performing a particular action and when we observe that action.[37] Thus, people in relationships become more emotionally similar over time. This similarity helps co-ordinate the thoughts and behaviours of the partnership; increases their mutual understanding; and fosters their social cohesion.

Relationship partners with less power (= team members) make more of the change necessary for convergence to occur. Thus emotional processes and their co-ordination across interaction partners are of central importance to relationship formation, functioning, and long-term outcomes. The emotional states and regulation strategies of others, especially those in positions of power, can have a real and enduring effect on individuals and groups. The existing evidence shows that while all emotions can be contagious, 'negative' emotions have greater power to influence.[38] This can lead to a negative organisational culture. The basic object is then for neurally-aware leaders to create a safe environment for all individuals within the organisation.

- *'Neurally-aware leaders' understand the mirror neuron footprint of emotional contagion and support a bottom-up approach to building safety. They down-regulate the firing of unhelpful neurotransmitters– adrenaline and cortisol – as well as up-regulate serotonin flow, dopamine release, and triggering of the parasympathetic nervous system.*
- *'Neurally-aware leaders' become aware of how their brains are interacting with others' brains, responses, and reactions. They extrapolate this to how others are thinking and feeling.*

Neurally-aware leaders build reflective practice into their leadership repertoire: 'Silencing the mind is the silver bullet'

A brain-centric leadership approach is anchored in the capacity to be mindful and reflective. Also known as silencing the mind, the neural correlates associated with this process of silencing the mind (or mindfulness) were recorded in a groundbreaking neuro-imaging study, where functional magnetic resonance imaging (fMRI) was used to examine the two neural modes of self-referencing: 'narrative' focus, or NF, and momentary experience, known as 'experiential' focus, or EF; as well as the neural systems supporting these 'modes' of awareness.[39]

The study revealed that mindfulness meditation enables a decoupling between the narrative mode and the experiential mode. These two forms of self-awareness are habitually integrated but can be dissociated through attentional training. The decoupling of these two forms of awareness enables one to choose which mode is required for the task at hand. The narrative focus equates to the conceptual world that is full of descriptions of events, memories, attitudes, and evaluations of people and things. The experiential focus is about tracking how the body, thoughts, and feelings change in an instant, to those of a judgement-free awareness of current experiences and intentions.[40]

Mindfulness practice is one way to integrate the various regions of the brain that facilitate psychological well-being. Not only does mindfulness practice have stress reductive effects but it also enhances cognitive functions and resilience, which are key behaviours for leaders.[41] Leaders can therefore be more in charge of the focus of their attention and can emotionally regulate disturbances (such as corporate change), because their brain's braking system is effectively recruited when needed. An additional benefit of mindfulness is that it enables easier adaptability to demanding situations and enhances emotional regulation – feeling the right emotion at the right time – a skill that is especially important in the workplace.[42]

> *'Neurally-aware leaders' make time and space in their work and in the work of others for sensitive reflection, knowing when to switch from analytical (hyperfrontality) to quiet mode (hypofrontality) by taking a walk, listening to music, silencing the mind, or journalising. This hypofrontality enables a broader 'field of view' instead of a myopic focus.[43]*

Neurally-aware leaders counter-balance mental shortcuts: 'The de-biased brain'

> *"Odd as it may seem, I am my remembering self, and the experiencing self, who does my living, is like a stranger to me."* – Daniel Kahneman

Executive attention is a finite resource. High cognitive load reduces leaders' ability to be empathetic towards others. This leads to a false consensus bias in that leaders develop tunnel vision and are not able to perceive a more accurate perception of reality that would allow them to be more flexible in how they respond to the world.[44]

Given that leaders are often under tough deadlines to churn out profits (and are thus under high cognitive load), they default to their own 'know how', or false consensus. This can have negative consequences for both business results and team effectiveness. To regulate the exhaustion of compounded, challenging decisions, the brain resorts to heuristics, cognitive rules-of-thumb, developed over time. These mental shortcuts are convenient but can also distort a leader's clear thinking. While it is difficult for leaders to detect and take control of their cognitive thinking errors, they can apply rational thought in order to detect others' faulty intuition and improve their decision-making.[45]

> - *'Neurally-aware leaders' aim to reduce the imminent negative impact of heuristics – an approach to problem solving that takes one's personal experiences into account – by adopting the perspectives of others.*
> - *'Neurally-aware leaders' counterbalance negative heuristics by identifying biases across the organisational landscape relevant to the decision-making process.*

Neurally-aware leaders cultivate resonant relationships – 'Survival of the nurtured'

When we imagine or are thinking about the intentional mental states of others (for example, their feelings, beliefs, needs) we use our own mental state as 'reference'.[46] Thus, mentalising about others is self-referential. Consequently, the leader's ability to understand and think about his/her team's dynamics effectively is directly interconnected to his/her ability to understand him-/herself. Accordingly, if the leader carries a lot of anxiety and unresolved conflict, he/she will project that onto the team or 'read' the team in the same way. He/she will not be able to create an environment where the team feels safe to drop their defences.[47]

Because mentalising about team members results in minimal output, it is tempting to try to rush through or short circuit this mental activity and rather to hope the group can achieve peak performance through task orientation only. Although seductive, this idea is dysfunctional insofar as it can lead to generalisations, 'group think', false consensus bias, or tunnel vision.

Given that thinking about self and others is inevitable, one way to help reduce the time needed for a new or changing team to be fully productive while minimising the tension, fear, or anxiety common in group development, is for the leader to ensure that the team engages in ways that will bring to the surface points of resemblance, strengthen resonances, cultivate empathy, and contribute to feelings of trust. Only *after* a sense of relatedness, or seeing others as part of the 'in' group, has been established, can social differences be effectively addressed.[48] [49]

Neuroscience research confirmed the business benefits of resonant leadership, finding a correlation between effective leaders and resonant relationships with others.[50] The study, using fMRI technology, indicated that when managers were asked to recall precise experiences with 'resonant' leaders, fourteen regions of the brain were triggered. When requested to recollect specific instances with 'dissonant' leaders, only six regions of the brain were activated, and eleven regions were deactivated. The regions of the brain triggered for resonant leaders were related to broadening attention and activating the social system; and other areas connected with 'approach' relationships. Dissonant leaders deactivated the social system and activated regions of the brain associated with narrowing attention, lowering compassion, and triggering negative emotions.

> - *'Neurally-aware leaders' recognise the brain as relational, meaning that our neural circuitry is in constant conversation with the firings of others' brains.*
> - *'Neurally-aware leaders' promote integration by cultivating both differentiation and linkage in themselves, and across the organisational landscape.*
> - *'Neurally-aware leaders' facilitate patterns of approach, by establishing a 'sense of control' perspective through non-directive conversations, reflective questioning, and acting as thinking partners.*

Neurally-aware leaders cultivate innovative thinking: 'From DUH to AHA moments'

Leadership requires both analytical problem solving and creative thinking. However, the business need for innovation emphasises the significance of understanding the neural distinctions of these two processes.

Creative cognition is a type of cognition that is exemplified by 'insight' as solutions to problems. These solutions are accompanied by a 'Eureka' experience. This mostly happens when a person does not even know he/she has been thinking about the problem. Positive mood is thought to enhance creative problem solving and performance relating to insight problems.[51]

Recent advances in neuroscience track the brain's process for generating insight, a precursor to innovation. Electroencephalography (EEG) that measures the electrical activity on the brain's surface in hertz (Hz) verifies that insight isn't a random occurrence. Insight is a predictable process which requires a 'rested brain', in terms of alpha wave dominance, and sensory gating; and then a predominant 'searching brain' where gamma waves take over in order to search for a possible solution among all the options held within the cortex.

It seems that the moment of insight signals the coming to consciousness of a newly integrated cognitive map, a momentary binding of a novel neuronal pattern, and creative thought. Research has shown that the gamma band wave spike and subsequent adrenaline/dopamine rush at the moment of insight is fleeting, perhaps lasting only ten minutes. Consequently, it can be said that insight is short term and provides motivation to act.

- *'Neurally-aware leaders' clarify the brain basis of insight. They demonstrate that insight is a process, and they cultivate creativity and innovation by valuing unstructured time as a key factor in insight creation.*
- *'Neurally-aware leaders' build a positive climate to boost creative problem solving and performance on insight problems.*
- *'Neurally-aware leaders' focus on enhancing solutions-focused actions through cognitive empowerment and supporting team members on an ongoing basis. In this way they ensure that new habits are activated, and strengthen new neural patterns.*

By cultivating these seven neurally-aware leadership behaviours, leaders can leverage their neural resources for optimal performance.

Brain Diagnostics: 'All Performance is Brain Performance'

The applied field of organisational neuroscience proposes a neural basis to behavioural variables. This neurological activity in various regions of the brain that is associated with specific behaviours can be gauged using neuro-imaging technology. It can therefore be said that all human performance is brain performance. Although we are far from using neuro-imaging techniques to gauge all leadership behaviour, there are brain-based self-report diagnostics available to infer brain functioning at work, and which aim to train the brain for optimal performance and wellbeing.

The MyBrainSolutions programme

The MyBrainSolutions web-based programme, developed by Brain Resource, leverages new insights in neuroscience in order to diagnose brain capacities across the four primary processing modes, as well as build personalised brain training applications that can improve brain health and facilitate change in behaviour. It deploys a validated, neuropsychiatric-based brain assessment and interactive games to target directly and improve the brain functions important in making healthy decisions and performing at peak.

The MyBrainSolutions programme provides:

- A validated assessment of four core capacities of brain function: Emotion, Feeling, Thinking and Self-Regulation. The assessment compares scores to a large database of healthy age-, gender- and education level-matched peers to produce meaningful scores

- A personalised report which profiles strengths and weaknesses in the four capacities, and defines an individual's style of brain function based on scores. The report also offers personalised recommendations for the training exercise most suited to a profile and based on an individual's personal goals
- A suite of interactive, online training games and exercises designed to train aspects of emotion, feeling, thinking and self-regulation capacities using validated approaches
- Gamification elements that support engagement over time. This includes a 'points' system that provides rewards for effort put into training.

More details on the MyBrainSolutions programme can be found on: http://www.mybrainsolutions.com.

The Neuro-diagnostic

Psychoneuro-endocrinology (PNE) refers specifically to the influence of mind states, either positive or negative, on immune and endocrine function. Based on the integration of the neurosciences with PNE, neurosurgeon Dr Ian Weinberg developed the Triangles Model. A unique feature of this application is the online Neuro-Diagnostic application which is used to quantify neuropsychological states and thereby the chemistry underpinning wellness, performance and leadership.

The Triangles Model[52] forms the foundation for accessing the chemistry of wellness, performance and leadership. In this way, appropriate intervention is designed to engage directly with the relevant neurophysiology. The online Neuro-Diagnostic application measures both stress profiles and PNE resilience in terms of wellness and performance, as well as the risk of developing raised pro-inflammatory cytokines that have been implicated in mediating chronic conditions such as type 2 diabetes, cardiac disease, osteoporosis, and even dementias.

The application of the Triangles Model is not restricted to personal coaching of the individual. Rather, it should be viewed as providing a comprehensive framework for the implementation of multiple modalities of intervention, including leadership training, team-building, management restructuring, and wellness enhancement.

To get more information on this application, see http://www.neuronostic.com.

The Neurozone-diagnostic for business brain-performance

According to Van der Walt (2013), at the core of human performance optimisation are eleven brain-performance drivers. The integration of these drivers and the observation that they can be individually and collectively enhanced is the foundation of the neurozone brain theory and diagnostics.

The Neurozone Model of brain performance offers insight into the brain's constituents for innovative performance. The model consists of real brain structures around a hypothetical axis from basic to most sophisticated. The model clusters the eleven key drivers into four major functionalities that determine brain performance. These are also structural (anatomical) and include (i) foundational drivers. (ii) emotional drivers, (iii) higher order drivers, and (iv) sensory drivers.

The neurozone diagnostic is a web-based self-report survey and allows for self-reliant brain performance development. Brain training is done via web-based brain seminars and workplace tools, three-month personal action plans, and the option to do frequent self-assessments over a year period. See www.neurozone.com

To get an overview of all the diagnostics that are anchored in the applied field of organisational neuroscience, see http://www.neurocapital.co.za

Conclusion

Emerging research has applied a social cognitive and affective neuroscience lens to reveal a deeper understanding of leadership behaviour. This new, quantitative science recognises that ultimately, to become a neurally-aware leader depends upon a deeper understanding of how the brain and body are receptive to the social, cognitive and emotional demands of the leader's world.

It is our view that applied organisational neuroscience will continue evolving, and its applications will expand. Providing evidence of how neuroscience applies to leadership behaviour in formal organisations can contribute to accelerating this evolution.

Glossary of terms

Allostatic load: A range of markers of stress, including cortisol and adrenaline levels in the blood, as well as immune system activity and blood pressure.

Amygdala: A small brain region that is part of the limbic system, which activates based on the strength of an emotional or motivational response.

Central executive network (CEN): Brain network responsible for high-level cognitive functions, notably the control of attention and working memory.

Default mode network (DMN): A large-scale network of brain areas that form a unified system of self-related cognitive activity, including autobiographical, self-monitoring and social functions. The DMN is typically deactivated during stimulus-driven cognitive processing.

Default network: A network of brain regions roughly in the middle areas of the brain, including the medial prefrontal cortex. It activates when you are not doing much else, and also when you think about yourself and other people.

Dopamine: One of the two main neurotransmitters involved in stabilising circuits in the prefrontal cortex (norepinephrine is the other). Dopamine is connected to feeling interested in something and is important for tasks that involve learning new things.

Functional magnetic resonance imaging (fMRI): A form of non-invasive neuro-imaging based on blood oxygen level-dependent signals in the brain in *vivo*.

Limbic system: A region in the centre of the brain important for experiencing emotions, memories, and motivations; includes the amygdala, insula, hippocampus, and orbital frontal cortex.

Mirror neurons: Neurons in the brain that help us directly experience other people's intentions, motivations, and emotions, by feeling the same way ourselves.

Neuroplasticity: The study of change in the brain, both moment to moment and in the long term.

Prefrontal cortex: A section of the outer layer of the brain, behind the forehead, involved in many types of executive functioning, planning and coordinating the rest of the brain.

Salience network (SN): A large-scale brain network involved in detecting and orientating towards salient external stimuli and internal events.

Ventrolateral prefrontal cortex: A region of the prefrontal cortex, beneath the right and left temples, that is important for all types of braking functions, including stopping physical movement and inhibiting emotions or thoughts.

Endnotes

1.	Ghadiri et al., 2012.	27.	Gordon et al., 2008.
2.	Schulyer, 2010.	28.	Cskikszentmihalyi, 1990.
3.	Lindebaum & Zundel, 2013.	29.	Boyatzis & Blaize, 2006.
4.	Fernandez-Daque et al., 2015.	30.	See endnote 26.
5.	See endnote 3.	31.	Spunt et al., 2011.
6.	MacLean, 1990.	32.	Payne, 2011.
7.	Henson & Rossouw, 2013.	33.	Arnsten, 1998.
8.	Maclean, 1990.	34.	See endnote 32.
9.	See endnote 7.	35.	Payne & Nadel, 2004.
10.	Ibid.	36.	Gross, 2008.
11.	Siegel, 2010.	37.	Badenoch, 2001.
12.	Grawe, 2007.	38.	See endnote 26.
13.	Rossouw, 2013.	39.	Farb et al., 2007.
14.	Gordon, 2009.	40.	Ibid.
15.	Cacioppo et al., 2014.	41.	Brown et al., 2007.
16.	Cozolino, 2010.	42.	Creswell et al., 2007.
17.	Sporns, 2013.	43.	Fredrickson, 2013.
18.	Bressler & Menon, 2010.	44.	Bauman et al., 2002.
19.	Ibid.	45.	Kahneman et al., 2011.
20.	Ibid.	46.	Mitchell, 2006.
21.	Gordon et al., 2008.	47.	Cilliers & Koortzen, 2005.
22.	Kandel et al., 2013.	48.	Lieberman, 2012.
23.	Gordon et al., 2008.	49.	Rock, 2009.
24.	Badenoch, 2001.	50.	Boyatzis et al., 2012.
25.	Gordon, 2009.	51.	Fredrickson, 2013.
26.	Ibid.	52.	Weinberg, 2007.

References

Arnsten, A, 1998. 'Enhanced: The biology of being frazzled'. *Science,* 280(5370):1711–1712.

Badenoch, B. 2001. *The brain-savvy therapist's workbook.* New York, NY: WW Norton.

Bauman, A, Sallis, J, Dzewaltowski, D & Owen, N. 2002. 'Toward a better understanding of the influences on physical activity: the role of determinants, correlates, causal variables, mediators, moderators, and confounders'. *American Journal of Preventive Medicine,* 23(2):5–14.

Boyatzis, R, Good, D & Massa, R. 2012. 'Emotional, social, and cognitive intelligence and personality as preditors of sales leadership performance'. *Journal of Leadership & Organisational Studies,* 19(2):191–201.

Boyatzis, R, Smith, M & Blaize, N. 2006. 'Developing sustainable leaders through coaching and compassion'. *Academy of Management Learning & Education,* 5(1):2–24.

Bressler, S & Menon, V. 2010. 'Large-scale brain networks in cognition: Emerging methods and principles'. *Trends in Cognitive Sciences,* 14(6):277–290.

Brown, K, Ryan, R & Creswell, J. 2007. 'Mindfulness: Theoretical foundations and evidence for its salutary effects'. *Psychological Inquiry,* 18(4):211–237.

Cacioppo, J, Cacioppo, S Dulawa, S & Palmer, A. 2014. 'Social neuroscience and its potential contribution to psychiatry'. *World Psychiatry,* 13(2):131–139.

Cilliers, F & Koortzen, P. 2005. 'Working with conflict in teams – the CIBART model'. *HR Future,* 113(10):51–52.

Cozolino, L. 2010. *The neuroscience of psychotherapy: Healing the social brain.* New York, NY: WW Norton & Company.

Creswell, JD, Way, BM, Eisenberger, NI & Lieberman, MD. 2007. 'Neural correlates of dispositional mindfulness during affect labelling'. *Psychosomatic Medicine,* 69:560–565.

Cskikszentmihalyi, M. 1990. 'Literacy and intrinsic motivation'. *Daedalus, Journal of the American Academy of Arts and Sciences,* 119(2):115–140.

Farb, NA et al. 2007. Attending to the present: Mindfulness meditation reveals distinct neural modes of self reference. *Social Cognitive and Affective Neuroscience,* 2(4):313–322.

Fernandez-Daque, D, Evans, J, Christian, C & Hodges, S. 2015. 'Superfluous neuroscience information makes explanations of psychological phenomena more appealing'. *Journal of Cognitive Neuroscoence*, 27(5):926–944.

Fredrickson, B. 2013. *Updated thinking on positivity ratios.* s.l.:s.n.

Fredrickson, B & Losada, M. 2005. *Positive affect and the complex dynamics of human flourishing.* American *Psychologist*, 60:678–686.

Ghadiri, A, Habermacher, A & Peters, T. 2012. *Neuroleadership: A journey through the brain for business leaders.* New York, NY: Dordrecht, DL; & London, UK: Springer Heidelberg.

Gordon, E, 2009. 'Neuroleadership and integrative neuroscience'. *Neuroleadership Journal*, 1:71–79.

Gordon, E, Barnett, KJ, Cooper, NJ, Tran, N & Williams, LM. 2008. 'An "Integrative neuroscience" platform: Application to profiles of negativity and possibility bias'. *Journal of Integrative Neuroscience*, 7(3):345–366.

Grawe, K. 2007. *Neuropsychotherapy: How the neurosciences inform effective psychotherapy.* Hillsdale, NJ: Lawrence Erbaum Associates Publishers.

Gross, J. 2008. 'Emotion regulation'. *Handbook of Emotions*, 3:497–513.

Henson, H & Rossouw, P. 2013. *Brainwise leadership: Practical neuroscience to survive and thrive at work.* Sydney, AU: Learning Quest.

Jung-Beeman, M, Bowden, EM & Haberman, J et al. 2004. 'Neural activity when people solve verbal problems with insight'. *PLoS Biology*, 2(4):500–510.

Kahneman, D, Lovallo, D & Sibony, O. 2011. 'Before you make that big decision'. *Harvard Business Review*, 89(6):50–60.

Kandel, E, Schwartz, J & Jessell, T. 2013. *Principles of neural science.* 5th ed. New York: McGraw-Hill.

Lieberman, M. 2012. 'Education and the social brain'. *Trends in Neuroscience and Education*, 1(1):3–9.

Lindebaum, D & Zundel, M. 2013. 'Not quite a revolution: Scrutinizing organisational neuroscience in leadership studies'. *Human Relations*, 66(6):857–877.

MacLean, P. 1990. *The triune brain in evolution: Role in paleocerebral functions.* New York, NY: Plenum Press.

Mitchell, M. 2006. 'Complex systems: Network thinking'. *Artificial Intelligence*, 170(18):1194–1212.

Rock, D. 2009. 'Managing with the brain in mind'. *Strategy & Business*, 56:59–67.

Rossouw, P. 2013. 'The neuroscience of talking therapies: Implications for therapeutic practice'. *The Australian Journal of Counselling Psychology*, 13(1):40–50.

Siegel, D. 2010. *The mindful therapist: A clinician's guide to mindsight and neural integration.* New York, NY: WW Norton & Company.

Sporns, O. 2013. 'Structure and function of complex brain networks'. *Dialogues in Clinical Neuroscience*, 15(3):247.

Spunt, R, Satpute, A & Lieberman, M. 2011. 'Identifying the what, why and how of an observed action: An fMRI study of mentalizing and mechanizing during action observation'. *Journal of Cognitive Neuroscience*, 23(1).

Weinberg, IR. 2007. *The last frontier.* Johannesburg, ZA: Interpak Books.

Chapter 5

ACTION SCIENCE

Andrew J Johnson

"Shall the practitioner stay on the high, hard ground where he can practice rigorously, as he understands rigour but where he is constrained to deal with problems of relatively little social importance? Or shall he descend to the swamp where he can engage the most important and challenging problems if he is willing to forsake technical rigour?" – Donald Schön[1]

Effective leadership is an important concern for ever-changing, modern, successful organisations.[2] At least this concern is so in theory, for consider how "innovation, ingenuity, and thinking outside the box are often cited as hallmarks of successful organizations, but in practice, their occurrence is rare. More likely, 'the way things work around here' is a litany of missed deadlines, low morale, strained relationships, and inept problem solving,[3] ... [and] defensive avoidance, hypervigilance, defensive blindness, ... rationalizations, denial, selective perceptions, and wishful thinking, ... [leading to] defective decision-making."[4]

It has become clear to me that examples of potential mismatches and gaps abound between the intentions and actions of leaders. These lead to leadership behaviour that is generally ineffective, and leaders showing a remarkable unawareness that they are not behaving according to their intentions. If leaders are unaware of the causes of these mismatches that lead to ineffective behaviour, there is potentially little that anyone can do to help them to change.

The gaps in what leaders say and do have always perplexed me, especially in relation to my experiences of well-meaning organisational leaders who at least express a desire to be effective, but who generally fare poorly in their execution of this desire (the latter statement is by their own admission). This leads to poor outcomes. Organisational leaders have many good ideas, very few of which are ever implemented. These mismatches between what leaders say and what they actually do in practice leads to leaders being ineffective. Eliciting these mismatches is intended to show what prevents leaders from being effective in their actions.

For purposes of defining effective leadership, I have chosen Argyris'[5] definition of effectiveness: "the degree to which one's intended consequences are accomplished." In applying this definition, one could broadly argue that it is the degree to which a leader's intention to create conditions that are favourable for employees to pursue actions to the benefit of themselves and their organisations is achieved. This ineffectiveness has remained, notwithstanding a large amount of advice to the leadership on what constitutes "good" leadership, and how to implement such advice. The advice and its implementation have a poor record. Argyris[6] is even more direct in his assessment of the advice of consultants: "[Consultants'] theory of action often makes [them] blind not only to the gaps and inconsistencies in their advice but also to the fact that they are blind. What they say, therefore, is not the result of ignorance, but of skilled unawareness and skilled incompetence. Professionally, they are very good at being wrong."

The advice of consultants is flawed in four areas:[7] "the advice represents espoused theory; the advice, as crafted, contains evaluations and attributions that are neither tested nor testable; the advice is based on self-referential logic that produces limited knowledge about what is going on; and the advice does not specify causal processes." At a very minimum, this advice fails because it is not possible to put it into action, and simply represents that which somebody else espouses, but cannot enact.

My chapter will therefore introduce a theory of action – Action Science (AS) – regarding leadership effectiveness as an epistemology of practice to produce knowledge that can inform action in the following ways: by eliciting mismatches and (counterproductive) leadership outcomes in organisational contexts; by briefly describing the historical roots of AS; by discussing a theory of action (AS) as an approach to leadership effectiveness and in so doing explore key elements of AS; by briefly discussing AS's value-add; and finally, by discussing theory-informed practical methods for leadership development.

Organisational Contexts of Leadership Practice

From personal experience, I would venture to say that a potential area where organisational leaders' effectiveness is most severely put to the test is in dealing with continuous *change* and improvement. Inability to do this successfully prevents them from building healthy *organisational cultures*. Success in these can lead to conditions that are conducive to *employee engagement*, positive outcomes in *effective customer service*, and, in turn, positive *business results*.

There is ample evidence that current executive leadership styles conform to the traditional hierarchical style, even though leaders believe in more transformational styles, but truly, are unaware of this.[8] This mismatch between leaders' intentions and actions leads to ineffective behaviour. The impact of this failure is apparent in organisational attempts to change their corporate cultures.

If culture is about "how we do things around here in order to succeed",[9] including a more engaged workforce to enhance greater customer orientation, the evidence is glaring that leaders have largely not been effective in this regard. A cursory scan of various organisational diagnostic sources (including culture/climate surveys, focus groups, exit interview analyses, and change interventions) appear to point to the fact that major challenges remain in the leadership styles of management, and that change interventions as proposed by consultants have largely been unsuccessful.[10]

If, however, you were to ask organisational leaders what they believe the cause of the ineffectiveness is, it is highly likely that they would cite extraneous factors such as the unreasonableness of customers, the vagueness of strategic goals, the unpredictability of the environment, or demonic competitors, and not their inherent insecurities or fears.[11] The gap between the professed cultures of organisations (in other words, its stated values) and the (old) behaviour of its leaders have serious (negative) consequences for their employees in, for example, employee engagement, resultant customer-orientated behaviour, and in turn business results.

It is clear that when employees are surveyed on their engagement levels, organisations generally fare poorly. Employee engagement is broadly defined as translating the inherent capacity of people into performance and business results,[12] and is expressed as the extent to which employees commit to something or someone in their organisation, how hard they work, and how long they stay as a result of that commitment.[13] Employees will invest their time and energy with a company that is committed to satisfying their expectations, both rationally – the extent to which managers satisfy an employee's financial and developmental self-interest – and emotionally – the extent to which employees value, enjoy, and believe in their work and managers.

The spin-offs of rational and emotional engagement are job satisfaction, job involvement, intrinsic motivation, attachment, loyalty, affective commitment, intention to stay, organisational citizenship behaviour, and discretionary effort: the willingness to walk the extra mile. Bowen, Gilliland and Folger[14] postulate that if employees experience a sense of courtesy, attention, responsiveness and respect from their managers (key elements of emotional engagement), they will in turn treat customers in a similar way – and so business results could be positively affected.

In sum, if what George[15] contends is the only valid test of a leader: the ability to bring people together to achieve sustainable results over time (in other words, achieving intended consequences), it appears that most organisational leaders would fare poorly. It is my opinion that AS offers real possibilities to provide answers to the challenges leaders face in effective (cultural) change, and in changing the behaviour of leaders in ways that address the root causes of ineffective behaviour, namely, mental models/master programmes.

Before I discuss these ideas in more depth, let me take a brief detour on the roots of AS. This is necessary because despite almost five decades of Argyris and Schön's writing – the fathers of organisational learning, teaching and practising AS, it has, as Dick[16] points out, produced little reaction, and has not led to much change.

Historical Roots

The concept of "action science" dates back about four decades – it was first used in 1976 by William Torbert, who was a student of Argyris. He envisioned a science that would be useful to an actor at the moment of action. Torbert[17] speaks of his "model of personal and social action and learning … [as] an integration of social action and scientific research – toward an action science."

Two social scientists who critiqued the separation of science and action and are highly regarded by Argyris for their contribution to the study of practical matters systematically, for generating knowledge to solve practical matters, and their commitment to creating conditions in society for the betterment thereof, are John Dewey and Kurt Lewin:

- *John Dewey (1859–1952):* Dewey contends that the researcher is not a spectator but an actor standing in a situation of action, creating the situation to which he or she is also responding. One could therefore reasonably conceive of organisational leaders creating the kinds of dilemmas they face in organisations, as they are simultaneously responding to them.
- *Kurt Lewin (1890–1947):* Argyris et al[18] describe Lewin's form of action research as a prototype of the kind of research AS is about, including his emphasis on experiments involving real problems, iterative cycles, his normative stance, democratic values of research, and his emphasis on both social science and social practice.
- *Action Science,* co-authored by Chris Argyris, Bob Putnam and Diana McLain Smith (1985) represents, to my mind, the seminal and most comprehensive exposé of AS. It ranges from its scientific approach juxtaposed to mainstream science, to its theoretical framework, to a description of how practitioners can learn AS skills (see also Putnam[19] for a brief exposition on the development of Action Science).

Action Science – a Theory of Action

A status quo of ineffective leadership and its concomitant negative impact on organisational life remains. This is so because there are defenders of that status quo. Action Science endeavours to produce knowledge that can inform action, with the intention of changing the status quo.[20]

Philosophical groundings

Action Science as an interpenetration between mainstream science and the counterview

The label AS raises an interesting challenge within the domain of social science: the combination of the primarily descriptive purpose of mainstream science (= theory) with action (= practice), implying a normative engagement with what has been described with the purpose of changing the context. Action Science therefore, while sharing several features of mainstream science (including intersubjectively verifiable data, explicit inferences, disconfirmable propositions and public testing), also has an appreciation of interpretation and meanings of the counterview; furthermore, the knowledge generated by science is used for purposes of changing the status quo (action research).

Action Science is a specific kind of action research. It locates itself in the context of the third scientific tradition of critical social science, following the critical theory tradition of the Frankfurt School, associated with the Institute for Social Research, founded in 1923 at the University of Frankfurt (including Habermas, Horkheimer and Adorno).[i] While AS is broadly classified under action research, Argyris and Schön[21] criticise it as not being capable of producing valid information, given the tacit rules that direct people's behaviour, preventing honest discussion from taking place. The methods should be fit for purpose, getting to the tacit reasoning that drives behaviour.

Action Science as an epistemology of practice

Action Science endeavours to generate knowledge in the service of action by engaging human agents (for example, executives in the workplace) in public self-reflection in order to create communities of (valid) inquiry in communities of practice, and to transform their world.[22] A community of practice of this type implies one characterised by norms such as valid information, free and informed choice, and internal commitment, requiring an epistemology of practice. In other words, it is a theory about the kinds of knowledge relevant to action. The kinds of knowledge that human beings use to construct pragmatic/practical explanations include:

- *Problem setting:* we name the things we will attend to and frame the context in which we will attend to them;
- *Tacit knowledge:* knowledge which informs actions of which we are unaware; and
- *Reflecting and acting:* reflecting-in-action makes explicit some tacit knowledge embedded in action so that we can figure out what to do differently.[23]

In sum, an epistemology of practice can be explained as follows:

> *"The human agent, confronted with a complex, puzzling, and ambiguous set of circumstances, draws on tacit knowledge to frame the situation and act. The consequences of this action generate information about the situation and about the suitability of the framing and action of the agent. The agent interprets this information, again drawing on tacit knowledge. If the action-as-probe generates information inconsistent with the original framing, if the action-as-move does not achieve intended consequences or leads to unintended consequences, or if the action-as-hypothesis is disconfirmed, the agent may be led to reflect on the tacit understandings that informed the original framing and action. This reflection may or may not lead to a reframing of the situation and a new sequence of moves."*[24]

An epistemology of practice implies that such knowledge must conform to its criteria. We must take effective account of the limited information-seeking and information-processing capabilities of the human mind (which I will discuss next); knowledge should be relevant to the forming of purposes as well as to the achieving of purposes already formed; and knowledge must take the normative dimension into account.[25]

---

i   cf Horkheimer (1982:244) for an exposition of critical theory, where he states that "a theory is critical to the extent that it seeks human emancipation, to liberate human beings from the circumstances that enslave them."

Information processing, socialisation and selective perception

The amount of information that human beings receive through their senses is so extensive and complex that if an individual were to attempt to process all such information, he/she would probably at best go insane owing to information overload, and at worst die. Human beings are programmed to filter information. Hence, our minds develop filtering systems in our present context, theories-in-use, to allow some information in while excluding other information, in an effort to develop a more simplified picture of all the information presented to our senses.

This conditioning/socialisation is well described by Argyris et al:

> "In social life, the status quo exists because the norms and rules learned through socialization have been internalized and are continually reinforced. Human beings learn which skills work within the status quo and which do not work. The more the skills work, the more they influence individuals' sense of competence. Individuals draw on such skills and justify their use by identifying the values embedded in them and adhering to these values. The interdependence among norms, rules, skills, and values creates a pattern called the status quo that becomes so omnipresent as to be taken for granted and to go unchallenged. Precisely because these patterns are taken for granted, precisely because these skills are automatic, precisely because values are internalized, the status quo and individuals' personal responsibility for maintaining it cannot be studied without confronting it."[26]

Additionally, we as individuals also make life manageable by socialising others into theories-in-use that are similar to ours.[27]

Over many years of socialisation through our parents, educational systems, religious affiliation, or communities in which we grew up, we have developed theories of action. These theories are "a repertoire of concepts, schemas, and strategies, and ... programs for drawing from [their] repertoire to design representations and action for unique situations",[28] in order to deal automatically and seamlessly with all new situations with which we may be faced. The problem of our inherited filtering system is brilliantly captured in this "knot" by the renowned psychologist, Daniel Goleman:[29] "The range of what we think and do is limited by what we fail to notice. And because we fail to notice that, we fail to notice there is little we can do to change until we notice how failing to notice shapes our thoughts and deeds."

Over time, the effects of selective perception have led human beings, including organisational leaders, to defensive reasoning that has been hard-wired in our minds. This is defensive insofar as all humans defend their own lines of reasoning as a position of "truth." They do so in a skilful and spontaneous way, especially in situations where the individual may feel embarrassed or threatened by an opposing view. What originally started as one person acting defensively becomes over time defensive acting on the part of the entire organisation. An organisational pattern of defensive behaviour has developed.

Organisational defensive routines

Like all human beings, leaders operate from defensive positions, including a desire to maintain a position of unilateral control, and also including self-censorship and face-saving. Organisations are replete with defensive types of reasoning.[30] How often do we encounter situations where, rather than being open and honest, we say/do one thing in public and another in private? We pretend that this is the rational thing to do. We then deny that we are doing this and cover up our denial.

Through continued use and internalisation, these develop into organisational defensive routines/patterns (ODRs). Argyris[31] explains ODRs as "… all the policies, practices, and actions that prevent human beings from having to experience embarrassment or threat, and, at the same time, prevent them from examining the nature and causes of that embarrassment or threat." What should also be clear from defensive routines is that they are intended to keep the status quo intact, by helping to avoid reflecting on the counterproductive consequences of the individual's behaviour. It should be noted that these ODRs operate at individual, group (consider Janus's "group-think"),[32] [ii] and organisational level.

Compare the behaviour of the executive who counsels his team on a company value of "treating each other with respect", when a moment before he had publicly attacked one of his subordinates. When confronted with the latter at a later stage, the executive could argue that he gave the subordinate "constructive feedback", or could claim amnesia: "I don't remember it, therefore it couldn't have happened."

This example of a defensive routine has the purpose of protecting one from embarrassment (or threat). Consider, for example, the embarrassment of having to explain such an inconsistency, which in turn stifles learning. Often others could feel uncomfortable in challenging such inconsistent behaviour, which potentially could be explosive: "challenging the boss could be career limiting." Therefore, the executive remains unaware of the impact of his behaviour, because others do not tell him. This is how "unspeakables" are created. Soon newcomers learn that "it is the way we do things around here." Therefore, the routines become entrenched in the organisational culture. "The purpose of this strategy is to avoid vulnerability, risk, embarrassment, and the appearance of incompetence."[33]

Theories of action

Senge[34] argues that the root causes of ODRs that create mismatches between what leaders say and what they do do not simply arise because of "weak intentions, wavering will, or even non-systemic understanding, but from mental models" (Argyris calls them master programs). Stated differently: "… [mental models] are simplified pictures of the world that have some characteristics of the real world but not all of them … [they] are a set of interrelated guesses about the world."[35] Argyris[36] argues that: "People may be said to develop theories of action to guide their behavior, to make it more manageable, to make it more consistent, and thereby to maintain their sense of being personally responsible – of being an origin of their behavior."

Theories of action are theories of governance, since "they explain how individuals or groups put their arms around reality in order to manage it effectively; they are at the core of human competence, self-esteem and self-efficacy, mastery and self-regulation, i.e., the more success they have in their endeavours, the higher the former outcomes."[37] Senge[38] is of the opinion that people trap themselves in defensive routines that insulate their mental models from examination. This then often results in these individuals developing what Argyris calls "skilled incompetence":[iii] managers use practised routine behaviour (= skill) to produce what they did not intend (= incompetence). As a result, they fail to learn how to produce the results that are really needed. Furthermore, these rules, or the underlying belief system of an organisational leader, can block the person from seeing or accepting facts that contradict it, leading to the "halo effect", which is a positive impression of one's company that can lead one to making positive

---

ii Groupthink is "a deterioration of mental efficiency, reality testing, and moral judgment that results from in-group pressures" (Janis, 1972).

iii 'Skilled incompetence' involves spontaneous, automatic, effortless behaviour which is not in the conscious attention of the individual, producing results that the individual did not intend. (Argyris, 2009) evaluations with regard to everything about it, even without evidence.[39] The halo effect is rooted in cognitive dissonance theory,[40] which states that people who want to have a cohesive picture of the world disregard facts that do not support their preconceived ideas. These mental models are used to design and carry out their actions. In other words, human beings are designers of action to achieve their intended consequences.

Design causality

The actions of human beings do not happen by chance. In other words, they are not accidental. They are deliberately planned according to rules that cannot be stated.[41] [42] In this sense, all human beings have theories of action. They have a particular picture, model or belief in their minds of how to view the world, and how to go about executing a particular task. Human beings also envisage the intended consequences they wish to achieve as an outcome of their actions.

For example, as a manager, I will have a particular image of what constitutes effective performance of my staff. I will also have a picture of what strategies to employ in helping them to become effective. I will then embark on a path to implement such a strategy, for example, by having sessions with employees to explain my concept of effective performance, and what actions need to be embarked upon to implement the concept, such as to set measurable performance objectives, tracking progress regularly, and measuring their impact on overall departmental performance. The effectiveness of my model of effective performance can be determined only insofar as it has the desired impact; in other words, that my staff achieve the performance objectives they have set in the first instance. Therefore, it should be clear that all human beings design actions to achieve intended consequences.

"Design" implies that human beings have agency: they are originators of their own actions. In this sense, AS speaks of "design causality" in making a connection between individuals' intentions and actions. Firstly, individuals design their own actions. Secondly, their actions are designed to achieve the consequences they intend.[43] Such design causality propositions could be as follows: "In situation S, if you want to achieve consequence C, under assumptions a_1 … a_n,[iv] do A."[44] This is in contrast to causal descriptions of mainstream science, where autonomous variables, of the kind "X causes Y" influence each other. In a different way, one could say that all reasoning is causal. In other words, it serves the purpose of achieving intended consequences. A theory-in-use proposition[45] acts as a hypothesis in that awareness of it could lead to behaviour that is more effective.

Figure 5.1 depicts diagrammatically the components of a theory-in-use. These rules, or mental models, which underlie all human action, are those that we espouse, and those that we actually use.

---

iv a_1 = assumption 1 to a_n = assumption infinity; it is almost like saying that causality is not linear, rather that it is conditional, depending on the assumptions we make

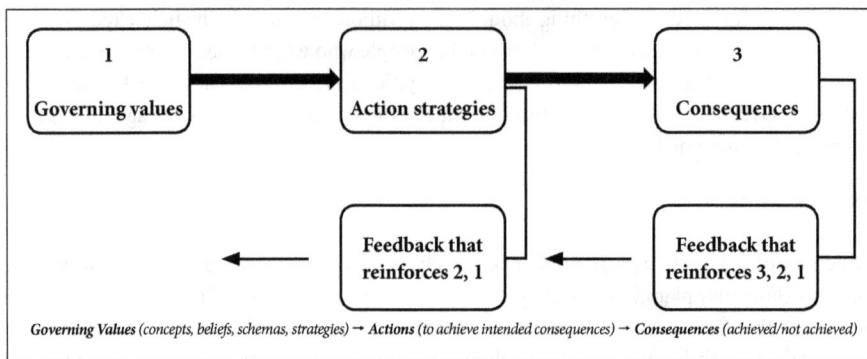

Figure 5.1: Components of a theory-in-use[46]

Espoused theory

Espoused theories are those to which individuals pay allegiance, believe they follow, and are able to state upon request. For example, when someone is asked how he would behave under certain circumstances, the answer one usually gives is the espoused theory of action of that situation.[47] Espoused theories could vary widely. They include values, beliefs and action strategies – for example: "We will build a smart organisation characterised by openness and transparency"). In other words, they are the things we believe in, claim to follow, and communicate publicly.

Theories-in-use

Espoused theory is different from 'theories-in-use', which are designs stored in our heads according to which we design actions to achieve our intended consequences (for example: "the CEO unilaterally appointed her executive team behind closed doors without consulting other senior members of staff, and informed management and staff about her decision without giving them an opportunity to comment or raise objections"). Note how this contrasts with the espoused values. This drives our actual behaviour according to our mental model.

Theories-in-use are tacit. They can be inferred only from actual behaviour. It is important to note that the difference between espoused theory and theory-in-use is not simply a distinction between theory and action. Both are theories of action. The distinction is rather that espoused theories are the values which individuals state guide their behaviour. Their behaviour or action is instead informed by values of theories-in-use of which they are unaware. Theories-in-use are the tacit assumptions individuals hold about themselves and others, as well as the situation and the connections between these.[48] The gap between the espoused theory and theory-in-use may also be tacit.

The central idea is that despite their espoused values, people rather follow unstated rules. These rules prevent them from behaving as they might consciously wish to do. The result is interpersonal and system processes in which many problems are concealed. Taboos prevent the problems, or their existence, from being mentioned. In effect, the unstated rules of the situation, and the unstated assumptions people form about each other, direct their interactions in both group and organisational settings.

There are two types of theories-in-use: Model I (MI) and Model II (MII).

Model I: Theory-in-use

Model MI is the default position from which all human beings operate. *Defensive* behaviour always has the purpose to win according to our own intent, but not according to the intent we state publicly (our espoused intent). We would rather act according to a model that drives our behaviour tacitly, our theories-in-use. Theories-in-use – both MI and MII, the latter of which I will discuss and juxtapose in a table format later (see Table 5.1 below), which are inferred from actual behaviour, can be understood in terms of their governing values, the action determined by such values, and the consequences which the actions produce. These may or may not be in line with the governing values. The governing values of MI theories-in-use are: be in unilateral control; win, do not lose; suppress negative feelings; and behave in a way you consider rational.[49]

The way in which a leader would achieve this, his *action strategy*, for example, would be to advocate his own position to remain in control of the situation and win – the primary behavioural strategy of MI – by making unillustrated attributions and evaluations; treating one's own views as obviously correct; and making covert attributions, evaluations, and face-saving moves such as leaving potentially embarrassing facts unstated.[50] Espoused theories vary a great deal from one individual to the next. However, theories-in-use do not. In other words, people act consistently with MI, irrespective of geography, age, socio-economic status, and level of education, gender, or ethnicity.[51]

The defensive consequences of MI theory-in-use are characteristic of current leadership practices, including miscommunication or misunderstanding; defensive interpersonal and group relationships; self-fulfilling prophecies; self-sealing processes; and escalating error. By implication, this results in decreased effectiveness.[52] Since these ways of operating are largely unconscious and automatic, they are difficult to change. Argyris[53] suggests that this "skilfulness" becomes tacit because of the way in which human beings reason, or make inferences. They jump from their premises to conclusions in a tacit way, based on their own beliefs; preconceived ideas; and ways of viewing the world in dealing with everyday problems. He proposes the "Ladder of Inference"[54] to explain this.

Ladder of Inference

The Ladder of Inference states that while we observe through our senses, information that we actually hear in a conversation is not necessarily the information on which we base our interpretations. In this instance, the lowest rung on a ladder would represent the actual conversation. Based on our tacit mental model, we automatically make inferences from that we have heard. In other words, we jump to a higher rung on the ladder. This is true insofar as human beings are programmed from early childhood to make sense of the world around them based on beliefs that have been hard-wired in our brains to the extent that we may no longer be aware of the influence of such beliefs. We have become unconsciously skilful in how we behave. It is a bit like the unconscious skilfulness that is required to drive a car.

Figure 5.2 gives a pictorial example of the Ladder of Inference.

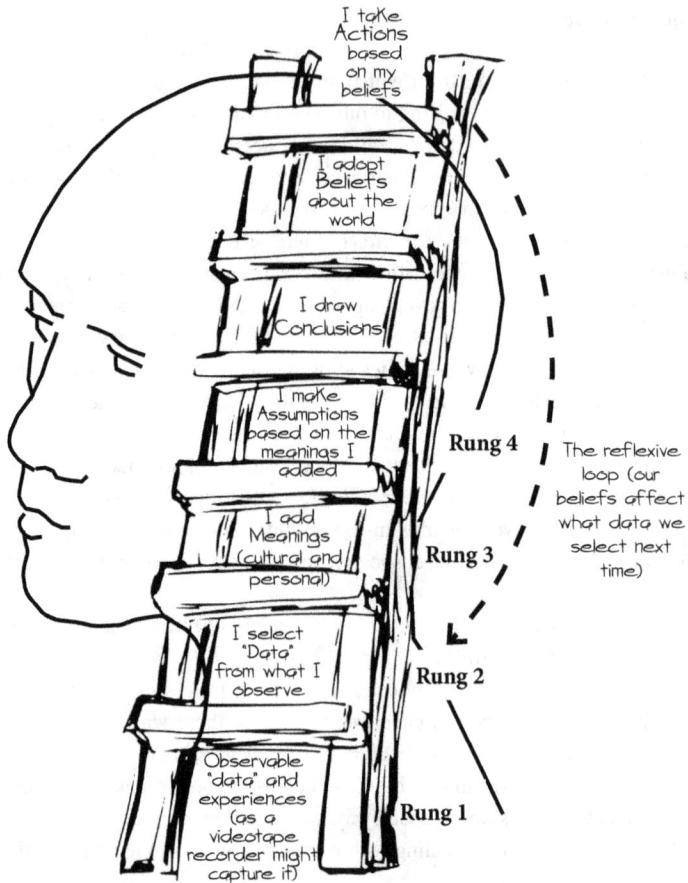

Figure 5.2: The Ladder of Inference[55]

Let me explain:

- When human beings experience some relatively directly observable data (= bottom of the ladder), such as a conversation (= Rung 1 of a ladder); for example, your colleague responds to your suggestion by pausing a moment and then saying, "[t]hat sounds like a rational approach", which you notice;
- You automatically (and selectively) make an inference (= assumption) about or impose meanings on your colleague's words, such as "Your colleague is saying that there is a problem with my suggestion" (= Rung 2);
- Then you impose meanings on the intended action of your colleague (= Rung 3), such as "Your colleague is covering her doubts about my suggestion"; and
- Finally you evaluate the action as good or bad in line with your own preconceived ideas/ beliefs (= Rung 4), along the lines of: "[s]he is uncomfortable criticising me directly, thereby avoiding conflict and subtly telling me not to make further suggestions. I have therefore decided not to make any further suggestions or recommendations."

What we ideally should do is to call for clarification instead of automatically drawing conclusions based on what we think was said, so that when we have pinpointed misalignment, which is always expressed as judgements at the top of the Ladder of Inference, we inquire back down the ladder to bring the underlying data to the surface. The defensive reasoning characteristic of MI – learned early in life and kept tacit by evaluations, abstractions and inferences far removed from observable data – provides the fundamental causal picture for ODRs. Organisational transformation requires changing the behavioural world (characterised by defensive routines, which in turn reinforce the MI theories-in-use and the ODRs). To do that, individuals must develop another theory-in-use.

Model II: Theory-in-Use

Action Science proposes a theory of action to overcome barriers to ODRs by correcting errors of mismatches, which fosters learning, and ensures that the corrections persevere.[56] Such learning is therefore about the detection and correction of errors. It is based on *productive* reasoning, in other words, the detection and correction of gaps between descriptive claims and practical outcomes or between intentions and results, thoughts and actions, theories and practices, or outcomes and expectations.[57]

If, by default, one's approach is to defend and win, it may appear that the situation is insurmountable. However, one could first develop awareness of this with the intent that while one's situation is still about winning, one could make public what is really behind one's reasoning, for purposes of scrutiny by others. Others will therefore have the opportunity to test the attributions one has made high up on the Ladder of Inference. MII theories-in-use suggests such an approach. While the action strategies are the same as MI – advocate, evaluate and attribute – it is done more transparently and openly, in ways where others can test such strategies. For example, a manager will feel free to point out the inconsistencies in a leader's action. The embarrassment the leader may experience because of an inconsistency is not covered up or bypassed, but is engaged. This facilitates learning, especially the kind that reveals the governing values behind the actions. Detecting these would be a first step to correcting errors.

For comparative purposes, Model I and Model II are juxtaposed in Table 5.1.

Table 5.1: Contrasting Models I and II[58]

	Model I	**Model II**
Governing values	• Be in unilateral control • Win, do not lose • Suppress negative feelings (showing ineptness, incompetence and a lack of diplomacy) and behave in a way you consider rational (objective and intellectual)	• Valid information • Informed choice • Vigilant monitoring of the implementation of choice in order to detect and correct error
Action strategies	• Advocate own position to stay in control of the situation and win • Evaluate the thoughts and actions of self and others • Attribute causes in ways that do not encourage questioning of one's own views and feelings	• Advocate, evaluate and attribute, however, it is done more transparently and openly, • In ways where others can test such strategies, for example, a manager will feel free to point out the inconsistencies in a leader's action.

	Model I	Model II
Consequences	• Miscommunication or misunderstanding • Self-fulfilling prophecies • Self-sealing processes and • Escalating error	• Embarrassment a leader may experience because of an inconsistency is not covered up or bypassed. It is engaged • This facilitates learning, especially the kind that reveals the governing values behind the actions • Detecting these would be a first step to correcting errors

Effectiveness ultimately constitutes moving from MI to MII.[59] How does one do this?

Single-loop and double-loop learning

It is proposed that learning which is about the detection and correction of errors – mismatches or gaps between intention and action, and between MI and MII theories-in-use – should move from single-loop learning (SLL) to double-loop learning (DLL). Behind such learning will reside either knowledge that inhibits or promotes learning as given in Table 5.2.

Table 5.2: Conditions inhibiting learning[v]

Knowledge that	
facilitates error (*anti-learning*)	inhibits error (*stimulates learning*)
Ambiguous	Unambiguous
Unclear	Clear
Inconsistent	Consistent
Incongruent	Congruent

Single-loop learning is about correcting a gap between one's action strategy and the consequences thereof, as shown in Figure 5.3. However, changing one's behaviour is not sustainable, because the tacit governing values underpinning behaviour are provoked when someone encounters threat or embarrassment (= stressful situations). What is required is to change the underlying governing values that drive one's action strategy.

---

v These conditions approximate Habermas's conditions of the "ideal speech situation": a) that what is uttered is comprehensible, b) that the content of what is said is true [that is, accurate], c) that the speaker is being truthful (the utterance is congruent with the speaker's intentions), and d) that the speech acts being performed are legitimate [that is, that the utterance is sincerely stated] (Argyris et al., 1985; Kemmis, 2006).

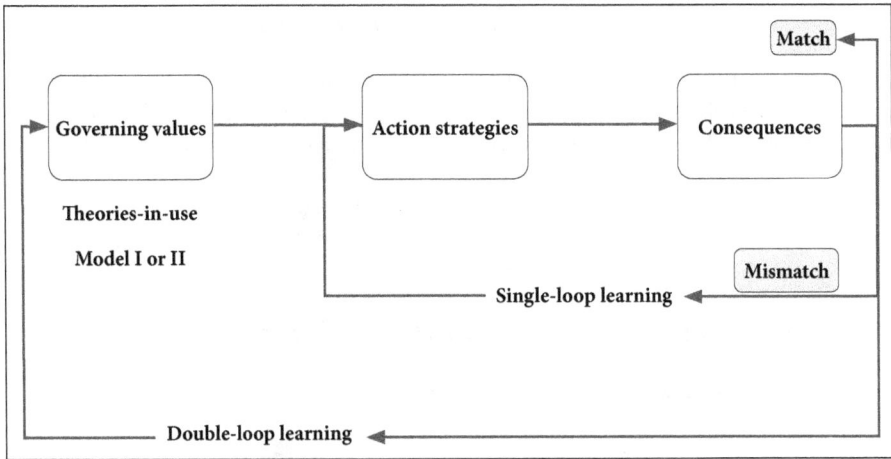

Figure 5.3: Effective learning[60]

Argyris[61] asserts that organisational DLL starts with effective leadership. Such leaders are able to discover the difficult questions; for example, "[i]s our corporate restructure driven by strategy or personalities?" They can create viable problem-solving networks to invent solutions to these questions, and generate and channel human energy and commitment to produce the solutions. MI encourages routine (= non-creative) learning and discourages non-routine (= creative/ innovative) learning that is intended to change the status quo.[62] The fundamental assertion is that the individual who aspires to reduce his or her ineffectiveness should shift from MI to MII theories of action,[63] as is depicted in Figure 5.4.

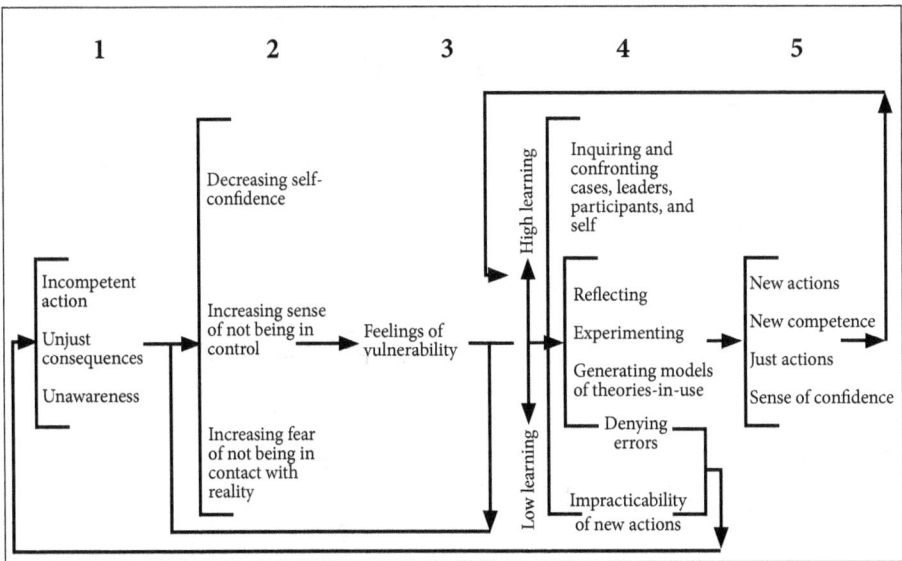

Figure 5.4: Unfreezing from Model I[64]

SLL and DLL also have parallels in family systems theory: first-order change is simple, negative feedback mechanisms to reduce tension in the family; and second-order change means intervening in the whole family as a single system. In order to do so, one needs to adopt third-order thinking.[65]

Implications for Leadership Development

A fundamental premise of AS is that talk implies data, providing a window to the logic of (= the reasoning lying behind) action,[66] because conversations are central to understanding reality and operating effectively in it. For the action scientist, the focus in collecting data is on what people say or do, and how this results in consequences. From such data the action scientist can begin to infer what is in people's heads; in other words, the tacit knowledge that drives what they say or do "to achieve consequences", and what their feelings and thoughts are when acting. Tacit knowledge can be inferred only from concrete illustrations.

The methodological strategy of Action Science

The methodological principle of AS is therefore that, because there is a mismatch between what people espouse and their in-use actions – of which they are unaware – they need to reflect on what they say or do. In so doing, action scientists will have to contend with: biased samples being retrieved; external attributions of causes; losing sight of the data on which inferences are based; elevating positive and diminishing negative evidence; skewing inferences in a self-protective direction; creating more defensive attributions with accompanying more severe consequences; testing their views privately; relying primarily on confirming strategies; and acting on the basis of private understanding which they hold to be true.[67]

The methodological strategy of AS therefore implies:

- Identifying a theory of action that underlies the action: the gap between espoused theories and theories-in-use being brought into awareness through intentional reflection on action;
- Critiquing its adequacy: effectiveness is seen to be critically dependent upon the ongoing testing of propositions; and
- Identifying pathways for learning and practising more effective theories-in-use.

All AS methods are intended to produce directly observable data: (1) on how individual thinking and behaviour contribute unintentionally to defensive routines, and (2) from which the theories-in-use can be inferred. In Argyris et al's[68] words, methods will have to be employed "to make known what is known so well that we no longer know it, ... so that it might be critiqued, ... and to make known what is unknown, [i.e.,] the discovery of alternatives so that they too might be critiqued." Hence, methods will have to be employed that elicit valid information about what individuals think and do, because the default pattern of individuals is to employ defensive reasoning. We espouse leadership effectiveness, but we lack the skills to produce such holistic inside-out development, AND we are unaware of this limitation.

How do we do this new learning? As indicated earlier, one cannot simply focus on changing the behaviour. New learned behaviours tend to break down when people experience stress, as stress triggers their default behaviours. One has to change the belief that drives the behaviour. For instance, if a manager believes people should be treated badly, one can train him as much as one likes, but until one has changed that belief, he will continue to treat people badly, particularly in stressful situations.

A "new" philosophical focus: an inside-out development approach

The new development approach is about taking an inside-out stance. It is about dealing with beliefs that prevent new learning from taking root, because the barriers to effectiveness, change and excellence reside fundamentally inside the individual. Therefore, the programmes that are designed to help develop people must go deeply into the space of helping managers see their blindness; to see their selective perception; to see how hypervigilant they are; to see how they rationalise issues; and so forth. If we cannot develop programmes that help people experience that, we are not going to be successful in our leadership development. The first angle one would take is to conceive "leadership" as more than theory. It is something that guides action. If leadership is action, it implies that such action can be effective or ineffective (*cf* the earlier definition of effectiveness, that is, 'the extent to …').

The knowledge we produce in our development programmes must be in the service of action. Two expressions of such learning are:

a) *Double-loop learning,* is learning that is not merely an insight, but also the detection and correction of errors. Errors are to be understood to be mismatches between our espoused strategic intent and what we actually do. Such learning should help someone to get to the underlying beliefs, attitudes and values that perpetuate ineffective behaviour intended to improve organisational processes, through an articulation of tacit reasoning processes and public disclosure:

   • *Basic principle:* leaders can improve their interpersonal and organisational effectiveness by exploring the hidden beliefs that drive their action (= long term change).[69]

b) *Action learning,* focuses on behavioural change through reflection on real business challenges:

   • *Basic principle:* leaders learn most effectively when working on real-time problems occurring in their work setting (= short-term change).[70]

Critical reflective developmental tools

In addressing both rigour and relevance, AS can provide a sound scientific basis for bridging the on-going science-practice integration gap. This is especially true for people and organisational development specialists who endeavour to develop effective theory-informed development practices in organisations. Over three decades ago, Argyris and Schön[71] lamented that: "… it has become a cliché to say that professionals must 'relate knowledge to effective action', or 'integrate theory and practice.'" All methods are intended to produce directly observable data on the following: how an executive's individual thinking and behaviour contribute unintentionally to defensive routines; and data from which an executive's theories-in-use can be inferred.

Advocacy and inquiry

Advocacy and inquiry are key skills in AS. They require that individuals (including development specialists) regard their views as subject to critique and testing. They must immediately make them public and invite others to inquire into them. Such reflective practice – reflecting-in-practice and reflecting-on-practice – is a core element of an epistemology of practice. Advocacy and inquiry could be utilised as ground rules for normal organisational practices, such as meetings/workshops or for self-reflection. Figure 5.5 depicts the process of balancing advocacy and inquiry.

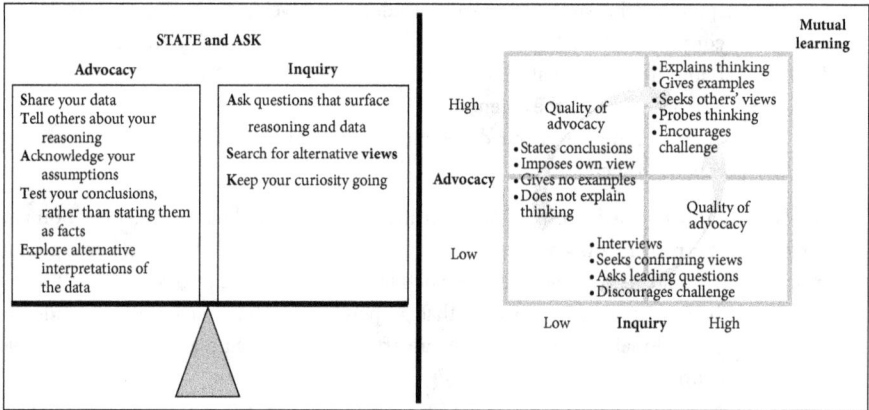

STATE and ASK				Mutual learning

Advocacy	Inquiry
Share your data Tell others about your reasoning Acknowledge your assumptions Test your conclusions, rather than stating them as facts Explore alternative interpretations of the data	Ask questions that surface reasoning and data Search for alternative **views** Keep your curiosity going

High Advocacy — Quality of advocacy:
• Explains thinking
• Gives examples
• Seeks others' views
• Probes thinking
• Encourages challenge

• States conclusions
• Imposes own view
• Gives no examples
• Does not explain thinking

Low Advocacy — Quality of advocacy

• Interviews
• Seeks confirming views
• Asks leading questions
• Discourages challenge

Low — Inquiry — High

Figure 5.5: Balancing advocacy and inquiry[72]

Left-Right hand column case method

The Left-Right hand column method represents a relatively easy method to make undiscussables discussable. This method is simply a blank sheet divided into two columns where the leaders capture an actual difficult conversation they had with someone else in the Right-hand column in narrative format. Simultaneously, they use the Left-hand column to reflect on their feelings and thoughts while having the conversation, but do not make this public.[73] Writing about a difficult incident allows leaders to take responsibility for both uncovering MI problem-solving methods, and creating more effective MII solutions to their problems.

This process helps leaders in developing a deep awareness of how much they are trapped in MI problem solving, because the information in the Left-hand column is bypassed, and the bypass is bypassed (= covered up). The written cases are then analysed according to the Ladder of Inference (see Figure 5.6 below, and Figure 5.7 in the next section).

Brief statement of context

I had diversity issues with my boss. Hence I felt a need to outline, from my perspective, key imperatives of diversity in the organisation, including the following tenets of proper transformation in the environment of the bank: the issue of culture, the issue of numbers in terms of the gap analysis (targets), the issue of remuneration and skills development (and all the other related issues).

What actually happened:

My thoughts and feelings	What we said
W's response was a bit sharp. He was very, a bit abrupt. He wanted the conversation to end quickly, while I wanted us to engage further. I'm pushing, I'm dragging him into something that he is not totally enthusiastic about.	**DM:** I hope you are very much aware [of] the challenges that we got with respect to our diversity forum and the culture within our environment [–] that we need to ensure that we have the proper culture, that proper skills development is taking place, that we are compliant in terms of the expectations from the Department of Labour [DoL]. So, I'd gone and worked out a programme where I felt we needed to reflect.
There was a gap between us, a wedge or a gap about where somebody is coming from, in terms of your experience, exposure to life, and what I deemed critical, and what is critical to his mind.	**W:** DM, I'm very much aware of what is happening, and my departure always has been "what needs to be done?" You know, maybe what you have set up to do, put it in 5-point plan, in terms of all the things that need to be done. Also come up with, highlight those areas you strongly feel we need to address, and I'll support you 100%.
There could be some pressure from elsewhere, he seemed to be absorbing pressure, you know, because he was not as committed or as vocal as he was before in terms of certain things he had strong (positive) feelings about, particularly in terms of equity and fairness in the work environment.	**DM:** I don't know whether you want me to discuss with you or you want me to extrapolate the information, so that I can present it to you. **W:** The ball is in your court, you do what you think is right. In terms of mentoring, I think we need to start identifying who can be the mentors, who are willing. It won't be just pick and choose, you need to do the matching process, in terms of who can be matched with whom in terms of mentoring and coaching. So I think that that's and exercise you need to do, and go and find out how best can we sum up the whole exercise to ensure that this happens.

Figure 5.6: Illustration of how the Left-right hand column is used

Ladder of Inference

The Ladder of Inference is used to help a leader reflect on how high up the Ladder of Inference she is, and to show that the inferences leaders do make are not directly based on observable data. Reflecting on the case presented previously, the following Ladder of Inference is generated for the leader (see Figure 5.7 below).

I adopt beliefs about the world *Top of the ladder*	When my manager responds in a way that I interpret as abrupt, I do not ask him what leads him to respond as he has and continues to advocate my view on the issue.
I draw conclusions *Rung 4*	He is covering up his lack of commitment.
I make assumptions on the meanings I added *Rung 3*	He is not committed to the diversity programme and is abdicating responsibility for driving this programme.
I add meanings *Rung 2*	He is under pressure from peers who believe they have something to lose in this process.
I select data from what I observe on the basis of what I believe *Rung 1*	My boss' responses are very abrupt to my suggestion to have an extensive discussion on the diversity programme.
Observable data (written case) *Bottom of the ladder*	A discussion DM had with his boss on what he perceived to be misalignment between himself and his boss on implementing a diversity plan for the organisation.

Figure 5.7: Illustration of how the Ladder of Inference is applied

Interviewing to elicit illustrations

Skilled interviewing is critical to elicit illustrations. If someone says that X is incompetent, probe the observable data that led him to this view. It is better to ask "what leads you to …?", rather than "why do you …?." The former helps to lay bare the reasoning behind his actions. The latter invites espoused theory. Others can then examine this.

In eliciting data for the leader to reflect on his MI theory-in-use, one could, for example, interview the leader to understand his specific strategy on effective leadership. What is critical in such an interview would be to guide the leader towards giving concrete illustrations of his strategy. Otherwise he may just be relating espoused theory. Here I report on an actual excerpt of an interview with a motor retail MD where he explains his "hands-off" leadership style as given in Figure 5.8 (below).

The interview is intended to establish the extent of leaders' counterproductive activities and causal explanations (Here is an example of the leader explaining his 'hands-off' management style)

Let me give you an example of that. I would walk into a sales manager and typically say, "Good morning. How was your day yesterday?"

"No, very good. We were busy."

"Excellent. Okay. Can you show what salesperson K did yesterday? Can we just see it quickly on your screen?"

"Sure."

"Mm, she wasn't so busy was she?"

"Mm, yes, you're right and she told me she had a hell of a busy day yesterday. No, it's okay. Don't worry about it. K is one of my better salespeople. No, she's fine."

"No. No-no-no-no, you need to call her in and discuss with her what did she do yesterday. Why are prospects not properly loaded? Where is she struggling with negotiations and at what stage is she in the sales process with negotiation A, B, C, D?" Because unless a sales manager is managing at what stage – let's just say you were the buyer. Okay.

And you were at a stage where we had done a demonstration of the car to you but we had been unable to take it to the next step. Then the sales manager should be saying, "But you saw customer C and you've done a demonstration, yes". And the salesperson would say, "Yes, I've done a demonstration."

"What is the next step?"

Figure 5.8: Example of an interview

Mapping complex interview data

Mapping can be used to systematise complex material for ongoing in-depth analysis by OD practitioners as a diagnostic and a solution generation tool. Mapping simply utilises the conceptual models MI and MII to analyse leaders' theories of action, including their governing values, action strategies, and consequences. These models also illustrate SLL or DLL. Figure 5.9 provides an illustration of mapping the previous interview.

Governing values	Action strategies	Behavioural consequences	Learning & effectiveness consequences
AT's theory-in-use is inferred from actual examples (and he provides many), also confirmed with him in the second interview): "When I want to steer my organization strategically, I tell myself I am adopting a hands off strategy while describing in minute detail what my people should do, with the result that I actually use a hands-on strategy."	• utilises a strategy that is very hands-on, looks at screen, what X has entered; • knows best (and maybe does) i.e., sole guardian of the definition of effectiveness in business and how task should be execute; • unilateral; does not inquire into other's reasoning, which may reduce effectiveness in achieving change in behaviour; "get him to do what I know is the right thing to do"; • advocates unilaterally the position that high-impact selling, i.e., making new contacts, properly recording them, ensuring a proper data-bank of prospects is route to success; makes attributions about people's personality and motives, e.g., "human beings, particularly selling human beings, tend to want to work in random ways"	• incongruence between his hands-off strategy, and on the other hand illustrating very hands-on behaviour; • hands-on approach, with many 1:1 interactions with sales managers, could contribute both to effectiveness and ineffectiveness. He may get the salespeople working more effectively, but he will not have time for focussing on the strategic issues as he defines them	• self-sealing, insofar as there is little public testing of his process theory • focus on changing behaviour of salespeople is an example of single-loop learning – no attempt to understand the governing values of salespeople that might be the real reason for their ineffectiveness

Figure 5.9: Illustration of mapping the interview

In sum, all development methods should help the leaders to surface the tacit mental models that stifle effective/sustainable learning.

The Value-add of Action Science

The value-add of AS can be summarised as follows:

- As a *critical-reflective tool* for application in managerial practice that enhances productive practices. Organisations have an interest in their leaders being effective. Action Science is an effective method of inquiry to surface gaps between what is espoused and what is enacted. Understanding the basic tenets of AS also provides leaders with a powerful tool to evaluate taking action with regard to the advice they receive from consultants.[74]

- As a *critical-reflective practical tool* for OD professionals to drive effective organisational change. Examining their own tacit theories-in-use, and designing interventions that could make public underlying individual and organisational defensive routines which hamper effective implementation of change, could go a long way to making them more effective[75] and thereby increasing their credibility.

Conclusion

Action Science endeavours to produce knowledge that can inform action, with the intention of changing the status quo. The theories of action of organisational leaders are characterised by skilled unawareness and incompetence, resulting in ODRs. The latter is not discussed publicly, and this undiscussability is not discussable.[76]

Action Science concerns itself with identifying mismatches between intention and action so that individuals are able to be effective in achieving their intended consequences. It proposes to do this by advocating methods such as MII that will help to derive valid information insofar as this method can tap into mental models that underpin behaviour (DLL). Moreover, it is not only about generating valid knowledge about the organisational dilemmas leaders face, but also about knowledge that it is possible to put it into action, which enhances effectiveness. Action Science as presented by Argyris, Schön and others makes a sound scientific-practice case as an effective inquiry, among other things, into the gaps of current leadership practices.

Endnotes

1   Donald Schön, 1983.
2   Hay Group, 2002.
3   Noonan , 2007, p. 3.
4   Argyris, 1993, p. 6.
5   Argyris, 1997.
6   Argyris, 2000, p. viii.
7   Argyris, 2000, pp. 93–95.
8   Argyris, 1992.
9   Schneider, 1994.
10   Beer, 2000 & 2001.
11   Martin, 1993.
12   PD Business Learning Consultants, 2007.
13   Corporate Leadership Council, 2004.
14   Bowen, Gilliland & Folger, 1999.
15   George, 2006.
16   Dick, 1993.
17   Torbert , 1976, p. 501.
18   Argyris, Putnam & McClain Smith ,1985, pp. 8–9.
19   Putnam, 2006.
20   Argyris, 1980.
21   Argyris and Schön, 1989.
22   Argyris et al., 1985, p. 2.
23   Argyris et al, 1985. pp. 45–54.
24   Argyris et al., 1985, p. 51.
25   Argyris et al., 1985.
26   Argyris et al., 1985.
27   Argyris, 1980.
28   Argyris et al., 1985, p. 81.
29   Goleman, 1985, p. 24.
30   Argyris et al, 1985.
31   Argyris, 1994, p. 81.
32   Janis, 1972.
33   Argyris, 1994, p. 80.
34   Senge, 1990, p. 174.
35   Argyris, 1980, p. 139.
36   Argyris, 1976, p. 3.

43   Argyris, 1993.
44   Argyris & Schön, 1974, p. 6.
45   cf. Argyris et al., 1985, pp .55, 169, 171, 244, 245, 248, 391–392, for actual examples.
46   Argyris, 1980.
47   Argyris & Schön, 1974.
48   Argyris & Schön, 1974.
49   Argyris, 1995, 1997.
50   Argyris et al., 1985.
51   Argyris, 1993.
52   Putnam, 1991.
53   Argyris, 1993.
54   Argyris et al, 1985; Argyris, 1993.
55   This image of the Ladder of Inference is available online at http://urbangrammars. blogspot.com/2009_04_01_archive.html
56   Argyris, 1993.
57   Argyris, 1993; Action Science Network, 2007; Argyris & Schön, 1996.
58   cf. Argyris 1993, 1995, 1997, 2000.
59   Action Science Network, 2007.
60   cf. Argyris 1999, 1993.
61   Argyris, 1976.
62   Argyris, 1999.
63   Action Science Network, 2007.
64   Argyris, 1982.
65   Watzlawick, Beavin & Jackson, 1967.
66   Argyris et al., 1985.
67   Argyris et al., 1985.
68   Argyris et al, 1985, p. 237.
69   Raelin, 1997.
70   Raelin, 1997.
71   Argyris and Schön, 1974.
72   Noonan, 2007, Available online at http:// www.iseesystems.com/Online_Training/ course/module5/5-04-3-0-balancing.htm

37	Argyris, 1993.		73	*cf* guidelines in Action Design, 2009.
38	Senge, 1990.		74	Argyris, 2000.
39	Rosenzweig, 2007.		75	Argyris, 1987.
40	Festinger, 1957.		76	Argyris, 2000.
41	Argyris et al, 1985.			
42	Argyris, 1980.			

References

Action Design. 2009. *Case guidelines.* [Online]. Available: http://www.actiondesign.com/resources/toolkit/case-guidelines. [Accessed 29 July 2016].

Action Science Network. 2007. *What is action science?* [Online]. Available: http://www.actionscience.com/actinq.htm. [Accessed 29 July 2016].

Argyris, C. 1976. *Increasing leadership effectiveness.* New York, NY: John Wiley & Sons.

Argyris, C. 1980. *Inner contradictions of rigorous research.* New York, NY: Academic Press, Inc.

Argyris, C. 1982. *Reasoning, learning, and action.* San Francisco, CA: Jossey Bass Inc.

Argyris, C. 1987. 'Reasoning, action strategies, and defensive routines: The case of OD practitioners'. In RA Woodman & AA Pasmore (eds). *Research in organisational change and development* (Vol 1). Greenwich: JAI Press. 89–128.

Argyris, C. 1992. *On organizational learning.* Cambridge, MA: Blackwell Publishers.

Argyris, C. 1993. *Knowledge for action: A guide to overcoming organizational change.* San Francisco, CA: Jossey-Bass Publishers.

Argyris, C. 1994. 'Good communication that blocks learning'. *Harvard Business Review,* 77–85, July-August.

Argyris, C. 1995. 'Action science and organizational learning'. *Journal of Managerial Psychology,* 10(6):20–26.

Argyris, C. 1997. 'Learning and teaching: A theory of action perspective'. *Journal of Management Education,* 21(1):9–26.

Argyris, C. 1999. *The next challenge for leadership: Learning, change and commitment.* Atlanta, GA: ASTD Lifetime Achievement Award.

Argyris, C. 2000. *Flawed advice and the management trap: How managers can know when they're getting good advice and when they're not.* New York, NY: Oxford University Press.

Argyris, C. 2009. 'Skilled incompetence'. *Harvard Business Review.* Boston, MA: Harvard Business School Press.

Argyris, C & Schön, DA. 1974. *Theory in practice: Increasing professional effectiveness.* San Francisco, CA: Jossey Bass Inc.

Argyris, C & Schön, DA. 1989. 'Participatory action research and action science compared: A commentary'. *American Behavioural Scientist,* 32(5):612–623.

Argyris, C & Schön, DA. 1996. *Organizational learning II: Theory, method, and practice.* Reading, MA.: Addison-Wesley Publishing Company.

Argyris, C, Putnam, R & McLain Smith, D. 1985. *Action science: Concepts, methods, and skills for research and intervention.* San Francisco, CA: Jossey-Bass Inc.

Beer, M. 2000. 'Research that will break the code of change: The role of useful normal science and usable action science'. In M Beer & N Nohria (eds). *Breaking the code of change.* Boston, MA: Harvard Business School Press. 415–427.

Beer, M. 2001. 'Why management research findings are unimplementable: An action science perspective'. *Reflections,* 2(3):58–62.

Bowen, DE, Gilliland, SW & Folger, R. 1999. 'HRM and service fairness: How being fair with employees spills over to customers'. In RS Schuler & SE Jackson (eds). *Strategic human resource management.* Oxford: Blackwell Business. 265–281.

Corporate Leadership Council. 2004. *Driving employee performance and retention through engagement: A quantitative analysis of the effectiveness of employee engagement strategies.* Washington, DC: Corporate Executive Board (CEB).

Dick, B. 1993. 'You want to do an action research thesis?" Thesis resource paper. [Online]. Available: http://www.scu.edu.au/schools/gcm/ar/art/arthesis.html. [Accessed 29 July 2016].

Festinger, L. 1957. *A theory of cognitive dissonance.* Redwood City, CA: Stanford University Press.

George, B. 2006. *Truly authentic leadership.* [Online]. Available: http://www.usnews/stylesheets/2006_leaders_article.css. [Accessed 29 July 2016].

Goleman, D. 1985. *Vital lies, simple truths: The psychology of self-deception.* New York, NY: Simon & Schuster Paperbacks.

Hay Group. 2002. *Fortune Magazine's 100 Most Admired Research.*

Horkheimer, M. 1982. *Critical theory.* New York, NY: Seabury Press.

Janis, I.L. 1972. *Victims of groupthink: A psychological study of foreign-policy decisions and fiascoes* [sic]. Boston, MA: Houghton Mifflin.

Kemmis, S. 2006. 'Exploring the relevance of critical theory for action research: Emancipatory action research in the footsteps of Jürgen Habermas'. In P Reason & H Bradbury (eds). *Handbook of action research.* London, UK: Sage Publications Ltd. 91–101.

Martin, R. 1993. 'Changing the mind of the corporation'. *Harvard Business Review,* 81–94, , Nov–Dec.

Noonan, W.R. 2007. *Discussing the undiscussable: A guide to overcoming defensive routines in the workplace.* San Francisco, CA: Jossey-Bass.

PD Business Learning Consultants 2007. 'Employee engagement'. *White Paper.*

Putnam, R. 1991. 'Recipes and reflective learning: "What would prevent you from saying it that way?"' In DA Schön (ed). *The reflective turn: Case studies in and on educational practice.* New York, NY: Teachers College Press. 145–163.

Putnam, R. 2006. 'Action science'. In R Thorpe & R Holt (eds). *Dictionary of qualitative management research.* London, UK: Sage.

Raelin, J. 1997. 'Action learning and action science: Are they different?' *Organizational Dynamics,* 202–222.

Rosenzweig, P. 2007. *The halo effect … and the eight other business delusions that deceive managers.* New York, NY: Simon & Schuster.

Schneider, WE. 1994. *The reengineering alternative: A plan for making your current culture work.* Burr Ridge, IL: Irwin Professional Publishing, Inc.

Schön, D.A. 1983. *The reflective practitioner.* New York, NY: Basic Books.

Senge, P.M. 1990. *The fifth discipline: The art and practice of the learning organisation.* New York, NY: Doubleday/Currency.

Torbert, W. 1976. *Creating a community of inquiry: Conflict, collaboration, transformation.* London, UK: John Wiley & Sons.

Watzlawick, P, Beavin, JH & Jackson, DD. 1967. *Pragmatics of human communication: A study of interactional patterns, pathologies, and paradoxes.* New York, NY: WW Norton & Co.

Chapter 6

PSYCHOBIOGRAPHICAL PROFILING

Roelf van Niekerk, Mark Perry and Paul Fouché

Psychobiographical profilers are storytellers who highlight interesting and important aspects of the life stories of extraordinary individuals. Generally, stories come in many forms and are not bound by societal, national, cultural, or historical boundaries. They form part of everyday conversations and are found in newspapers, magazines, books, theatres, television programmes, and films. The entertainment value of stories is readily acknowledged. But stories are not only for entertainment. They also inform, educate, enlighten, and inspire.

Not surprisingly, storytelling has infiltrated the organisational world in recent decades. Stories have become a cornerstone of organisational life, where they appear in different forms and play important roles, particularly in programmes aimed at education, training, development, motivation, empowerment and marketing. During such programmes, emerging leaders are required to analyse case studies; identify key challenges and motives; debate issues and situations from multiple perspectives; reconcile the interests of different stakeholders; develop appropriate strategies; and share relevant personal experiences.

This chapter deals with storytelling that focuses on the lives of leaders. It demonstrates that storytelling, or psychobiographical profiling, is a useful strategy to develop or improve leadership. Profiles of leaders are useful methods for illustrating the multitude of factors that contribute to effective and ineffective leadership. They illustrate, among other things, that leadership is the product of a multitude of causal factors, and that the best way to make sense of leadership is to approach it from many different perspectives.

This chapter focuses on six aspects of psychobiographical profiling. In the next two sections psychobiographical profiling is defined and the underlying philosophy and purpose are presented. This is followed by a brief review of the history of psychobiographical profiling. Thereafter, the psychobiographical profiling process and its value and benefits, as well as a critique, are explicated in detail. A chapter summary serves as a conclusion.

Before we turn in more detail to psychobiographical profiling, consider the following brief anecdotes which describe the life experiences of five prominent leaders. Do you recognise them?

- *A* was a prominent South African political leader. A's mother died when he/she was two weeks old. The first time A saw a photograph of his/her mother was when A was 55 years old. During A's early career, he/she lectured economics at a university for eight years.
- *B*, a South African pioneer who achieved international prominence at the age of 45, lost his/her first job when colleagues requested him/her to leave as a result of irreconcilable differences. At the time, B was in his/her early thirties.
- *C*'s parents divorced when he/she was seven years old after which he/she was placed in the custody of his/her father. C was retrenched when he/she was 35 years old (this happened shortly after the death of C's father). C survived the retrenchment crisis, re-established his/her career, and within a few years emerged as one of South Africa's prominent leaders.
- Following *D*'s death, a panel of leadership experts cautioned young leaders not to try to emulate D's style. They stated: *"If they do and do not possess his personality, they will have problems. None of our theories encompass D."* The panel also urged those involved in leadership development to consider revising theories to ensure that provision is made for the distinctive behaviours and contributions of leaders such as D.

- During his/her childhood, *E* was a sickly child. He/she had been diagnosed with polio in the first year of his/her life. This illness left him/her with an atrophied right hand which forced E to write with his/her left hand. At the age of 14 years, E contracted tuberculosis and spent 22 months at the Rietfontein Sanatorium. Initially, E dreamt of becoming a medical doctor. However, owing to limited financial resources, E qualified as a teacher, but resigned from his/her first teaching job.

Who are these leaders? How did the experiences described above influence their lives, careers, and leadership? The identities of the five leaders appear at the end of the chapter.[1]

Definition and Description

Two distinct disciplines are represented in the term *psychobiography*, namely psychology and biography. The first, psychology, is recognised as a scientific discipline that values empirical evidence and uses theoretical models to describe behaviour. Biography, on the other hand, emphasises the uniqueness of individuals (rather than the commonalities among them) and denotes a more subjective, intuitive, and literary approach. The alliance between biography and psychology, based on their common interest in life stories and biographical material, benefits both disciplines. Psychobiographical profilers agree that psychology improves biography as much as biography improves psychology. However, because of the different methods employed, the interdisciplinary relationship between psychology and biography is also characterised by a degree of tension and uneasiness.

Generally, psychobiographical profiling refers to any biography that involves the systematic application of psychological theory. In its simplest form, psychobiographical profiling incorporates at least three elements: (a) a biographical account, or life story of a notable individual; (b) an analysis of contextual factors, developmental processes, and accomplishments; and (c) a theoretical interpretation of the life story.

Psychobiographical profiling has several characteristic features. It is an inter-disciplinary approach that invites contributions and perspectives from several scientific disciplines (for example, business science, economics, psychology, political science) and the humanities (for example, history, philosophy, sociology, and spirituality). It typically approaches life stories from a longitudinal perspective. Psychobiographical profiling comprises in-depth studies of extraordinary individuals in the contexts in which they made their contributions. Psychobiographical profiling does not afford anonymity or confidentiality to participants. Instead, it requires that profiled leaders be identified by name. Furthermore, psychobiographical profiling employs indirect methods to analyse the development or characteristics of individuals. Usually, extensive use is made of biographical material available in the public domain and originally compiled by writers, journalists, or researchers. This material is not collected primarily to solve a scientific problem, but rather to answer questions and describe phenomena that are inherently important, particularly from psychological and historical perspectives. Lastly, psychobiographical profiling often focuses on completed lives.

Philosophy and Purpose

Psychobiographical profiling overlaps with the philosophy and intentions of social learning theory, the narrative approach, and positive psychology.

Social learning theory

This well-known theory emphasises the importance of observational learning, or learning from others. The original author, Canadian psychologist Albert Bandura, proposed that most human behaviour is acquired by observing others. Bandura suggested that observational learning occurs intentionally or accidentally. This is how, for example, children learn to play with toys, perform chores, develop skills such as riding a bicycle, or learn to speak, and how children and adults alike acquire important leadership competencies. In many cases, the behaviour that is being learned is the same as the modelled behaviour (for example, imitating the behaviour of an experienced presenter). However, original behaviours can also be learned through observation. Observers are often able to solve problems correctly even after the models they had observed failed to solve them. Thus, observational learning exceeds mere imitation of behaviour.

Bandura proposed that three factors influence modelling, namely the characteristics of the model, the attributes of the observer, and the consequences associated with the modelled behaviour. This implies that we are more influenced by models who appear competent and relatively similar to ourselves, that our level of motivation will determine how likely we are to imitate models, and that we are more likely to copy behaviours if we believe that such actions will lead to positive outcomes or if we believe that it is in our best interest to do so.

Narrative approach

The narrative or storytelling approach relates to the natural tendency of human beings to express themselves through stories. Stories fulfil important psychological functions. The primary function of the narrative approach is probably integration, or the organisation of diverse aspects of our experiences. Stories represent a natural and spontaneous way to organise information. In a sense, we describe and explain the meaning of our lives through our life stories. As such, stories play an important role in our attempts to experience continuity and meaning in terms of our past, present, and future. But stories also explain, educate, entertain, convince, and inspire. In addition, stories play an important role when we try to gain understanding of difficult life experiences. Ultimately, stories help to organise life experiences into a more-or-less comprehensible narrative form. Currently, the narrative approach is very popular in a number of disciplines, such as education, history, philosophy, psychology, sociology, and theology. The approach represents a co-ordinated interdisciplinary attempt to describe, analyse, and interpret life stories in their natural contexts. In a sense, it has become a *root metaphor* for the study of lives in their social contexts.

Positive psychology

The emergence of positive psychology at the turn of the century provided scientists with renewed impetus to study extraordinariness in all its facets. Psychobiographical profilers are attracted to life stories that are in one way or another eminent, distinguished, exemplary, illustrious, or extraordinary. Indeed, in some cases, profilers focus on lives that are contentious or notorious. However, such profiles are outnumbered by those that focus on psychological strengths and human potential.

Psychobiographical profilers are fascinated with optimal human functioning. Therefore, they focus on individuals who occupy the upper end of the distribution of commendable qualities such as influence, talent, charisma, or innovation. Profilers investigate how individuals acquire extraordinariness and the factors that contribute to the development of extraordinariness. In fact, psychobiographical profiling probably counts as the most popular current approach to the study of optimal functioning.

Furthermore, following the democratisation of South Africa, there has been a drive among South African psychobiographical profilers to study the lives of South African leaders who have made an exceptional impact on their citizens. Naturally, within a young democracy there is a need to acknowledge remarkable contributions and celebrate excellence. Psychobiographical profiling is positioned favourably to enhance awareness of, and pride in, compatriots representing different fields and contrasting cultural backgrounds. The progress made by profilers in this regard is acknowledged in Table 6.1, which provides a summary of a number of completed South African academic studies. These studies focus on leaders who have made contributions in the arts, literature, music, entrepreneurship, politics, religion, and sport.

Table 6.1: South African psychobiographies to date

Leader	Author	Degree, Year, Institution	Context in which leader made contribution
Cornelis Jacobus Langenhoven	MPO Burgers, A Jacobs	MA (1939) Wits, MA (2005) UPE	Literature, Politics
Louis Leipoldt	MPO Burgers	D Litt. (1960) Wits	Literature
Ingrid Jonker	LM van der Merwe	PhD (1978) UFS	Literature
Jan Christiaan Smuts	JP Fouché	D Phil (1999) UPE	Military, Politics
Helen Martins	L Bareira, D Mitchell	MA (2001) UPE, MA (2013) RU	Art
Bantu Stephen Biko	D Kotton	M.A. (2002) UPE	Politics
Wessel Johannes (Hansie) Cronje	A Warmenhoven	MA (2004) UPE, PhD (2006) RU	Sport
Chris Barnard	R van Niekerk	MA (2007) UStell	Medicine
Hendrik Verwoerd	M Claasen	MA (2007) NMMU	Academia, Politics
Herman Mashaba	MA McWalter	MA (2008) UJ	Entrepreneurship
Emily Hobhouse	C Welman	MA (2009) UFS	Philanthropy
Mahatma Gandhi	K Pillay	MA (2009) UPE	Politics
Ralph John Rabie	HMG Uys	MA (2010) NMMU	Music
Frans Martin Claerhout	M Roets	MA (2010) UFS	Art
Alan Paton	M Greeff	MA (2010) UFS	Literature
Christiaan de Wet	R Henning	PhD (2010) RU	Military, Politics
Bram Fischer	DK Swart	MA (2010) UFS	Politics

Leader	Author	Degree, Year, Institution	Context in which leader made contribution
Desmond Tutu	LM Eliastam	M Soc Sci (2010) UFH	Religion
Brenda Fassie	O Gogo	MA (2011) UFS	Music
Olive Schreiner	M Perry	PhD (2012) UFS	Literature
Ellen Kuzwayo	Z Arosi	MA (2013) NMMU	Literature, Politics
Helen Suzman	C Nel	PhD (2013) UFS	Politics
Beyers Naude	B Burnell	PhD (2013) UFS	Politics, Religion
Charlize Theron	T Prenter	MA (2015) RU	Performing arts

The use of psychobiographical profiling to analyse and interpret the life stories of extraordinary individuals allows for the exploration of both overt and covert aspects of human behaviour, including private motives and the causes underlying behaviour. The ultimate aim is to discover the core themes in life stories of exemplary individuals. In the process, life stories are transformed into informative narratives, and the circumstances and qualities that set exceptional individuals apart from others are highlighted.

Historical Overview

Approximately a century ago, psychobiographical profiling was introduced to the discipline of psychology by Sigmund Freud. Although earlier informal applications of psychology in biographies have been documented, Freud established psychobiography with the publication of an influential profile entitled *Leonardo da Vinci and a Memory of His Childhood* in 1910. This profile is credited as being the first formal or scientific psychobiography. In it, Freud provided a set of methodological guidelines. For example, he urged profilers to base conclusions on adequate biographical material, investigate the validity of biographical anecdotes, compare life stories with the behaviour of contemporaries, and resist attaching value to isolated acts, events, and circumstances. Freud also completed other psychopbiographies on historical figures such as Moses and Dostoyevsky.

Psychobiographical profiling also benefited from the development of the case method at Harvard University a century ago. At the time, the case method represented a step forward in making business education more relevant and interactive. Since then, exploration of real-life problems and case studies have taken up increased time in business education and leadership development. Case studies, in particular, are now widely employed to bring the realities of complex business and leadership issues into training and development situations. They offer leaders opportunities to immerse themselves in decision-making processes and extrapolate from case studies to the realities they face. Business school cases tend to highlight the best practices of organisations. For obvious reasons, organisations rarely acknowledge their experiences as ineffective in public. Here, psychobiographical profiling takes a different stand. Profilers believe that it is in the interests of learning to analyse and highlight both exemplary and unsuccessful behaviours and outcomes.

Since the publication of the first formal psychobiography, it has not only developed into an established method and genre, but has also gained international interest and support. Psychobiography has also spread across psychological sub-disciplines, to the extent that Joseph Ponterotto[2] refers to a *renaissance* of psychobiography, and describes psychobiography as a *mainstay* in psychological enquiry. In-depth profiles of extraordinary individuals are becoming more common. Psychobiographical profiling also extends beyond academic use and application. For example, it is noteworthy that the United States Central Intelligence Agency employs psychobiographical profilers to produce data for use in policy development.

In South Africa, psychobiographical profiling is well established. The first academic profile was published almost eight decades ago (see Appendix A). Following a slow start (during the middle of the twentieth century, case study research was viewed as inferior), there has been a revival since the turn of the century. Currently, psychobiographical profiling is conducted at various South African institutions, including the Nelson Mandela Metropolitan University, University of Fort Hare, University of Johannesburg, University of South Africa, and the University of the Free State. The recent revival is reflected in the increase in academic psychobiographies.

Process

The process of psychobiographical profiling poses characteristic methodological challenges. This section addresses these challenges and recommends guidelines for improving the quality of profiles. Interested readers are also referred to the methodological guidelines provided by several international experts.[3]

Step 1: Set objectives

One set of objectives of psychobiographical profiling is academic, while another pertains more specifically to leadership training and development. Academically speaking, the objectives of psychobiographical profiling include the formulation of an accurate and coherent biographical description, an interpretation of the life story in terms of a particular theoretical framework, and the informal evaluation of the applicability of the theoretical framework to the life of the leader. In addition, profiling provides a useful means of testing and refining aspects of existing theories, or even developing new theories.

In terms of leadership training and development, the objectives of psychobiographical profiling focus on learning opportunities that challenge emerging leaders to review key aspects of the profiles, consider personal experiences that relate to the profiles, and debate the style, decisions, actions, or ethics of profiled leaders. Psychological profiling is not just about acquiring knowledge, or mapping new information into existing cognitive structures. It brings real life situations to leadership development programmes. Profilers understand that provocative life stories are often better suited to exploring new terrain than detailed theoretical maps.

Information that is contextually embedded is easier to learn. We learn quickly in situations that are true to real life. If we are assisted in connecting learning experiences to our personal lives, we learn in ways that are relevant. New experiences are linked to existing ones and to our constructions of the world. Therefore, learning situations that resonate with our previous experiences and/or are relevant to our current situation are more likely to promote engagement and embedding of learning.

Such learning opportunities allow for multilevel learning through reflection, discussion, and situation analysis. These learning opportunities are consequently associated with a number of benefits:

1. Emerging leaders are afforded opportunities to step into the shoes of other leaders and to explore the situations they encountered.
2. The learning tends to dig deeper in order to explore what is underneath the surface, and consequently raises awareness of important issues relating to leadership.
3. Emerging leaders are confronted with the perspectives of others on the issues in the case and are given opportunities to contest issues.
4. Emerging leaders are able to reflect on the outcomes depicted in the profile and draw lessons from a retrospective point of view.
5. Emerging leaders are given opportunities to receive feedback on their perspectives and the implications of their decisions and actions.
6. Emerging leaders are able to reflect on how leaders achieve extraordinariness over extended periods of time (or even the entire life course).
7. Leaders are given opportunities to generalise from the case and employ different conceptual frameworks to further their understanding of leadership issues.

Step 2: Decide on format

Psychobiographical profiling requires that the life stories of leaders should be approached from a longitudinal perspective. Essentially, this implies the in-depth investigation of leadership embedded within historical, social, cultural, economic, and political contexts. Psychobiographical profiling also requires life stories to be written in such a way that they effectively engage readers. They must focus on relevant and compelling leadership issues that raise, rather than answer, multiple questions. Profiling must make an appeal on the emotions of emerging leaders and should offer them opportunities to embark on personal journeys of exploration and discovery. Ultimately, profiles that effectively engage readers, and focus on captivating leadership issues, serve as provocative vehicles for personal and leadership development.

Step 3: Make choice of profiles

It has been mentioned that psychobiographical profiling focuses on the lives of extraordinary individuals. Typically, a purposive approach is employed to identify leaders for study. In other words, profilers are required to use their judgment to select leaders who best meet the purposes of the investigation. Leaders are usually chosen on the basis of the interest value, uniqueness and significance of their lives. Leaders that are capable, original, ingenious, and accomplished are more likely to grab attention. Sometimes, psychobiographical profiling focuses on the lives of historical leaders such as Adolf Hitler, Albert Luthuli, or Mahatma Gandhi. If the chosen leader is not a contemporary of the profiler, care should be taken to interpret the life within the historical and socio-cultural circumstances that prevailed at the time.

Profilers are drawn to leaders for reasons that may be conscious and/or unconscious. Usually, profilers are fascinated by particular aspects of leaders. Because of this fascination effect, it is important to foreground the relationship between the profiler and the leader whose life is investigated. The accuracy, objectivity, and credibility of findings are undermined if profilers do not acknowledge the role they themselves play in knowledge creation. Attitudes and emotions may influence not only the choice of leader, but also the collection of material, and the interpretation of findings. Naturally, well-known individuals tend to be prime targets for projections and may elicit strong emotions. Profilers should therefore approach leaders with awareness of their own preferences and prejudices.

Step 4: Collect biographical material

A large amount of information is usually available on extraordinary individuals. The collection of material therefore presents profilers with a considerable challenge. Profilers source biographical material from primary or first-person sources (for example, diaries, autobiographies, letters, interviews) and secondary sources produced by others that are available in the public domain (for example, biographies, newspaper and magazine articles, Internet documents).

Some researchers are reluctant to acknowledge the usefulness of documentary data. However, documents are valued by profilers because of their stability (they can be viewed repeatedly) and convenience (they are freely available). Documents are also useful for validating the accuracy of material obtained from other sources. Profilers acknowledge that documents may be influenced by author bias and therefore they deem it necessary to review multiple documents to minimise the impact of bias and enhance the credibility of the biographical material. Importantly, psychobiographical profilers should co-operate with researchers representing disciplines such as history, literature, management, and political science, who also employ biographical material.

Step 5: Analyse and integrate

Profilers usually face large volumes of biographical material of varying quality and therefore have to employ strategies to extract significant and useful material. South African profilers extract and analyse material according to established international guidelines.[4] Usually, a theoretical framework is required to condense material and guide the ordering of relevant information. During this process, profilers typically employ matrices to display material accurately. Matrices fulfil a number of functions. Firstly, they permit the collection, ordering, and easy viewing of material. Secondly, they suggest preliminary trends and identify gaps in the existing material. Thirdly, matrices facilitate detailed analyses.

During data extraction and analysis, the focus should be on biographical material emphasised by the particular theoretical framework. For example, profiles of Steve Jobs, Raymond Ackermann, and Nelson Mandela could employ theories focusing on entrepreneurial personality, career development, and charismatic leadership respectively.

The credibility of interpretive processes depends to a large extent on the clarity, coherence, attention to detail, in-depth theoretical knowledge, and appropriate contextualisation of the life story. This is referred to as 'thick description', which goes beyond factual material and incorporates personal experience, history, theory, and meaning into the sequences of behaviours and events.[5] Psychobiographies that include thick description draw readers into the life stories and allow them to identify with the behaviours and experiences of a leader. Because of the focus on individual life stories, the scientific rigour of psychobiographical profiling is sometimes questioned. The following four criteria are recommended to assess the value of competing interpretations:[6] logical soundness, comprehensiveness, credibility, and consistency. The ideal psychobiographical profile is one that is meticulously investigated, holistic in coverage, and balanced in interpreting both strengths and weaknesses.

Step 6: Consider ethical issues

Several ethical issues require consideration during psychobiographical profiling. Firstly, leaders who are still alive should consent (preferably in writing) to being profiled. In cases where consent is not possible, it is advisable to use only material available in the public domain. Secondly, profilers should take steps to reduce the risk of invading the privacy of leaders and embarrassing them. All life history material must be treated respectfully. Thirdly, profilers must strive to remain as objective as possible throughout the profiling.

Value and Benefits

As a form of storytelling, psychobiographical profiling aspires to inform (transmit knowledge), engage (capture attention), and inspire (motivate). It appeals to three levels of learning, namely thinking, feeling, and action. Moreover, storytelling appeals to diverse audiences who may have a range of interests and different learning styles. As such, psychobiographical profiling has the potential to play an important role in organisations and business. In this section, the value and benefits of psychobiographical profiling are reviewed.

Historical record

To start off with, few would argue against the historical function of psychobiographical profiling. At a very general level, the study of extraordinary individuals fulfils a societal function, in that it provides a historical record of noteworthy people and events. Through studies of this type, we learn about the commonalities shared by people and the factors and experiences differentiating them, as well as the ways in which they develop and express potential.

Individuality

Unlike the approach to leadership that emphasises and highlights general, shared characteristics, psychobiographical profiling places the individuality of the leader at the centre of theoretical analysis and interpretation. It reminds us that although generalisation is important, the uniqueness of and differences between individuals are at least equally important.

Longitudinal perspective

Psychobiographical profiling has value because it focuses on behaviour patterns that develop and evolve over extended periods of time, or even the entire life course of the leaders (or other persons) who are profiled. This perspective facilitates an in-depth understanding of developmental processes. It reminds us that although cross-sectional snapshots of the behaviours and characteristics of leaders are important, leadership should also be studied longitudinally to reflect life events as they unfold over time.

Contextualisation

Closely related to the previous benefit, psychobiographical profiling asserts that leadership development takes place and is influenced by its context. This context includes a complex combination of personal, social, cultural, economic, historical and political factors. Profilers accept that we cannot understand development and behaviour without being sensitive to contextual influences. By incorporating a wide range of influences, psychobiographical profiling replicates and portrays real-life situations that enable readers to empathise with profiled leaders, their experiences, and the events they encountered. In this sense, profiles of leaders can act as reality tests that allow emerging leaders to confront the complexity of business situations and decisions.

Self-knowledge

This benefit is related to contextualisation because it focuses on the development of self-understanding. Psychobiographical profiling offers leaders a route to self-understanding and self-acceptance. For example, a recent study[7] described and interpreted the leadership development of a prominent South African leader, Brand Pretorius, from the perspective of authentic leadership theory. This study had an obvious academic purpose. However, the profiling process required that Brand Pretorius reflect on his career; explore the influencing factors, events, and experiences; and consider his leadership development and style in the light of contemporary leadership principles and theory. For a leader who approaches the end of his formal leadership career, this same process is likely to assist the leader in gaining insight and integrating pieces of the leadership puzzle. In contrast, a leader whose leadership career is still in progress may benefit from a facilitated learning process such as coaching in order to develop insight and consider changes aimed at increased influence and impact.

Theory development

Another major benefit of psychobiographical profiling is that it provides a valuable method for developing, evaluating, and refining existing theoretical frameworks. Individual life stories are ideally equipped to investigate and extend theoretical frameworks through the confirmation or refutation of constructs. Here, the term *analytical generalisation* is important. This type of generalisation occurs when a particular set of findings is generalised to a broader theory. Profiling enables emerging leaders to identify closely with a life story, analyse the relevant issues, acquire new concepts, and ultimately understand leadership in a coherent and meaningful way.

Flourishing

This benefit relates to its association with the positive psychology movement. Some profilers are particularly interested in optimal human functioning, or the life stories that reflect exemplary traits demonstrated by individuals (for example, exceptional talent, charisma, creativity, and wisdom). Psychobiographical profiling allows them to analyse the life stories of eminent individuals in an indirect and non-invasive manner (that is, without the constraints imposed by experimental methods or psychological measures). These life stories demonstrate that extraordinary achievements, human strengths, and virtue are within our reach and have the potential to motivate us to strive towards similar achievements. Inspiring psychobiographical anecdotes may encourage individuals to follow the example, take action, change their ways, or try harder.

Training and development

It should be clear by now that psychobiographical profiles are effective training tools. Profiles increase awareness and understanding of leadership behaviours, skills, styles, or underlying theories. They help us to understand the qualities or circumstances that set leaders apart from their ordinary counterparts; demonstrate how leadership develops; and allow emerging leaders to identify the value that profiling holds for their own leadership journeys. By using profiles to analyse decisions, actions, circumstances, or interventions that promoted performance or enhanced leadership, emerging leaders may be helped to understand important leadership lessons. Also, by highlighting particular concepts or principles in a profile, trainers may provide new perspectives on the lives of profiled leaders. When emerging leaders find content in psychobiographical profiles that resonates with their own experiences, beliefs, values, preferences, or goals, they will be more open to learning.

It is important to acknowledge the existing competence and experience of emerging leaders involved in leadership development. They bring accumulated experience to development programmes and often require less skill building, but more path-finding and execution. They will benefit more if the learning taps into their wealth of experience. Psychobiographical profiling exposes individuals to new ways of doing things. It is high-impact learning that challenges world views and fundamental assumptions.

Profiling links content to context and generates changes in attitudes, beliefs and behaviours that can be applied outside the learning situation in the workplace. In the process, profiling challenges us to construct new mental models and approaches that integrate our learning. Essentially, profiling challenges us to determine how new information fits with our existing approach, how it is similar and different to what we already know and do, what we need to change, and the implications for our beliefs and behaviours.

Critique

Despite the increased popularity of psychobiographical profiling, it continues to attract mixed reviews. The most important criticisms and methodological challenges are outlined in this section. It is important to note at the outset that although the amount of criticism has decreased in recent years, psychobiographical profilers heed the criticism and remain aware of the shortcomings and limitations of their approach. They recognise that psychobiographical profiling is one of the tools from the toolbox and not a standalone answer to important leadership questions. They also acknowledge that psychobiographical profiling is unable to fully capture the complexity of leadership. However, there is a growing recognition of the importance of psychobiographical profiling for generating knowledge that cannot be obtained through other approaches. Thus, profilers confidently offer their interpretations as complementary to existing ones, and maintain that profiling has the potential to make an important and meaningful contribution to the study of leadership.

The following characteristics of psychobiographical profiling receive most criticism: contact between profilers and profiled leaders, reductionism, insufficient consideration of social and historical context, and biased interpretations.

Contact between profilers and leaders

Profilers often have no personal contact with, or direct knowledge of, leaders. This limits opportunity to verify biographical material or interpretations. However, it must be noted that there are also several advantages to studying the life stories of *absent* subjects. These include the range of data sources collected and analysed by profilers, the opportunity to collect biographical material across the lifespan resulting in a balanced description on a broader scope of behaviour, and the opportunity to retrospectively analyse the intended and unintended consequences of behaviour.

Reductionism

Psychobiographical profilers are often accused of being reductionistic, in other words, of using inadequate data to interpret complex phenomena or processes. More specifically, critics accuse profilers of over-interpreting adult behaviour in terms of earlier experiences, reducing human motivation to a single or limited range of denominators, or emphasising personal factors at the expense of social and historical factors. Profilers acknowledge the risk of approaching life history material in a restricted, narrow-minded, or formulaic manner. They value methodological rigour and follow widely accepted guidelines to counter reductionism.

Context

One of the difficult challenges facing profilers is giving sufficient consideration to biographical material as well as the socio-historical contexts, including cultural, economic, historical, political and social factors. Profilers often study the life stories of historical leaders, or leaders from different cultures. This adds complexity to the task of profilers, and emphasises the importance of in-depth engagement with several types of data. It is important to acknowledge that psychobiographical profiling cannot come close to the true complexity of the real world.

Bias

The manner in which psychobiographical profilers select leaders and the amount of time spent with single life stories make it very difficult for profilers to remain objective throughout the project. Prolonged and in-depth engagement with biographical and contextual data challenges profilers to remain open-minded, impartial and to employ systematic methods to collect, order, and interpret the vast amount of material. Admittedly, some profilers may be tempted to omit material that contradicts their theoretical preferences or preliminary interpretations. Such omission undermines the accuracy and objectivity of the profile and will inevitably compromise its credibility.

Conclusion

This chapter presented an overview of the characteristics, purpose, development, process, and value of psychobiographical profiling. It demonstrated that in-depth descriptions of the lives of leaders in all their complexity and contradiction provide leadership practitioners with comprehensive and life-like perspectives on leadership. Psychobiographical profiles are intended for use in a variety of settings where leadership development is presented ranging from business schools to in-house programmes.

One of the main benefits of psychobiographical profiling is its potential to raise questions regarding the utility and applicability of various leadership theories and kindle the formulation of new hypotheses concerning leadership. Underlying psychobiographical profiling is a fascination with human behaviour, particularly how and why some individuals stand out from the rest. Psychobiographical profiling offers emerging leaders opportunities to examine the lives of exceptional leaders to gain a deeper understanding of what makes some leaders exceptional and the dynamics at play in the process.

Endnotes

1   The five prominent leaders are/were: (A) Helen Suzman; (B) Prof Christiaan Barnard;
     (C) Raymond Ackerman; (D) Steve Jobs; (E) Archbishop Desmond Tutu.
2   Ponterotto, 2014.
3   Alexander, 1990; Elms, 1994; Runyan, 1984; Runyan, 1988; Schultz, 2005.
4   Alexander op cit; Huberman & Miles, 2002.
5   Denzin, 1989.
6   Runyan, 1984.
7   Harwood, 2015.

References

Alexander, I.E. 1990. *Personology: Method and content in personality assessment and psychobiography.* Durham, NC: Duke University Press.

Denzin, N.K. 1989. *Interpretive biography.* London, England: Sage.

Elms, A.C. 1994. *Uncovering lives: The uneasy alliance of biography and psychology.* New York, NY: Oxford University Press.

Fouché, J.P. & Van Niekerk, R. 2010. Academic psychobiography in South Africa: Past, present, and future. *South African Journal of Psychology,* 40(4):495–507. doi:10.1177/008124631004000410.

Fouché, P. 2015. The 'coming of age' for Southern African psychobiography. *Special Edition of Journal of Psychology in Africa (Psychobiographical Research),* 25(5):375–378. doi.org/10.1080/14330237.2015.1 101261

Fouché, P., Nel, C. & Van Niekerk, R. 2014. Helen Suzman: A psychobiographical-psychosocial developmental trajectory study. *Journal of Psychology in Africa,* 4:351–360. doi.org/10.1080/14330237.2014.980622.

Harwood, C.S. 2015. 'A psychobiographical study of Sybrand Gerhardus (Brand) Pretorius'. Unpublished Master's thesis. Nelson Mandela Metropolitan University, Port Elizabeth.

Huberman, A.M., & Miles, M.B. (Eds.). (2002). *The qualitative researcher's companion.* Thousand Oaks, CA: Sage.

Ponterotto, J.G. 2014. Best practices in psychobiographical research. *Qualitative Psychology,* 1(1):77–90. doi:10.1037/qup0000005.

Runyan, W.M. 1984. *Life histories and psychobiography: Explorations in theory and method.* New York, NY: Oxford University Press.

Runyan, W.M. 1988. Progress in psychobiography. *Journal of Personality,* 56(1):295–326. doi:10.1111/j.1467-6494.1988.tb00470.x.

Schultz, W.T. (ed). 2005. *Handbook of psychobiography.* New York, NY: Oxford University Press.

Van Niekerk, R., Vos, H., & Fouché, P. 2015. The career development of Christiaan Neethling Barnard: A psychobiography. *Special edition of Journal of Psychology in Africa (Psychobiographical Research),* 25(5):395–402. doi.org/10.1080/14330237.2015.1101268.

Chapter 7

KEGAN'S COMPETING COMMITMENTS

Ian Lawson

Some of the greatest opportunities available to organisations are created by how leaders construct their roles, and their ability to adapt to changing circumstances. This chapter gives an overview of how the Immunity to Change process, created by developmental psychologists Robert Kegan and Lisa Lahey,[1] helps leaders to change in order to meet new organisational demands. Kegan's approach broadly fits into a consensus today among cognitive scientists that the operation of the brain can be distinguished by two different types of cognition, each with different strong and weak points.[2]

The purpose of the chapter is to elucidate Kegan's competing commitments approach as expressed in the Immunity to Change process as a lens to look at leadership. To this end the following topics are addressed: the difficulty of change; adaptive versus technical change; the 'Immunity to Change' process; features and efficacy of this process. Throughout a case study of a leader involved in overcoming his immunity to change is presented. It offers a key piece of the puzzle on how people change, what Kegan calls the 'mental mechanism of transformation,'[3] by overcoming their mental blocks to change.

Neo's Story

Neo's drive and energy had helped grow *Power Drives*, where he worked, into one of the most successful dealerships for high-end cars in South Africa. He had been made general manager within two years. Sales flourished as cars sold by the company added prestige to the new elite, and new showrooms were built.

But circumstances among the new elite changed as the economy failed to grow, and they dried up as potential buyers. Sales were markedly down. Neo developed different plans to attract additional buyers, but they were not coming together. His problems did not stop there. His bull-headed pursuit of schemes which no longer worked worried his chairperson, and his dismissive approach to ideas from his staff on how to improve sales demoralised them.

The chairperson had championed his rise to eminence in *Power Drives*. She knows he is creative, hard-working, charismatic, and gets results. But now she worries that Neo's trademark strategy to grow the business is floundering under the strain of a changing market. She wonders how much of this has to do with his leadership, or is it the market? He continues doing the same things, as though he is on autopilot. His *internal* 'GPS' habitually takes him on the same, well-worn route.

I SEE NO REASON NOT TO TRUST MY G.P.S

Figure 7.1: Driving on a road to nowhere[i]

The chairperson wants him to change the road he is on and find more expansive routes to improve the business. In her mind it is not that Neo does not have the power and authority to make changes; he does. She thinks the question is more about whether he can *reset* his GPS. She knows the market demands a different approach and style of behaviour, but Neo is not responding to these dynamic circumstances. She had never thought much about this before, but suddenly it is an important question to her: is it possible just to flick a switch?

Change is not Easy

But Neo's GPS is well and truly set by what has led to his success and kept him out of harm's way. It has championed his cause so well that it is now second nature to him. It works automatically and quickly, effortlessly, and as though he has no control over it.

His GPS is doing its job – stopping him from getting lost. Over the years it has worked out the best route for him. It works so well to protect him that it even invents reasons to explain away the dwindling sales, ensuring he stays on its programmed track. But now it is putting him in harm's way. Neo does not understand any of this. He sees his GPS as internal. It tells him that changing is a hazard. Not only that, it does not show him the new roads that will improve his capabilities in order to meet his new goals.

Adaptive versus Technical Changes

In 1948 Einstein had some advice for Neo, and the rest of us, relevant to when we repeatedly fail to solve our problems.[4] He wrote that when our situation is unlike anything we have previously experienced, it is pointless to carry on doing what worked in the past. Instead, we need to transform our 'thinking, actions and relations', to *reset* our internal GPS Almost 50 years later Ron Heifetz echoed Einstein when he described 'adaptive' challenges, which can be met only "through changes in people's priorities, beliefs, habits, and loyalties".[5] Adaptive challenges can be distinguished from technical ones in the following way: technical changes do not require that you change, only that you learn a new skill. As you have probably seen in your own life, learning a new skill is a lot easier than changing your own priorities, beliefs, habits, and loyalties.

The point Einstein and Heifetz make is that when the demands we face change significantly, there is a good chance that our 'truths' will no longer help us to find solutions. In his 1994 book, *In*

---

i   Illustration by Lisa Mellows, inspired by the *The New Yorker*, 'Daily Cartoon', 5 January 2015 issue. [Online] Available: http://www.newyorker.com/cartoons/issue-cartoons/cartoons-january-5-2015-issue. [Accessed 29 August 2016].

Over Our Heads, Kegan makes the case that the changing expectations that businesses and work contexts in general place upon us are often beyond our understanding and capacities.[6] This is what is happening to Neo – he had set his own course, followed it, and sold cars. He is good at being master of his own destiny. But he is now called upon to question all that he perceives as true and certain about selling cars, and perhaps even his world – and it is not as easy as 'flicking a switch'.

The kind of change Einstein, Heifetz and Kegan talk about is not easy because of the way our brains work: they are a living representation of our history. The main task of most of our brain is to protect us. One of the ways it does this is by signposting what has brought us both success and danger.[7] Over time we cohere around these signals and our mindsets: our 'truth' is established. We feel our signs; we act on them; but we do not know they are there –it happens automatically. This is our built-in Immunity to Change – the deep-rooted drivers of our behaviour, which undercut our progress when circumstances around us change.

The work of Kegan and his colleagues shows our brains may develop new signposts to help us navigate the uncharted routes of change. We do this by trying out novel experiences to compete with *what our brains are telling us to do*. He notes that 80 years of research point to 'optimal conflict' as the lever for doing this.[8] It is perhaps best brought to the surface through facing a series of tests which are posed as probing questions.

In Neo's case the questions are:

- Are the falling car sales a big enough problem for him that they constantly nag at him, and frustrate him?
- Is there a way to show him that it may be his uncertainties which are stopping him from moving forward?
- Is there a way to support him in trying out new possibilities in a way that does not scare him or let him off the hook with regard to making the changes he seeks for the business?

The 'Immunity to Change' Process

In two books published in 2009 Kegan and Lahey offer their 'Immunity to Change ' process, outlining its central concepts and processes, and integrating elements of their theoretical framework, which 'illuminates'[9] the set of relationships that drive the change needed by Neo and others who are facing adaptive challenges.

Table 7.1:Four phases in overturning immunity[10]

Unconsciously 'immune'	Consciously 'immune'	Consciously 'released'	Unconsciously 'released'
In the beginning of the process we do not know that we have deep-seated beliefs which can derail our strongest desires to change – we resist the very change that is actually good for us *because we are immune.*	We become aware that we are unable to change by creating our own, intriguing and convincing immunity map. It shows the hold our GPS has over us. At this phase we can see our resistance to change, but there is not much we can do about it.	Through a series of tests we learn what our GPS may be doing to mislead us. We consciously work at learning new behaviours because we feel and think differently about our GPS – often for the first time in our lives.	Finally, when our new ways of thinking and behaving are automatic and easy, we are on the road to being unconsciously released.

Source: Kegan and Lahey, 2009b

Figure 7.2 illustrates how this awakening develops.

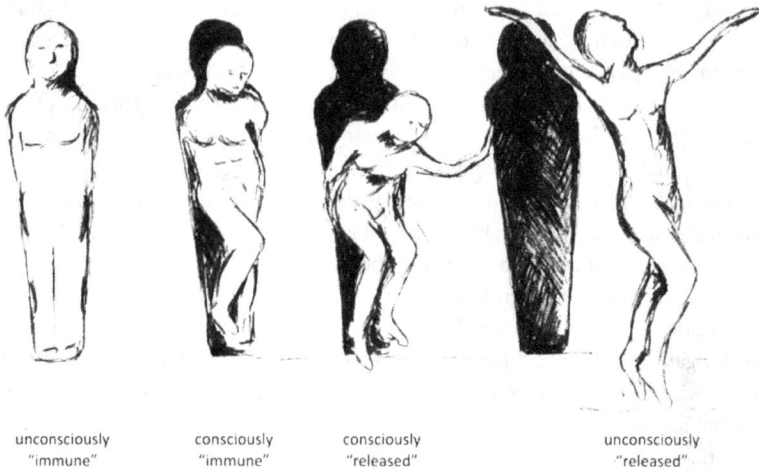

unconsciously   consciously   consciously   unconsciously
"immune"   "immune"   "released"   "released"

Figure 7.2: Illustration of how awakening develops[ii]

In a series of cautious exercises, the 'Immunity to Change ' arc helps us to travel these four phases of overturning our immunities, and moves us to help re-programme our GPS with new capabilities to meet our new goals.

Each of these phases is contextualised, generally and through the lens of the case study, below.

Phase 1: Unconsciously immune: the desire to improve personally

The best way to begin with the 'Immunity to Change ' is with an important goal at which a person, or team, is failing. The goal needs to be a 'big deal' which supports an organisational imperative. The process also calls for an appetite to look at doing things in new – perhaps as yet unimagined – ways, based on a realisation that working harder and more efficiently will not lead to desired results. This leads to a strong desire to improve, and creates 'optimal' conflict.

The chairperson decided to act before it was too late. She spoke to Neo about her concerns. He acknowledged he was also worried. They looked at technical issues, and his leadership style. The chairperson suggested to him that his unilateral approach could be a stumbling block. He was not convinced but agreed to assess it, using the Immunity to Change approach. They agreed that a useful goal for him would be to 'have the courage to explore new ways to increase sales'. Thus, his improvement goal would be 'to explore new ways'. 'Increase sales' is an outcome and not a personal improvement goal.

His map 'X-rays' his Immunity to Change, laying bare the contradiction in his thinking and actions between his 'first' and 'second' jobs, and clearly illustrating that the second job puts the brakes on change. It also shows that his 'big assumption' governs his meaning-making, and leads to his symptomatic behaviour of what he 'does and does not do'.

---

ii   Illustration by Lisa Mellows, inspired by the *Zenos Frudakis* – Public Monuments and Portrait Sculptures. [Online] Available: http://www.zenosfrudakis.com/. [Accessed 29 August 2016].

IMMUNITY TO CHANGE MAP

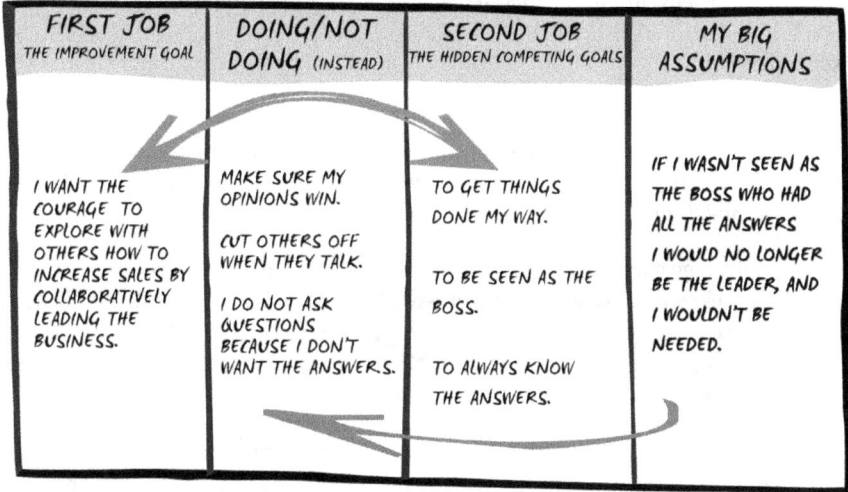

FIRST JOB THE IMPROVEMENT GOAL	DOING/NOT DOING (INSTEAD)	SECOND JOB THE HIDDEN COMPETING GOALS	MY BIG ASSUMPTIONS
I WANT THE COURAGE TO EXPLORE WITH OTHERS HOW TO INCREASE SALES BY COLLABORATIVELY LEADING THE BUSINESS.	MAKE SURE MY OPINIONS WIN. CUT OTHERS OFF WHEN THEY TALK. I DO NOT ASK QUESTIONS BECAUSE I DON'T WANT THE ANSWERS.	TO GET THINGS DONE MY WAY. TO BE SEEN AS THE BOSS. TO ALWAYS KNOW THE ANSWERS.	IF I WASN'T SEEN AS THE BOSS WHO HAD ALL THE ANSWERS I WOULD NO LONGER BE THE LEADER, AND I WOULDN'T BE NEEDED.

Figure 7.3: 'Immunity to Change' map

It is important to note the process for developing an 'Immunity to Change' map:

1. It is completed from left to right, starting with an area of improvement that has big-time implications, and which is not being met.
2. In the second column, Neo lists his behaviours which work against his improvement goal, making sure to not concern himself with reasons and fixes.

The first two columns are standard management approaches: identify a goal and generate the barriers to it; columns three and four are different.

3. There are two steps in the third column.
   3.1. Neo reflects only on the negative feelings that come up when he imagines himself doing the opposite of the behaviours listed in the previous column. For example, he gets a strong feeling in his stomach that if he does not 'cut others off when they talk', they will 'walk all over me'. The feeling is visceral.
   3.2. This feeling that 'they will walk all over me' is translated into a commitment he holds: 'to be seen to be the boss', the person in charge whom no-one dares to walk over.
4. The final column describes what he fears will happen if he can no longer meet his hidden column 3 commitments. His GPS immunises him to make sure his fears do not materialise. This leads to his column 2 behaviours being inevitable.

Column 4 is the lever into Neo's incapacity to achieve his improvement goal and trigger his change.

Phase 2: Consciously immune: rattling the GPS

Neo is in a catch-22 situation. The map starkly lays out for him that the opposing commitments between his 'two jobs' take him away from his improvement goal:

- Yes, he is openly working on improving sales and doing the logical work he is called upon as a leader to do; business goals are in place and he has a strategy.

- BUT, underground, his values are shielding himself from anything counter to his view of reality, the 'reality' that his GPS has set for him.

As Kegan puts it:

> "*Most people at work, even in high-performing organisations, divert considerable energy every day to a second job that no one has hired them to do: preserving their reputations, putting their best selves forward, and hiding their inadequacies from others and themselves.*"[11]

While Neo still has no alternative to the path he is on, he now realises that what he can do or not do is limited by his own thinking. It can be gut-wrenching to know that our 'truths' – which have guided us for years and got us to where we are – may not be the 'complete truth'.

The 'Immunity to Change' process gives Neo, and us, three more exercises[12] to help us judge if we are immune to change that is in our interests:

- *Observe ourselves in action*: For a few weeks, Neo keeps a close eye on himself. He notes when he automatically does his 'second job', and what the costs are to him; and he looks at the role his 'truths' or 'big assumptions' played in his actions.
- *Picture a progression of how we will act* when we are: (i) taking a very small step away from our big assumption. While 'small', it is quite different from what we normally do and think. Imagine how we will act later when we are (ii) consciously abandoning, even rejecting, our old way of doing things; and still later (iii) no longer thinking and behaving as we did: we are 'new', even though we may now incorporate some old behaviours when they are appropriate.
- Look at our past, particularly when we were growing up, and think about happenings that may be related to the big assumption and how they affect our life now. This is not a navel-gazing exercise; instead, it is a means to reflect and develop insights into why our living GPS was programmed in a certain way.

BUT I LIKE LIVING IN THE PAST – IT'S WHERE I WAS SUCCESSFUL.

Figure 7.4: Immunity to Change[iii]

When doing these four exercises, Neo, and we, make no attempt to change our behaviours. The purpose of the exercises is to help us inspect the path of our GPS to assess its usefulness.

---

iii Illustration by Lisa Mellows, inspired by the *The New Yorker*, 'Daily Cartoon', 5 January 2015 issue. [Online] Available: http://www.newyorker.com/cartoons/issue-cartoons/cartoons-january-5-2015-issue. [Accessed 29 August 2016]..

It is a deliberative process that also opens the choice to more optimal, mindful ways to adapt to changing, challenging or coping with different situational realities. It moves us away from automatic modes of feeling and doing.

1. The immunity map is like an 'X-ray' of our personal anxiety managing system. It helps us to see that we create false beliefs about our own inabilities to do that which **'is completely possible for us to do'**.
2. Observing ourselves helps us to clearly see **the costs** to ourselves and others of not doing *that* which we think is impossible, and the benefits of doing the impossible.
3. Picturing our progress helps us to build signals for ourselves, in a small way, of our new path.
4. Looking back at our history may help us realise that our brain is a living representation of the past. And, the dangers it long ago signposted for us might no longer exist. Yet we act as though they do, creating our artificial boundaries so resisting change.

Taken together, these four experiences help Neo to understand better how his 'second' job works against his goal.

Neo's next steps are to dig up the signposts that are working against him, and to replace these with ones which will help him to work collaboratively, consistent with the improvement goal he has set.

Phase 3: Consciously released: new signposts

Creating new signposts is part of the process and the engine that drives overcoming Immunity to Change . Developing the map is quick and insightful; creating signposts is the hard work. It is best understood as a continuum:

1. Neo starts off testing the 'truth' of the signposts which automatically point him to his 'second' job. Only if these tests lead Neo to know the signposts are probably no longer true, does he move onto the second part.
2. The second part involves building a new set of signposts to guide him to a key part of his 'first' job – having the courage to explore new ways of increasing sales.

Digging out signposts is delicate work and needs patience. The four exercises already described – developing the immunity map, observing ourselves, picturing our progression, and looking at our past – do a good job of slightly slackening the signposts' grip on us. But we are still attached to their signals because they continue to help us make sense of our world: any attempt just to rip them out is doomed to fail; our gut response would be to fight off the attack. And we would end up reinforcing the truths of our second job, undoing and retarding our efforts to change.

Kegan and Lahey use their own version of the 'SMART' acronym to safeguard us against the fragility of change when designing these lived experiments:[13]

Table 7.2: Using the SMART acronym

Safe	People must feel that the experiment is not putting them in harm's way and that they *can* live with the worst outcome.
Modest	They should take small steps that do not try to prove or disprove the big assumption, and even though they are small steps, they should be clearly conceptualised to test the big assumption.

Actionable	The task can be carried out in the next two weeks. This practical time horizon keeps the momentum going.
Research	Information is collected on each person's thoughts, feelings and actions arising from the test. Diaries are a practical way to record this data.
Test	The task provides valid data to test the big assumption. The research record should be analysed in the light of the big assumption.

For Neo, whose big assumption is *that if he was not seen as the boss who had all the answers he would no longer be needed as the leader*, a safe first test could be:

- To change his behaviour by simply having a chat with knowledgeable industry outsiders on options to improve sales. In the discussion he simply listens. His purpose is to be curious about the views and approach of other leaders.
- He collects his thoughts and feelings about himself as the leader: before the discussion, during, and after it.
- These thoughts and feelings provide him with data, in a small way, about his ability to be open to the views of others.

At fortnightly intervals Neo will conduct further tests in order to lose his signposts gradually.

Almost imperceptibly, digging up old signposts turns to planting new ones. This can never be, first or last, only an *intellectual* exercise. It has to tug at our heartstrings; bring butterflies to our stomach – strike at our gut.

In Neo's next exercises he increasingly turns up the heat on his tests of his big assumption by finding ways to test his response to collaborating more actively. Again, there is a series of appropriate 'smart' experiments. For example, in our case study, Neo changes his behaviour by directly asking his staff their opinions of his ideas in order to increase sales, but does so without replying to their responses. When he feels safe with this behaviour, the experiments could be turned up a notch and he could discuss the merits of his staff's opinions.

In the experiments, Neo collects information to assess how happy he feels about himself – as the leader – when he does not know all the answers. The process of experimenting continues until Neo fully discards his 'second' job, and slips into his 'first' job like a hand into a glove.

Over time, Neo moved from his old behaviour to his new behaviour, as shown in Table 7.3.

Table 7.3: A comparison between old and new behaviour

Old behaviour	New behaviour
If I am not seen as the boss who has all the answers, I will no longer be the leader, and I won't be needed.	I now have the courage to explore together with others how to increase sales.

Let us now analyse what has happened with Neo. In one way the challenge he faced is the same as that of many leaders – a call to, change. A Google search for 'change + South Africa' brings up over 50 000 hits. There are calls for transformation in higher education, in the judiciary, in social and race relations, in the economy and in the way business is done. There are many ways in which transformation can happen, where the *form* of something changes. It can, for example, be skin deep, or it can alter the very form of a person's meaning-making which is the subject of this chapter.

What the chairperson was calling on Neo to do was transform in such a way that his 'second' job no longer got in the way of his main job. Getting more knowledge or skills, for instance, being 'trained in listening', would not help him be an open communicator because the commitments of his 'second' job – the automatic settings in his GPS – were powerful blocks. This approach to transformative learning, according to Kegan, occurs when a person changes "not just the way he behaves, not just the way he feels, but the way he feel– not just what he knows but the way he knows".[14] Such transformation is helped when people are able to 'get onto the balcony' and take a different perspective in order to reflect on what they are doing, and how they think and feel about, and how they understand it.

Neo's series of experiments put him safely onto the balcony so that he could try out new behaviours that increasingly pushed the credibility of his 'truths' for him. The data Neo got from taking on these new perspectives – his thinking and feeling about them – led him little by little to decide that he was safe as a leader if he did not know everything and that his staff had, for example, some good ideas on how to increase car sales.

Phase 4: Unconsciously released: GPS reset

Neo's relations with his staff are now different. He regularly involves them in decision-making, and even wants to hear what they have to say. Nonetheless, after weighing advice that he is given, he still feels comfortable doing it his way when it makes the most sense to him. He has become much closer to the chairperson, with whom he is now able to share some of his inner concerns. He feels his old self as being part of a distant, and strange, past with which he does not identify much although, oddly, he realises he can now make better sense of this past. He may face new areas of change, and will have to draw on a different way of operating in order to apply his new capacities to different challenges. He feels confident that he can revisit the steps and work with a GPS that will not get him stuck 'in bad traffic' or an endless loop, but which has opened up energising pathways that are better suited to the complexities of a changing world.

Neo decides he is going to talk to his staff about their practising Immunity to Change as a team effort. In observing those around him, he has slowly come to realise that it wasn't just he who was unaware that he was blocked from changing by his own outdated beliefs. Others, too, seem to limit their own success, and would benefit from unblocking their Immunity to Change .

Features of the Immunity to Change Process

The process offers a practical developmental framework for leaders to explore new, more fitting behaviours. In a marketplace where there is a shortage of leadership skills it offers the capacity for organisations to home-grow leadership talent.

This chapter seeks to show, to use Kegan's words, that a foundational assumption of development is that leaders

> "... can grow; that not only is attention to the bottom line and the personal growth of all employees desirable, but the two are interdependent; that both profitability and individual development rely on structures that are built into every aspect of how the company operates; and that people grow through the proper combination of challenge and support, which includes recognising and transcending their blind spots, limitations and internal resistance to change. For this approach to succeed employees must be willing to reveal their inadequacies at work – not just business-as-usual, got-it-all-together selves – and the organisation must create a trustworthy and reliable community to make such exposure safe".[15]

Efficacy of the Immunity to Change process

A recent study of the efficacy of the Immunity to Change process found that participants reported an average improvement of close to 70% toward improvement goals, whereas the control group reported no progress, "despite reporting that they actively worked on these goals for an average of 37.5 hours ... with the 3-month comparison period".[16]

Other studies clearly show that greater mental complexity – the outcome of the Immunity to Change process – is associated with improved business success. Eigel, for example, assessed 21 CEOs of large and successful organisations, and 21 middle managers from the same companies. His findings show a clear link between increasing mental complexity and increasing performance.[17]

Conclusion

The above discussion, and as illustrated by research, the Immunity to Change process is a step forward in the leadership development field. It is a genuinely developmental approach to how people learn and grow, and why they hunker down and resist change. It is based on a rigorous, scientific approach to the gradual development of new strengths to fit changing leadership demands. It offers a significant leap forward in developing leadership potential to better cope with today's increasing unpredictability and complexity.

Endnotes

1 Kegan & Lahey, 2009b.
2 Stanovich, 2012.
3 Kegan & Lahey, 2009a p. 434.
4 Einstein, 1950.
5 Heifetz, Linsky & Grashow, 2009.
6 Kegan, 1994.
7 Siegel, 2012.
8 Kegan & Lahey, 2009b Op. Cit. [See endnote 1 or 2.]
9 Kegan & Lahey, 2009b. [See endnote 1.]
10 Kegan & Lahey, 2009b. [See endnote 1.]
11 Kegan et al., 2014.
12 Kegan & Lahey, 2009b Op. Cit. [See endnote 1 or 2.]
13 Ibid.
14 Kegan, 1994. [See endnote 6.]
15 Kegan et al., 2014 p. 4.
16 Markus, 2013.
17 Eigel & Kuhnert, 2005.

References

Eigel, K & Kuhnert, K. 2005. 'Authentic development: Leadership development level and executive effectiveness'. In L Gardner, B Avolio & F Walumbwa (eds). *Authentic leadership theory and practice. Vol 3: Origins, effects and development (monographs in leadership and management)*. Bingley, England: Emerald Group Publishing.

Einstein, A. 1950. *Essays in humanism*. New York, NY: Philosophical Library.

Heifetz, R, Linsky, M & Grashow, A.2009. *The practice of adaptive leadership: Tools and tactics for changing your organization and the world*. Cambridge, MA: Harvard Business Press.

Kegan, R. 1994. *In over our heads: The mental demands of modern life*. Cambridge, MA: Harvard Business Press.

Kegan, R & Lahey, L. 2009a. 'From subject to object: A constructive-developmental approach to reflective practice'. In N Lyons (ed). *Handbook of reflective practice*. Cambridge, MA: Springer. p. 434.

Kegan, R & Lahey, L. 2009b. *Immunity to Change : How to overcome it and unlock the potential in yourself and your organization*. Cambridge, MA: Harvard Business Press.

Kegan, R, Lahey, L, Fleming, A & Miller M. 2014. 'Making business personal'. *Harvard Business Review*, R1404B.April Reprint.

Markus, I. 2013. 'Efficacy of Immunity to Change coaching for leadership development'. *The Journal of Applied Behavioral Science*.doi:10.1177/0021886313502530.

Maxwell, JA. 2005. *Qualitative research design: An interactive approach*. London and New Delhi: Sage Publications.

Siegel, D. 2012. *The developing mind*. New York, NY: The Guilford Press.

Stanovich, K. 2012. 'On the distinction between rationality and intelligence: Implications for understanding individual differences in reasoning'. In K Holyoak & R Morrison (eds). *The Oxford handbook of thinking and reasoning*. New York, NY: Oxford University Press.

Chapter 8

ARBINGER'S CHANGING MINDSET

Cobus Pienaar and Jim Ferrell

Recently we were engaged by a world-renowned company that we will call PY Systems. PY had suffered from a recent string of scandals and negative media reports. As a result, an organisation whose very name had historically garnered great respect had become a bit of an embarrassment, and they were suffering from unprecedented low employee morale.

PY did what many organisations in similar circumstances do. They gathered leaders into committees tasked to diagnose the organisation's problems and prescribe solutions. One committee, for example, was working to fix what they believed were failed communication practices throughout the organisation. Another was trying to figure out how to improve alignment and accountability throughout the organisation. Still another was rethinking their customer service efforts.

These leaders had nothing but the best of intentions. Each one of them was committed to the company's success. Individually and collectively they had done significant and important work in thinking about potential solutions to the organisation's problems, and they had identified a number of changes that definitely needed to be made. Their suggestions were deeply informed by their collective years of experience and success in the industry, and their ideas were good. In short, they were a decent, professional, hardworking, and diverse group of people whose efforts were about to amount to much less than they hoped.

These and similar initiatives resulted in far less impact than their proponents intended because they rested upon a model of human behaviour and performance that is incomplete and misleading. As we describe in the next section, this incomplete model, which we call the Behavioural Model, is misleading because it fails to account for the impact of mindset. We will begin by contrasting the Behavioural Model with Arbinger's Mindset Model. Then we will explore two distinct mindsets from which leaders and organisations can operate – an *inward mindset* or an *outward mindset*. These two mindsets form two ends of what we call the *mindset continuum*, and we argue that behaviour change efforts become increasingly effective as a leader or organisation moves more towards an outward mindset. We will consider the case of a fairly common leadership approach in order to demonstrate the importance of mindset.

The Arbinger Mindset Model

At the most basic level, a leader's or organisation's results are driven by the behaviours of the leader or the collective behaviours of those in the organisation. We will represent this understanding with a simple diagram, shown in Figure 8.1. The triangle in Figure 8.1 represents the behaviours – that is, the initiatives, actions, and activities – being performed that add up to the current level of achieved results. As the diagram depicts, behaviours drive results.

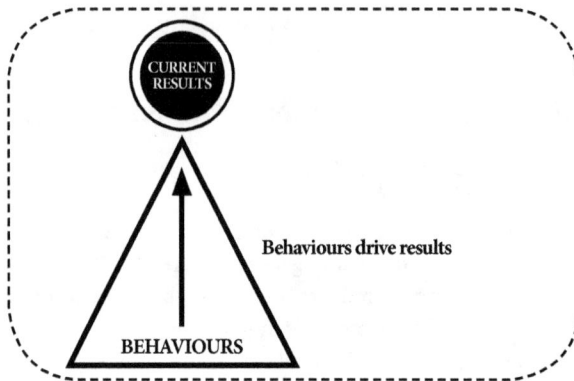

Figure 8.1: The Behavioural Model

While clear, this rendition is incomplete and fundamentally misleading because one's choice of engaging in this or that behaviour is itself driven by something that is deeper than behaviour. Which is to say that a leader's or an organisation's results are driven not merely by their behaviours but by a deeper, determining factor as well – one's mindset. The term 'mindset' will be used in this chapter to refer to the individual and collective mindset of everyone in the organisation.

Mindset

The way we use the term *mindset* is more than a prevailing belief about oneself or others. It refers to the way one sees and regards the world – how one sees and regards others and oneself, for example, as well as how one sees challenges, opportunities, circumstances, and so on. Every choice is made from the context of the mindset of the person who is choosing, and the person's possible choices are limited by how and what he or she sees. The possible strategies for a company, for example, are bound by the mindset of the CEO and other executives. Likewise, the success of a behavioural plan that an executive team may put together, even a good one, will still depend on the execution efforts of the broader team, and how individuals respond will be a function of their own mindsets, not of the behavioural plan itself.

Mindset model

So while an organisation's results are driven by the collective behaviours of those in the company, those behaviours are themselves driven by the organisation's prevailing underlying mindset. We capture this reality in the modified diagram of the Mindset Model, shown in Figure 8.2.

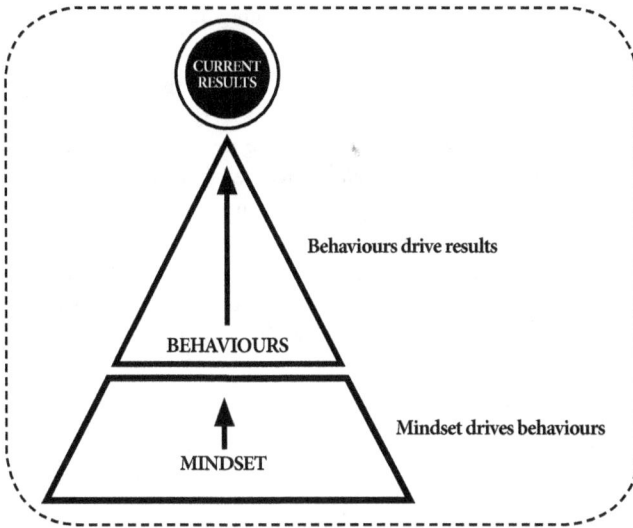

Figure 8.2: The Mindset Model

Mindset deficit

Now let us consider PY, and any other organisation that wants to improve its performance significantly. How can it successfully move from its current level of performance to its target level of performance?

The prevailing approach is to determine what actions and activities will be necessary in order to achieve the increased level of results and then to prescribe those behaviours across the system, pushing the organisation to make the necessary behavioural changes, as depicted in Figure 8.3.

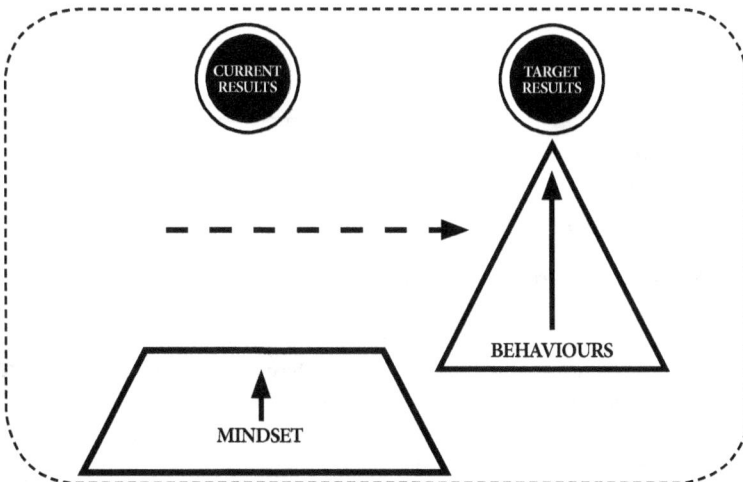

Figure 8.3: The Mindset deficit

This is what PY leaders were planning. They were going to roll out a whole host of new communication protocols and other behavioural initiatives – most of them very well conceived –

in order to rescue the company from its current doldrums and elevate it to new levels of success and performance. But should they have expected that this would work? Would prescribed behaviours that were not supported by the underlying mindset of an organisation produce the desired results?

We recently posed this question to an executive team of one of the largest healthcare organisations in the world. Immediately the team realised that this could not work. They had seen the proof of it over many years in their own organisation: behavioural solutions that are unsupported by the underlying mindset of an organisation will fail – every time. One of these executives voiced the strongest argument any of them could make to the contrary: "Some leaders, through charisma or sheer willpower, may be able to drive this kind of change in the short term," he said. "But it won't last. When he or she leaves, for example, if not sooner, it will snap right back to where it was."

Mindset and culture

It is popular to talk of culture as being the deep lever that determines which behavioural initiatives will stick and which will not. You may find it helpful, however, to think of culture not as the foundation of the diagram, where we place mindset, but rather as the entire diagram, as shown in Figure 8.4.

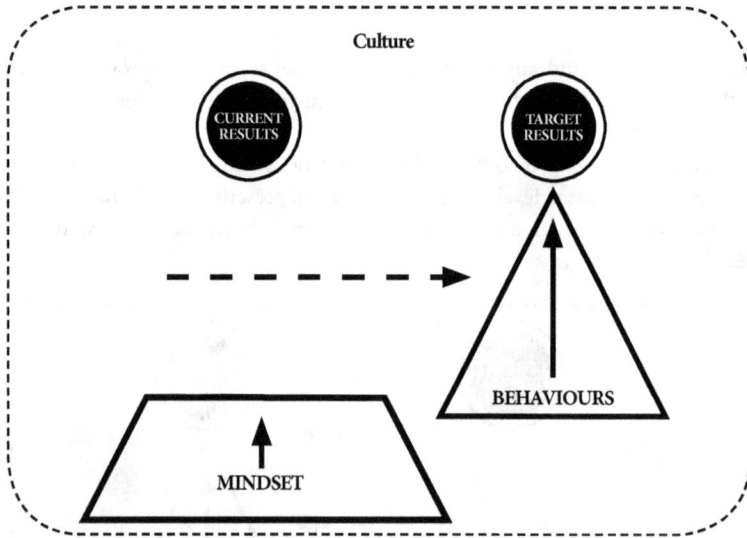

Figure 8.4: Culture includes Mindset and Behaviours

The organisation depicted in Figure 8.4 has a culture where behaviours are frequently mandated and where those mandates are resisted. The culture will be characterised by a lack of trust and a corresponding lack of accountability. Leaders will blame the organisation's poor performance on the lack of execution by the workforce, and employees will blame the results on poor leadership. What this boils down to is that an organisation's culture is comprised of both the prevailing mindset in the organisation and the behaviours that are or are not happening in the organisation.

Mindset gap

In the case of PY, leadership had not yet confronted the cause of most of the culture challenges they were facing – what we at Arbinger call the *mindset gap*. The mindset gap is the difference between an organisation's prevailing mindset and the new mindset required to execute effectively the behaviours necessary to produce an improved level of results. This gap must be bridged in order to turn goals from mere dreams to realities. Over the medium and longer terms (and in most cases the shorter term as well), an organisation's performance will be limited by the prevailing mindset of the organisation. In order to stick, attempts to change behaviour must be preceded or accompanied by efforts to change mindset.

So long as the mindset gap remains, attempts to get people to change behaviour will be resisted, twisted, complained about, undermined, and ultimately discarded and forgotten. This is why potentially helpful behavioural training so often fails to deliver its promised results. Attempts to prescribe behaviours that do not comport with the underlying mindsets of both the training participants and the larger organisation will necessarily fail. Any positive changes will be marginal rather than transformative. Potentially helpful ideas fade away as just the latest flavour of the month.

The good news, however, is that when you sufficiently improve the prevailing mindset – either of an individual or an organisation – you no longer have to manage many of the behaviours you previously thought would have to be mandated. As mindset changes, so does behaviour, without having to prescribe it. And where you still need to prescribe certain behaviours, the suggestions would not be systemically resisted, as when there is a mindset deficit. Achieving mindset change gets you much of the way towards achieving behavioural change.

In order to understand the kind of mindset change that can have this kind of impact, we also need to explore the two extremes of what we call the *Mindset Continuum* – an Inward Mindset and an Outward Mindset.

Two Types of Mindset

An understanding of the Mindset Continuum starts with a fundamental observation: *People are different from objects*. This is hardly a revelation, of course. Until, that is, one sees the extent to which individual behaviours and organisational structures and practices are built upon precisely the opposite assumption. Let us begin by thinking about what is different between people and objects, between a person and an object such as a chair, for example. To start with, people have feelings. Chairs do not. People have intentions – things they want to do. They have wills and objectives and goals, and so on.

For purposes of illustration, we will use a triangle to capture one of the dimensions of these differences between people and chairs. In the Figure 8.5, the person on the left represents you, the reader. The triangle immediately to your right represents the objectives you have and the things you are doing to try to achieve them. The figure on the right represents one of your co-workers. She has things she wants to do and accomplish as well, so we have placed a similar triangle to *her* right.

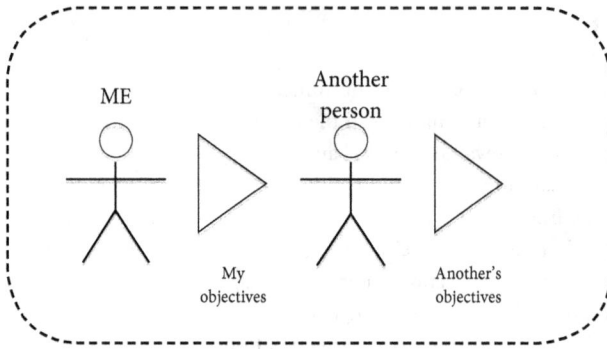

Figure 8.5: How we see People

When we see others as people, they matter to us. And because they matter to us, what they are trying to do matters to us as well. They have their own goals, challenges, hopes, and headaches, just as we do, and we are alive to and interested in what they are caring about. In fact, this aliveness to others' needs and objectives is what it means to see others as people. Contrast this with the way we see objects, depicted in Figure 8.6.

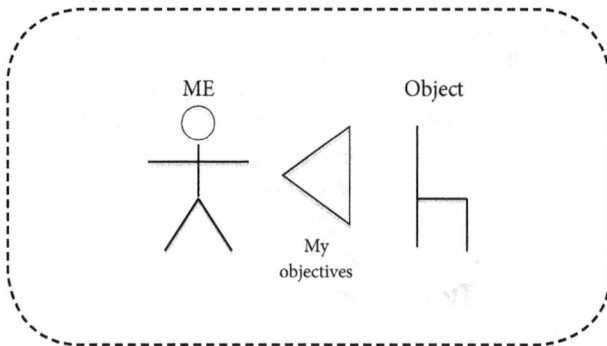

Figure 8.6: How we see Objects

Objects do not have things they want to do or accomplish. Because of this, we care about them, if at all, only to the degree to which we think they can help us with what we are trying to accomplish. We have reversed the direction of the behaviour triangle in this case to illustrate the egocentric way in which we relate with objects. Things get interesting when we see that we can see *people* the way we see *objects* – that is, only in terms of what we think they can do for us.

Outward and inward mindsets

Think of these different ways of seeing others as two distinct mindsets – an *Outward Mindset* on the one hand, and an *Inward Mindset* on the other. Think about the version of you depicted in the Outward Mindset diagram given in Figure 8.7. In a workplace setting, you may think of the triangle immediately to your right (what we call an *inside triangle*) as representing the objectives and activities that comprise your job, or the things that you do in your home or other relationships. The triangle to the right of your colleague (what we call an *outside triangle*) represents your colleague's objectives and activities.

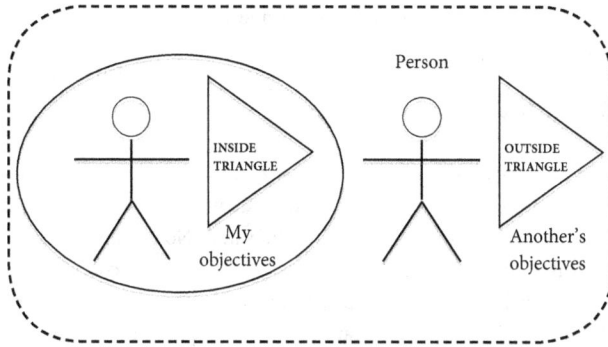

Figure 8.7: Illustration of the Outward Mindset

With an outward mindset, you feel the obligation to nail your own job (your inside triangle objectives), and to do so in a way that makes it easier for your colleague to accomplish his or her job (his or her outside triangle objectives). You feel responsible both for what you do and for your impact on what your colleague is trying to do.

When our mindsets are inward, on the other hand, we focus only on what we ourselves do. Others may be negatively affected by what we do, but this is not very important to us. Although a colleague has his or her own objectives, we do not really care about those objectives when our mindsets are inward. For this reason, we omit the outside triangle, which displays what the other person wants and is trying to do, from the Inward Mindset diagram in Figure 8.8.

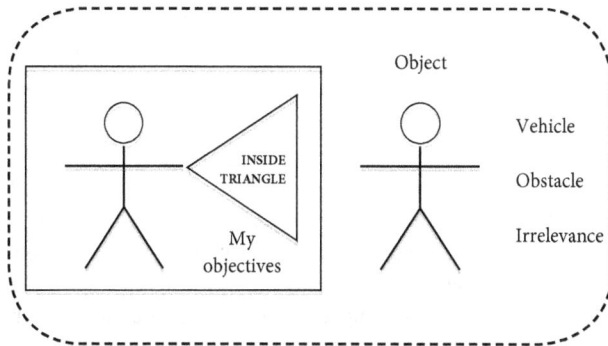

Figure 8.8: Inward Mindset diagram

The person to the right of you on in Figure 8.8 could be your customer, your work colleague, your partner, your child, your neighbour, your parent, or a stranger on the street, the person who waits on you in a restaurant, or the person in the car next to you. In this mindset, these and others exist for us only in relation to what we think they can do for us. If we think they can help us with our objectives, we see them as vehicles. If they make it more difficult for us to do what we want to do, we see them as obstacles. If we don't think they can help us one way or the other, they are irrelevant to us.

The inward mindset may sound and look sinister, but very often it is simply a person who has his or her head down, thinking only about his or her own lane, as it were. Such a person may not have ill feelings towards others, and very often has no malicious intent. He or she may also be hardworking. However, when his or her mindset is focused inward, such a person is systemically unaware of (and in some cases uninterested in) his or her impact on others. Organisationally, workplaces like these show up as siloed and non-co-operative. At home, an inward mindset may lead to cold indifference.

The mindset continuum

These two mindsets – inward and outward – form two ends of a continuum. Consider, for example, an organisation in which every leader and others operate with an inward mindset and where the practices, rules, and processes continually invite the same. No organisation is completely like this, but consider this extreme case as the left end of the mindset continuum. Then consider an organisation comprised of leaders, people, processes, and practices that are entirely of an outward mindset. Once again, no single organisation will display a completely outward mindset, but let that possibility form the extreme right end of the continuum, as depicted in Figure 8.9.

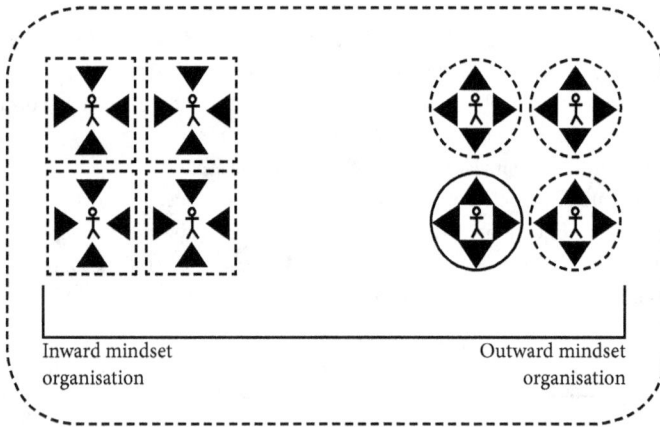

Figure 8.9: *The Mindset Continuum*

In our work we both assess clients and invite them to self-assess where they are on this continuum. We do this to get a baseline against which to measure progress. We have been surprised in our research to discover how people rate their own organisations. If an entirely inward mindset is 0 on the scale and an entirely outward mindset is 10, on average, a relatively small fraction of groups assess their own organisations at higher than 5 on this continuum, with many of them self-assessing at somewhere between 2 and 4. Interestingly, this same research shows that, on average, people rate themselves more highly on this continuum than they rate their organisations. So you end up with the conundrum of companies rated as, say, a 3 by employees who, on average, rate themselves as a 7.

Wherever one is on the continuum – even if an organisation self-assesses one as an 8 out of 10, for example – the project is still to move the organisation to the right on this continuum – more and more towards an outward mindset. Why? Because collaboration, innovation, leadership, culture, and value to customers all improve as organisations increasingly apply an outward mindset in their strategies, structures, systems, processes, and day-to-day work.

Exercise

1. Where would you as a leader position yourself on this continuum, when thinking about mindset?

2. Where would you as a leader position your organisation (the employees in your organisation) on this continuum, when thinking about mindset?

3. What would happen if the majority of the employees in your company had to operate from an inward mindset?

4. What would happen if the majority of the employees in your company had to operate from an outward mindset?

5. Think of a time when you've functioned from an inward mindset – a time when you were more concerned about others' impact on you rather than your impact on them. Consider what traits you exhibited, and the emotions you cultivated. What were your interactions like with others? What sort of thoughts crossed your mind? Consider the following questions:

    a) What am I like when I am functioning from an inward mindset at work?
    b) What effect do I have on others when I'm functioning inward?
    c) What am I like when I am functioning from an outward mindset at work?
    d) What effect do I have on others when I'm functioning outward?

The preceding thoughts are echoed and supported by research conducted by McKinsey.[1][2]

> *"Many companies move quickly from setting their performance objectives to implementing a suite of change initiatives. Be it a new growth strategy or business-unit structure, the integration of a recent acquisition or the roll-out of a new operational-improvement effort, such organisations focus on altering systems and structures and on creating new policies and processes. To achieve collective change over time, actions like these are necessary but seldom sufficient. A new strategy will fall short of its potential if it fails to address the underlying mindsets and capabilities of the people who will execute it."*

The same McKinsey research indicates that if companies can identify and address pervasive mindsets at the outset, they are four times more likely to succeed in organisational-change efforts than are companies that overlook this stage.

Interventions wishing to deliver results must include a focus on improving the mindsets of organisational leaders.

An Illustration of Mindset in Action in Everyday Life

To illustrate the difference between these two mindsets, picture a leader hard at work in his office, who is suddenly interrupted by the members of a work team who want advice on some aspect of their project. The leader is busy, but the team members seem to have an urgent need. How is this leader likely to see these team members in this situation? What meaning might they have for him? Will he see them as problem employees who have disturbed and disrupted him in his important work? Or will he see them instead as employees with a problem, who can use his help?

If this leader were to see them with an outward mindset, he would see them empathetically, in terms of their own needs instead of just his own. If he were to see them with an inward mindset, they would be objects to him rather than people – obstacles who are keeping him from what he needs to do. The team members would be obstacles to this leader even if he indulged them and spent the time they wanted him to, but did so while feeling victimised or burdened by their presence.

More rides on this choice of mindset than simply how the leader views these team members. His view even of himself will be determined by his mindset. To see his team members as irritating obstacles, for example, is to view himself as the-person-who-is-so-important-and-so-busy-that-he-should-not-be-troubled; while to see them in terms of their own needs instead of just his own is to see himself as someone who can and ought to help, if not this minute, then soon.

It is common to switch back and forth between these two mindsets. Yet these are fundamental categories, for in any given moment we are seeing others and ourselves either as people who count in the same way as we do, or as people who don't. Sometimes we can carry mixed mindsets at the same time – seeing some people as people and others as objects – alive to and interested in what some are trying to do, while being dead to the reality and hopes of still others.

Effectiveness has less to do with what we do than with our underlying mindset. The reason for this is that we cannot hide an inward mindset towards others, and others will feel invited by us in our inward mindset moments to resist us reflexively. However impressive the outward display of manners and interpersonal techniques we employ to conceal it, who we really are and how we are seeing will always bleed through. As the poet, TS Eliot, wrote: "The man that is shall shadow the man that pretends to be."

Take the case of 'Gordon', a well-read, enlightened and conscientious leader, who was the founder of his company. He possessed a clear vision of his company's future and its mission, and was blessed with uncommon intelligence and charisma. He was clear about the functions of each person reporting to him, and was exceedingly precise in his communications. He carefully instructed everyone in the way he wanted things done, and he delegated and followed up with clarity and consistency. He was explicit in his corrections of others, but always friendly and polite. Much of Gordon's time was spent listening, sharing, explaining, encouraging, persuading, and cajoling. In his eyes, Gordon met all the criteria of effective leadership. He was involved, proactive, knowledgeable, committed, visionary, and even kind. According to all outside his team, he was the role model leader.

Unfortunately, Gordon's team members did not share Gordon's view of himself. Despite his great skill, it was obvious to Gordon's people that he just did not like, or trust, them. Gordon was like many leaders in that those who worked for him always felt that he was being nice out of sheer grit – that it was something required of him, but unnatural. His manner said to them: "I am in charge here. You aren't able to do this work without me. Look how much I must do and how hard I must work to put up with you. And I even do it cheerfully!"

Despite Gordon's strenuous efforts, he could not conceal his mindset. His people felt devalued by him because he did in fact devalue them. His mindset came across in countless subtle ways – in the tone of his voice, in the look on his face, in his posture and his gestures. And what was conveyed in those subtle ways was more important to Gordon's people than all the things he attempted to convey to them – his plans, his dreams, his instructions, and even his outwardly kind manner. What Gordon knew, and even what he implemented in the way of sound managerial and leadership principles, were both less important to his people than his mindset was.

People have a notion of how leaders feel towards them, and they react to this. Employees can usually sense when leaders treat them primarily as objects. Given a little time and experience, people can tell when there is no real feeling or authenticity behind a leader's behaviour or words, when they are being manipulated or outsmarted, or when their interests are not really at stake. In other words, they know when they are being treated as objects in order to serve a particular purpose.[3] It would not matter if a leader tried to manage by walking around, sitting on the edge of a chair to practise active listening, enquiring about family members in order to show interest, or by using any other skill learned in order to be more effective. It would not matter if such a leader did all the 'right' things interpersonally, even applying all the latest leadership skills and techniques to his or her communications and tasks. People ultimately resent them and their tactics. They fail as leaders because they provoke resistance in people.[4] Employees respond primarily to the mindset of a leader, and not necessarily to the words (that is, behaviours) that leaders sometimes use in order to try to impress followers.

Examples could go on and on. What they do illustrate is that genuine improvement in leadership and ultimately to the organisations they lead is not primarily a matter of behaviour and skill alone. Mindset is always primary. This is why the many efforts that attempt to alter behaviour – but which do not also alter the mindset of leaders and employees – ultimately make little difference.

Conclusion

Leadership training and development is a billion-dollar industry worldwide. Organisations spend considerable time, money and energy on building their leadership capacity in order to gain a competitive advantage, but the various approaches to building leadership capacity are failing to hit the mark.[5]

The ideas in this chapter suggest that organisations and those responsible for leadership and management development should consider the effectiveness of training initiatives and interventions that merely focus on skills transfer on a behavioural level,[6] without addressing the mindset of leaders. Kets de Vries (2006:1–2) provides a powerful narrative to illustrate this:[7]

> *"There once was a person who noticed a disturbing bump under a rug. This person tried to smooth out the rug, but every time he did the bump reappeared. In utter frustration, he finally lifted up the rug, and to his great surprise, out slid an angry snake."*

This metaphor resembles those occasions when organisations agree to leadership development interventions and training that only deal with the behaviours of leadership. These programmes attempt to smooth things over, while the snake beneath – the underlying cause (the mindset) – keeps working its mischief. Unless training starts to pull out the 'snake' and deal with it, it will confound efforts to improve leadership efficiency and, ultimately, organisational growth.

The first step of any leadership development programme requires leaders to examine their greatest asset and liability, namely, themselves. Leaders however are rarely trained how to explore their strengths and assets, let alone their flaws, weaknesses, shadow sides, or their mindsets.[8][9] Blakely also shares this notion when he argues for more intensive training in understanding the underlying drivers of behaviour (mindset).[10] This is substantiated by Kaiser and Kaplan who are of the opinion that MBA programmes – which are supposed to develop the leaders of tomorrow – tend to focus exclusively on such curricula as functional business knowledge and behaviour, while neglecting the deeper, harder to develop competencies, aspects that will ultimately most determine the success of leaders and their respective companies.[11]

There is an urgent need to change the focus in leadership training and development in the coming years to facilitate more intensive development processes and programmes for leaders than what is currently found in most leadership training programmes and business schools.

(This chapter is based in part on a chapter in the forthcoming book called *The Outward Mindset*, published by The Arbinger Institute.)

Endnotes

1   Barsh & Lavoie, 2014, April.
2   Boaz & Fox, 2014, March
3   Dotlich & Cairo, 2003.
4   Ibid.
5   Weiss & Molinaro, 2006.
6   Kaiser & Kaplan, 2006.
7   Kets de Vries, 2006.
8   See endnote 6.
9   Locander & Luechauer, 2006.
10 Blakeley, 2007.
11 See endnote 6.

References

Barsh, J & Lavoie, J. 2014 (April). *Lead at your best*. McKinsey & Company. [Online]. Available: http://www.mckinsey.com/global-themes/leadership/lead-at-your-best [Accessed 21 April 2016].

Blakeley, K. 2007. *Leadership blind spots – and what to do about them*. San Francisco, CA: Jossey-Bass.

Boaz, N & Fox, EA. 2014 (March). *Change leader, change thyself*. McKinsey & Company. [Online]. Available: http://www.mckinsey.com/global-themes/leadership/change-leader-change-thyself [Accessed 21 April 2016].

Dotlich, DL & Cairo, PC. 2003. *Why CEOs fail: The 11 behaviors that can derail your climb to the top – and how to manage them*. San Francisco, CA: Jossey-Bass.

Kaiser, RB & Kaplan, RB. 2006. 'The deeper work of executive development: Outgrowing sensitivities'. *Academy of Management Learning & Education*, 5(4):463–483. doi:10.5465/amle.2006.23473207.

Kets de Vries, Manfred FR. 2006. *The leader on the couch: A clinical approach to changing people and organizations*. San Francisco, CA: Jossey-Bass.

Locander, WB & Luechauer, DL. 2006. 'Leadership paradoxes: It takes courage to look within'. *Marketing Management*, 15(1):46–48.

Weiss, D & Molinaro, V. 2006. 'Integrated leadership development'. *Industrial and Commercial Training*, 38(1):3–12. doi:10.1108/00197850610700763.

Chapter 9

LEADERSHIP PSYCHODYNAMICS

Pieter Koortzen

Consultants and coaches often assist with the development of leaders in organisations. They would often report to me that they were aware of 'under the surface' behaviour which tended to appear from time to time without any rational stimulus in the environment. They also reported that this sometimes irrational behaviour tends to appear unexpectedly and often has a negative effect on the leader's self-perception, relationships, and brand in the organisation. This type of behaviour is also not explainable by any of the well-known leadership perspectives, theories and models, and is often misdiagnosed as some form of pathology by consultants who are less familiar with the System Psychodynamic approach. While it may be true that some of the behaviour may have its roots in past experiences, these are by far not the only dynamics (motives or drives) which may contribute to the behaviour manifested.

Leadership behaviour can more accurately be viewed as the interplay between the person, the role he/she occupies, and the team and organisational dynamics operating in his/her environment. In this chapter the stance is therefore taken that leadership behaviour can be viewed as a process, which results from the dynamics of the individual and the system of which he or she is a part. Leadership development from this perspective therefore implies assisting the leader and his or her team in exploring and making conscious the personal, team, and system dynamics operating at a certain point in time. In general, one can say this approach requires understanding the functioning of the person in his/her role, in the team, in the organisation, and in the external environment, as presented in Figure 9.1. Consulting and coaching from this perspective, with all its complexity, brings a richer understanding of leaders' experiences and provides various lenses through which the behaviour can be explored and understood in order to yield better outcomes.

Figure 9.1: A system psychodynamic view of leadership in organisations

In order to introduce this perspective (or lens) to a wider audience the chapter contains, firstly, an overview of the System Psychodynamic perspective and its origins. Secondly, key concepts in the system psychodynamic perspective of leadership are presented, whereafter a number of important processes and concepts in the system psychodynamic perspective of leadership are described. This includes the consultancy stance and the concepts which are explored in the leadership development process.

The System Psychodynamic Perspective and its Origins

In order to understand and to give justice to this perspective, this section starts with a short overview of the psychodynamic perspective, which forms the basis of the system psychodynamic perspective. This is followed by a more detailed discussion of system psychodynamics.

The psychodynamic perspective

Leadership is about the way people behave in organisations, with effective leaders taking responsibility for meeting the needs of their followers, paying attention to group processes, calming the anxieties and acknowledging the aspirations of members of their group while liberating energy and inspiring positive action.[1] These authors, however, point out that many of the drivers of behaviour are irrational and that attempting to explore these in a rational way yields very few results. Exploring these unconscious drives leads consultants and practitioners into the complexities and messiness of power relationships, and many of these dynamics therefore stay unexplored and unresolved. Consultants working from the psychodynamic perspective focus on both the rational and irrational dynamics inside and between individuals in the organisation and attempt to explore and understand the myriad motivational drivers, and decision-making and interaction patterns. As an example, leaders are sometimes impacted on by their own anxieties and fears in making significant changes in the organisation, or they may be immobilised by the dynamics and power plays between members of their teams.

If we are to understand the changes in behaviour of leaders and their teams, it requires the acceptance and exploration of the hidden undercurrents that affect human behaviour in organisations.[2] In order for you to understand the basic assumptions of this clinical view of behaviour,[3] we have summarised them in four points:

- *Firstly*, they argue that there is a rationale behind every form of behaviour, even for actions that seem irrational. This means that all behaviour can be explained even though the explanation may not be obvious at first and results from unconscious needs, drives and desires. This requires consultants and coaches to explore different angles to the behaviour in an attempt to, what I sometimes call, "make sense of non-sense" or seemingly irrelevant detail. Uncharacteristically, irrational behaviour of leaders can be explained if consultants and coaches take the time to explore and understand the unconscious needs, desires and fears of leaders.
- *Secondly*, it is assumed that a great deal of mental life (feelings, fears, motives and drives) operate at the unconscious level but still affect the conscious reality and physical wellbeing. Building on this, people are not always aware of how and why they are behaving in a certain way, and consultants and coaches can assist in exploring these blind spots or shadow sides of leaders. This implies that leadership development involves developing an acute self-awareness and a continuous exploration of the unconscious material which forms part of the leader's personality.
- *Thirdly*, it is believed that nothing is more central to who a person is than the way in which they regulate and express emotion. Our emotions colour our experiences with positive or negative connotations, and this in turn creates preferences in the choices we make and the

way in which we interact with the environment. Emotions furthermore form the basis of how we view ourselves and others, and consequently have an impact on our relationships. With the necessary guidance and development, individuals can fortunately change the way they perceive and express emotions. Developing the emotional intelligence of leaders can, for example, be done at a conscious skills level only, or by also exploring the unconscious emotions and drives which create some of the seemingly more irrational behaviours.[4]

- *Lastly*, human development is seen as an inter- and intrapersonal process in which our past experiences, including the developmental experiences offered by our early caregivers, play a role. These experiences continue to influence us throughout our lives. In developing leaders from this perspective, attention will have to be given to both inter- and intrapersonal processes. By attending only to the intrapersonal experiences, an opportunity to understand the impact of the leaders on others in the team will be lost. A combination is therefore suggested.

These premises of the clinical paradigm form the basis of the psychodynamic perspective and represent the complex and unique nature of the perspective. The origins of the system psychodynamic perspective can, however, also be traced back to a number of other perspectives and consultants, and coaches working from this perspective should receive intense training in the theories, models and techniques.

The origins of the System Psychodynamic perspective

System Psychodynamics is "a term used to refer to the collective psychological behavior within and between groups and organisations. Systems psychodynamics, therefore, provides a way of thinking about the leader's task of energizing or motivating forces resulting from the interconnection between various groups and sub-units of a social system."[5] This includes the interactions between leaders and their team and the motivating forces which result from these interactions. The origins of this perspective can, however, be traced back to a number of perspectives which can be explained in the following way.

Psychoanalysis

As mentioned before, the psychodynamic theory forms the basis for the philosophy of the systems psychodynamic perspective.[6][7][8] Although Freud, the father of the psychoanalytical theory, wrote very little on the subject of work, it is believed that attachment to work can be considered as a way for a leader to satisfy his or her conscious and unconscious needs, desires and fantasies, which may already have developed in childhood. These fantasies may involve the leader's needs to have power over his or her siblings (peers at work) or parental figures (senior leaders in the work context). In this way, employees and leaders can satisfy unfulfilled, unconscious needs from their family contexts.[9] It is further suggested that by exploring these fantasies with a leader or a leadership team, great insight can, for example, be gained into the way in which leaders may prevent an organisation from changing by holding onto their power. Exploring and gaining insight into the conscious and unconscious needs and drives of the collective leadership team can also provide valuable information on the leadership philosophy and strategy of the leadership team. As an example, one can compare a leadership team that is open to change and growth in which a strategy of empowerment innovation and taking responsibility is facilitated versus a leadership team which is controlling and creates numerous rules, regulations and policies in a bureaucratic fashion.

- ### *Object relations*

A further contribution to the systems psychodynamic perspective is Klein's Object Relations Theory.[10] [11] [12] This theory focuses less on instincts and sees an individual as object-seeking, which results in a specific culture in a system.[13] In a similar fashion to the way in which young children seek significant objects (including people) to attach to and build relationships with, employees and leaders seem to continue this in adult life. According to object relations theory, people use one another as objects to create safety and stability for themselves at work, and by studying these relationships, consultants and coaches can gain insights into how psychodynamic processes within people shape the relationships between leaders and employees and eventually lead to a specific culture.[14] As consultants, we, for example, study the relationships which leaders have with different individuals in their teams as well as the lack of relationships with others. This often assists in understanding the inner world and turmoil of leaders. The lack of attachment to certain objects and individuals deserves special attention in an attempt to explore what these can possibly represent to the leader. In a diverse country like South Africa, assisting leaders in understanding the relationships they develop across gender, race, age and culture seems even more important.

- ### *Social systems*

The system psychodynamic perspective also incorporates the idea that groups or organisations are social systems in which the collective (groups or organisations) becomes a unique social organism with an identity of its own, which is greater than the elements of which it is made up. Individuals who form part of these work systems are increasingly more aware of complex relationships which operate in work systems and leaders especially have the responsibility of navigating these relationships to the benefit of all. This perspective therefore includes the idea that a work system is not purely a rational system through which production and services are delivered, but that it is also a social system with complex sets of social relations.[15]

In this regard,[16] it is mentioned that this represents a rejection of the economic reason for work within a group or organisation. Employees and leaders therefore do not work purely to make a living, but also to satisfy their social needs and be part of a social entity for the greater good. These relationships often also form the cornerstone of effective organisational cultures, and leaders take responsibility in facilitating these relationships and in creating effective networks. It is also explained[17] that there is growing support from within organisations of the limitations of the logical/rational models and it is believed that non-rational forces influence leadership, group behaviour, and organisational culture. As consultants and coaches, we often assist leaders in exploring the relationships between the different members in the team and also the relationships between the leader and team members. The quality of these relationships often forms the basis of the climate and culture that exists in the team, and leaders need to understand the important role they play in creating this.

- ### *Open systems theory*

Finally, the system psychodynamic perspective also incorporates the idea that an organisation is an open system[18] which interacts with the environment in which it operates, and requires leaders to manage the boundaries between what is 'in' and what is 'out'. Apart from the fact that a system mostly exists by exchanging materials with its environment, some authors[19] [20] also believe in the idea that a final outcome can be reached through various different means and routes. In the organisational context, the use of the open systems theory implies that the functioning of the organisation can be studied through the relationships between the social and technical elements of the organisation as well as the relationships between different parts and the whole, and also includes the whole and the external environment.[21] This requires leaders to focus constantly on the technical and social elements of the organisation, the relationships between different teams or departments, and the relationship the organisation has with its environment. This implies that no event in the organisation happens in isolation and that leaders need to understand relationships, relatedness, and interconnectedness in order to guide their teams effectively in such an open system.[22]

In the following section the key concepts in the system psychodynamic perspective of leadership will be presented.

Key Concepts in the System Psychodynamic Perspective of Leadership

In this section, the key concepts and ideas that have emerged from the system psychodynamic field, as it relates to leadership and organisation study, are presented. The different authors believe that each of these lenses provide a way of looking at the hidden dynamics and undercurrents of leadership and organisational behaviour. The section is divided into an individual leader and a group relations section.

Individual leader dynamics

The "inner theatre" of an individual is described as one of the core concepts of the psychodynamic perspective.[23] [24] This inner theatre is filled with memories of the people who have influenced us, for better or worse, and all of the core conflictual relationship dynamics which have resulted from these. Our early experiences with key individuals (such as parents and teachers) contribute significantly to the creation of response patterns and even styles, which are repeated in different contexts and with different people. These patterns often represent attempts to reduce our anxiety and elicit complementary behaviour from others, and in this way, certain relationship themes develop over time. These resulting themes are often rooted in our deepest wishes, needs and goals, and therefore represent our unique personality styles. These themes play out in the work context.

In the context of the workplace, and in relationships with employees, peers and executives, leaders also act out these themes and rightly or wrongly anticipate how others will react to them. Unfortunately, leaders also tend to react to the *perceived* reactions of others, and not to their *actual* reactions. This often leads to ineffectual and even dysfunctional interactions. Consultants and coaches therefore have the responsibility of assisting leaders in understanding the motivation behind their behaviour, identifying the key relationship conflicts affecting their ability to live and work productively, and aligning these deep wishes to create more productive and mutually enhancing interpersonal relationships. This clearly implies working under the surface at the unconscious level with unconscious motives and drives and assisting the leader in developing an acute level of self-awareness.

Group relations dynamics

The system psychodynamic perspective does not focus only on the dynamics of the individual leader, but also describes leadership from a systems perspective.[25] It is also explained that understanding leadership behaviour also requires a strong focus on the leader–follower relationships[26] as described in theory on the psychology of groups (Group Relations Theory). Bion[27] identified three basic assumptions to be studied in the individual (which he called the microsystem); the group or team, department or division (the mesosystem); and the organisation (the macrosystem). These assumptions have been accepted by consultants working from this perspective as the cornerstones for the study of organisational dynamics.[28]

- *Dependency.* This assumption revolves around the idea that the worker, in the same way as a child, unconsciously experiences dependency on an imaginary parental figure or system.[29] In the organisational context, these needs for parenting, acceptance, and love are not always met, which leads to the worker experiencing frustration, helplessness, powerlessness, and disempowerment.[30] Employees often assume, at an unconscious level, that the leader or organisation can and should provide protection and guidance similar to that offered by parents. Some employees perceive the leader as an omnipotent force and they therefore readily give up their autonomy. Although this may contributes to goal-directedness and cohesiveness, it also impairs followers' critical judgment and leaves them unwilling to take initiative. These expressions of dependency[31] are projections of the worker's own anxiety and insecurity, and indicate work and emotional immaturity. Furthermore, this defence against anxiety can also be seen as a manipulation of the leader "out of role", into becoming a supervisor or parental figure, so that the team can feel safe and cared for. Consultants and coaches should assist leaders in exploring and understanding the ways in which they take up their roles and fall into the 'trap' of dependency. Leaders are expected to facilitate opportunities for employees to become interdependent rather than stay in the dependency mode. This typically requires the development of an understanding of group processes and dynamics and effective feedback, mentoring and coaching skills.
- *Fight or flight.* This assumption suggests that the everyday life of organisations is filled with anxiety and that employees, in an attempt to cope with the anxiety, use fight-or-flight defence mechanisms.[32] Fight reactions can, for example, manifest in aggression against the self, team members (with envy, jealousy, competition, elimination, boycotting, sibling rivalry, and fighting for a position in the group and privileged relationships with leaders), and even leaders.[33] Flight reactions, on the other hand, can manifest in avoidance of others, illness, or resignation. Psychological flight reactions can include defence mechanisms such as avoiding threatening situations or emotions in the present, rationalisations, and intellectualisations. These behaviours generally lead to a break in cohesion, identity and productivity, especially when leaders encourage the fight–flight assumption, inflaming their followers against real and/or imagined enemies, and using the in-group/out-group division to motivate people and to channel anxiety outwards.[34] Consultants and coaches should assist leaders in exploring and managing underlying anxiety and in shaping the group's identity by creating meaning for followers. The resulting sense of unity will be highly reassuring.
- *Pairing.* This assumption presumes that in order to cope with the anxiety, alienation, and loneliness in organisations, individuals and teams attempt to pair up with other perceived powerful individuals or subgroups. The unconscious need[35][36] is to feel safe and secure and to create. This pairing is based on the unconscious fantasy that creation will take place in pairs. This, however, also implies the splitting up of the group between individuals who

are similar and excluding those who are different. These pairings can be observed in, for example, all the males or all the females getting together in a group. In the South African context, one can also observe different races or age groups functioning in isolation from other individuals. This happens when anxiety is experienced because of differences. The individual or team therefore tries to split up the whole and build a smaller system in which they can feel secure. Pairing can also manifest itself in ganging up against the leader, who is perceived as the aggressor or authority figure.[37] In these situations, leaders will need to address the anxiety, feelings of insecurity, and fantasies in order to build effective relationships with different team members.

- *One-ness.* Two additional assumptions were later added to Bion's original assumptions.[38] The one-ness assumption implies that individual team members often seek to join a powerful union with an omnipotent force in which they are willing to surrender the self for passive participation, thereby experiencing existence, well-being, and wholeness. These are experienced by individuals as oceanic feelings of unity. This wish for salvationist inclusion can be seen in a team striving towards cohesion and synergy and may not seem problematic on the surface, but may lead to a group operating in isolation and not having sufficient contact with other groups in the rest of the organisation. This may even lead to a total denial of differences, with behaviour of group-think and a resistance to interaction with the outside world manifesting itself. Leaders need to address this 'silo' mentality and facilitate relationships with other teams and departments in order to create a co-operating and collaborative environment.

- *Me-ness.*[39] The me-ness assumption can be seen as the opposite of the one-ness assumption and seems to result from the fact that we are living in a modern and turbulent society in which individuals are pressed more and more into pulling back into themselves in order to cope with the disturbing reality of the external world. In this way, they are attempting to create an inner, comfortable world in which the external environment can be avoided. This can easily lead to the group being perceived as a non-group, with a number of individuals functioning on their own. This also creates a culture of selfishness, in which the individual is concerned only with his or her personal boundaries, which have to be protected from others. This resistance of individuals to integrate effectively in the team can affect the team's performance negatively, and leaders need to facilitate the exploration of related feelings, processes, and dynamics in order to achieve more cohesion.[40] Apart from these basic assumptions, a number of other concepts are also important in understanding leadership dynamics from this perspective.

How does the System Psychodynamic Perspective of Leadership Work?

In this section, the basic approach which is followed in the leadership development process is discussed. The goal is also to describe the task of the consultant or coach in more detail.

The development process and consultancy stance

In consulting and coaching leaders from this perspective, consultants should have a very good knowledge of individual psychological processes and the covert behaviour which operates in systems.[41] [42] The primary task of the consultant or coach is to heighten the awareness of the leader so as to understand better the covert meaning of organisational behaviour, and thereby understand the deeper and unconscious challenges faced by leadership. These can include challenges originating from the "inner theatre" of the leader, the role which he or she occupies, and the dynamics of their team or the organisation in which they operate (see Figure 9.1). While the unconscious can often be a source of destructiveness, it can also be the source of great creativity, and by allowing the unconscious to emerge, acknowledging it and linking it to the conscious aims of the leader and his or her team, a generative organisational environment can be created.[43] This requires the consultant or coach to assist in:

- Helping the leader to gain self-awareness and an understanding of their own functioning.
- Assisting leaders in exploring and making sense of the way they take up their roles in the organisation.
- Understanding the relationships between him- or herself and the members of the team, as well as the unconscious and sometimes destructive dynamics which may operate in the team.
- Optimising the way in which the leader creates a creative atmosphere of trust and collaboration in which the aims of the team can be achieved.

In summary, the system psychodynamic consultancy stance can be viewed as one that 'makes sense out of non-sense' – interpreting behaviour (verbal and non-verbal) in the 'here-and-now', without presumption of coincidence, without memory or desire.[44] Consulting from this stance implies "licensed stupidity."[45] More specifically, it is suggested that the consultant will work with the following behaviour:[46]

- The way in which individuals, leader and groups manage their anxiety in the organisation by using various defence mechanisms
- The way in which authority is exercised by leaders and others in different systems
- The nature of interpersonal relationships within the organisation and between the leader and team members
- The relationships and relatedness with authority, peers and subordinates
- Leadership practices and the management of boundaries and culture of the organisation
- Inter-group relationships between sub-systems or departments
- Identity, roles, tasks, space, time, and structures as boundaries and the management thereof in coping with anxiety.

Some of these concepts are explained in more detail in the following section as they are used in the leadership development process.

Dynamics which are explored in the leadership development process

The systems psychodynamic consultant or coach engages in an analysis of, among others, but not limited to, the interrelationships between such constructs as anxiety, social defences, projection, transference and counter-transference, valence, resistance to change, boundaries, role, authority, leadership, relationship and relatedness, and group-as-a whole.[47] [48] [49]

In consulting to and coaching the leader, consultants formulate working hypotheses or interpretations of the unconscious dynamics which operate inside the individual leader or the systems of which he or she is part, with special focus on relatedness, representation, and authority.[50] These concepts seems to play a prominent role in the way that leaders **take up their**

roles. Apart from having direct relationships with others in the team, the leader also needs to have relatedness to team members and other parts of the system. This implies that the leader considers others' perspectives, feelings, needs and aims even when they are not present, and makes decisions with them in mind, or involves them when necessary. It also implies that the leader is a representative of the team and represents them in different systems and also manages the boundary between the team and other systems in the organisation. Failing to represent effectively may lead to a team feeling unsafe or unprotected and not being taken care of in the organisation. With regard to authority, leaders need to understand that their authority to lead comes from different sources including the top (executive), the sides (peers), the bottom (subordinates), and from within themselves. In order to lead effectively and be authorised by these groups, leaders need to build strong, trusting relationships with the different role players and have confidence in themselves.

Apart from assisting leaders in the way in which they take up their roles, consultants and coaches also explore the **dynamics in the systems** in which leaders operate. This involves taking cognisance of attitudes, fantasies, conflicts and anxieties prevalent in these systems which may trigger social defences and certain relationship patterns, and which affect the way in which the task is performed.[51] [52] When teams feel anxious they may, for example, project unwanted feelings onto the leader ("he does not know what is going on"), and if the leader has the valence for incompetence (picking up feelings of incompetence from others), he or she may become completely ineffective by containing this sense of incompetence on behalf of the group.

Furthermore, consultants and coaches also assist in understanding how unconscious anxieties are reflected in the **structures and organisational design** of the organisation and in exploring these with the leader.[53] [54] [55] In this perspective, the system is studied as a reality and as a 'system in the mind' / 'group as a whole'.[56] It can also be said that[57] organisations live within us and are part of our identity. This creates a paradox in which we are part of the system we want to change. Wells also mentions that we are not objective observers of an outside organisation, but instead are emotionally involved and part of the organisation. This makes what happens in the organisation very personal, and the structures and policies we create in organisations are often a representation of our inner emotional lives. Consultants and coaches are therefore able to assist leaders with exploring complex organisational dynamics by studying how the structures and policies or lack thereof represent unconscious dynamics in the team or organisation. As an example, leaders may not realise how ineffective some of the structures and policies have become over time because these are often used to contain anxiety. Consultants and coaches, on the other hand, approach with an objective perspective and often challenge these conventions in order to facilitate change.

The CIBART Consulting Model

Cilliers and Koortzen[58] describe a consulting model called CIBART, which allows consultants and coaches who are starting out in working with this perspective to focus on the most important constructs in the consulting or coaching process. Applying the CIBART model also allows coaches to study, explore, analyse and intervene in the way leaders take up their roles in the organisation. This model, which is presented by means of the CIBART mnemonic incorporates a number of constructs, namely Conflict, Identity, Boundaries, Authority, Role and Task, which represent some of the most important areas to address in system psychodynamic coaching.

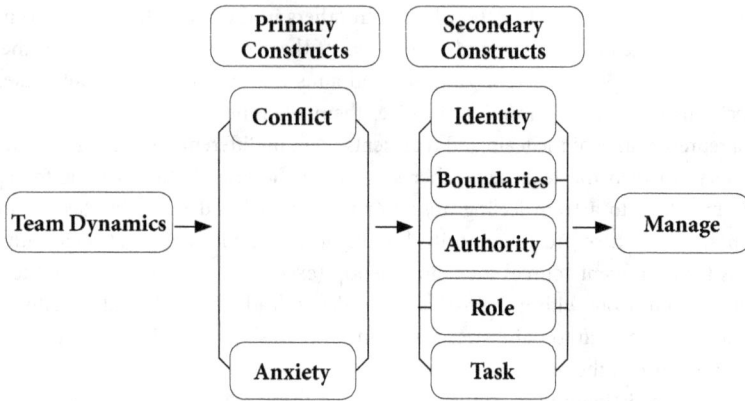

Figure 9.2: The CIBART consulting model

As indicated in Figure 9.2, team dynamics can be analysed by studying the conflicts and anxiety, which operate at the conscious but more often unconscious levels in teams. The anxiety (fear of the future) and conflict function at both the conscious and unconscious levels with leaders and teams often not aware of the full extent of these. Leaders also function within the team context and often contribute to the conflict and anxiety or are the receivers of anxiety, anger and aggression from the team. They also have the responsibility of containing the conflict and anxiety in the team by managing the secondary constructs, which represent different forms of boundaries. Coaches offering coaching from this perspective often assist leaders in analysing and understanding their roles within the context of the team. This implies that these coaches assist leaders in studying the unconscious dynamics (forces) in the team and the way in which they contribute to these dynamics or are involved in them.

- *Conflict.* According to this framework,[59] conflict can be seen as a very natural and human condition, which serves as the basic driving force or dynamo for the team's performance, creativity and innovation. Teams can't exist without conflict, and it may even assist them in coping with change and transformation. Conflicts often result from anxiety and can be viewed as any type of split which exists between the different parts of the system (team). Conflicts in and between members can manifest intra-personally (in the individual, between ideas and feelings); interpersonally (the experience of differences between two or more team members); intra-group (between factions or subgroups); and intergroup (between one team/department and others in the larger organisational system). As coaches we often assist leaders and teams in exploring and understanding the anxiety, which they or their teams may experience as well as the accompanying conflicts. Finding ways to address the conflicts can often be found in one or a number of the other constructs (secondary constructs) of the CIBART model. These secondary constructs not only offer possible sources of conflict, but also identify areas in which changes need to be made in order to resolve conflicts and contain anxiety. As consultants and coaches, we therefore often attend to the identity, boundary, authority, role and task conflicts which manifest in a team.
- *Identity.* Identity[60] can be described as the characteristics of the team and includes its members, their task, and the climate and culture which make them different from other teams and unique. The identity of the team is, however, directly influenced by the personality and style of the leader, the team's experience of leadership, and how personal leadership is exercised by members of the team. A lack of identification with the team's nature and performance, and unclear identity boundaries, create a high level of anxiety in

the team. In coaching leaders, their relationships with the members of the team are often explored, and team members are often included in the coaching sessions in order to explore how they identify (or not) with the leader (or manager) and his/her goals, values, and the organisation's vision, mission, goals, and brand. Discrepancies between the identity of the leader and team members often lead to an unstable identity, and coaches often need to find ways of integrating the leader and team members into a unit with a collectively defined culture.

- *Boundaries.* With regard to boundaries, it is suggested that the leader manage the difference between what is inside the boundary in relation to what is outside the boundary.[61] It therefore requires both inward and outward focus from the leader. When boundaries are poorly designed and managed, they can cause a great amount of stress and anxiety for both the leader and the team. The task of leadership is therefore located on the boundary between the organisation and the external environment, and by standing at the boundary, a leader can create a more controllable environment in which the team can achieve their objectives. Basic boundaries, which need to be managed by the leader or others taking up a leadership role, are time, space (territory) and task.

- *Authority.*[62] Authority can be viewed as the level of power to perform roles and tasks. Authority also refers to the formal and official power that the leader and team members receive to perform their tasks, as it is given (1) from above (by the organisation, executives, colleagues), (2) from below (by subordinates), and (3) from within (by the leaders themselves). The authority of leaders can, however, also be removed or limited when the team perceives the leader as misusing or abusing the power. As consultants and coaches, we often assist leaders in exploring the ways in which they receive and exercise their authority in the team. The ways in which they authorise and sometimes de-authorise others also form an important part of the discussion.

- *Role.* Role forms the boundary around work and refers to the description of what needs to be done in order to perform.[63] Taking up a specific role implies being authorised to do so and knowing the boundaries of what will be rewarded and what not. Coaches assist leaders and team members not only in clarifying their roles but also in agreeing on and adhering to their roles. The way in which leaders take up their roles often receives a great deal of attention, with the goal of optimising their functioning in the role and in eliminating and delegating roles and tasks which are not in line with their level of work.

- *Task.* Leadership is also directly related to the pursuit of the organisation's aims and primary task.[64] It is through monitoring the primary task (sometimes referred to as the purpose or mission of the team) that the leader is able to avoid abuse of power, maintain on-task behaviour, and minimise off-task and anti-task behaviour. By focusing on the task, leaders ensure that the team deliver on their mandate and contribute effectively to the success of the system.

Case study

The following case study is presented as a way of illustrating the way in which the CIBART model is used in consulting to and coaching leaders.

In consulting with a senior member of an executive team, the person indicated that he was considering resigning after only six months in the organisation. It was clear that the personwas experiencing serious intrapersonal **conflicts** about staying or leaving the organisation.

In exploring these conflicts, the person explained that as a medical specialist, he is committed to delivering quality medical care in the public sector, where he has worked for most of his life. His current role, however, was in a private hospital group, in which he was responsible for community investment. This role seemed to be in line with his personal values, and he had accepted the role with great enthusiasm and vigour. After a few months, however, it became clear that the organisation's motive for community investment did not correspond with his, and after being unsuccessful in implementing a number of community projects as a result of low return on investment, he started to experience intense emotional reactions and conflict.

Using the CIBART model, we were able to analyse the origins of the conflict, and the coachee identified an **identity** conflict as one of the main contributing factors. It seemed that his identity (who he is and what he stands for) was not aligned to the identity and values of a profit-driven organisation. Furthermore the normative **role** (the job description) was significantly different from the experiential role (what he experienced on a day-to-day basis), which also differed from the phenomenal role (what he thought others were saying about him in the role). On a day-to-day basis he ended up having to convince his team members of the importance of community investments and that these are not always profit driven. This resulted in his becoming more and more **de-authorised** over a period of time. In obtaining support from his team members, he had to explain repeatedly the importance and the long-term impact of community investment. This was necessary because the executive team did not see community investment as part of the primary **task** (mission) of the team or the organisation, and the strategy on community investment had received very little attention before he had joined the team. The coaching process with the whole team also focused on managing time, space (territory) and task **boundaries** which the team struggled with. Some members consistently interfered with the executive's tasks and engaged members in the public sector on community investments without involving him. This left him even more de-authorised. In coaching the team, a lot of time was spent on the way they were working as a collective, and developing relationships and relatedness received special attention.

Conclusion

The Tavistock Consulting Executive Coaching Programme summarises coaching from a Systems Psychodynamic perspective in five points.[65] Miller starts by indicating that coaching from this perspective allows coaches to work at or under the surface and to tackle the hard-to-reach dynamics that limit the performance of organisations, teams and leaders. This method of executive coaching therefore allows one to uncover "what's really going on." The five tips Miller offers to coach successfully from this perspective can be summarised as follows:

- *Emotion is data:* As professionals we can't ignore these emotions which are stirred up by coaching and consulting processes. This includes the irrational feelings our clients experience during the process. Employees, for example, can feel excited, competitive, miserable, angry or happy during and after a conversation with a peer or boss. These emotions provide important clues on what is happening between individuals in a system. As coaches and consultants, we need to attend specifically to the emotions we experience in the room with a client. We believe they are a communication that needs attention.[66]
- *Remember the Person, Role and Organisation triangle.* As systems psychodynamic coaches and consultants, we work with what is being referred to as the *PRO Model*. If we fail to attend to all three contexts, we are missing a crucial part of the context of our coaching

work. While focusing on the Person, the Role and the Organisation, we also need to pay attention to the personal 'small talk' (for example, where a client is going on holiday, or has personal difficulties at home). These may shed light on the current situation that a client is facing.

- *Working below the surface:* While the concrete, visible and factual information such as the organisational structure, reporting lines, how long a client has been in the team, and so on, are important, we also need to pay attention to the more deeply hidden material. In "Johari Window" terms, this material may fall in the "unknown to self and unknown to others" quadrant. Working in this way allows the coach or consultant to draw attention to a client's blind spots and derailing behaviour, which may trip the client up.

- *Have courageous conversations:* Courageous conversations are the hardest but often also the most important to have with our clients. Our clients often come to coaching because of a difficulty in understanding complex dynamics in a system and an inability to verbalise these with the people in their teams.[67] It is also suggested that a good rule of thumb is that if it feels difficult to say, it's exactly what needs to be said. Because of the difficulty of these conversations, they need to be handled sensitively, and the timing and pace should be considered carefully. If handled well, they can lead to new insights and very creative outcomes.

- *Coach as accompanist:* The coach serves the client and therefore needs to work at the client's pace and respect that there may not be a simple solution to the problem. The coachee is the expert in terms of the organisation and culture, and our job as coaches and consultants is to help them harness their expertise in a way that works for them.

Endnotes

1	Kets de Vries, & Cheak, 2014.	35	Bion, 1961.
2	Newton, Long & Sievers, 2006.	36	Lawrence, 1999.
3	See endnote 1.	37	Kets de Vries & Cheak, 2014.
4	Beck, 2012.	38	Turquet, 1974.
5	Neumann, 1999.	39	Turquet, 1974.
6	Cilliers, 2005.	40	Koortze & Cilliers, 2002.
7	Czander, 1993.	41	Cilliers, 2005.
8	DeBoard, 1978.	42	Czander, 1993.
9	Czander, 1993.	43	Krantz, 2005.
10	Ibid	44	Cilliers & Koortzen, 2005.
11	Miller, 1993.	45	Czander, 1993.
12	Rice, 1965.	46	Koortze & Cilliers, 2002.
13	Czander, 1993.	47	Bion, 1961.
14	Hirchhorn, 1993.	48	Bion, 1962b
15	Czander, 1993.	49	Hirchhorn, 1993.
16	Koortze & Cilliers, 2002.	50	Cilliers, 2005.
17	Kets de Vries, 1991.	51	Czander, 1993.
18	Gharajedaghi, 1985.	52	Hirchhorn, 1993.
19	Czander, 1993.	53	Czander, 1993.
20	Von Bertalanffy, 1950.	54	Hirchhorn, 1993.
21	Czander, 1993.	55	Krantz, 2005.
22	Cilliers, 2005.	56	Wells, 1980.
23	Kets de Vries & Cheak, 2014.	57	Armstrong, 2005.
24	McDougall, 1985.	58	See endnote 23.
25	Kets de Vries & Cheak, 2014.	59	Cilliers & Koortzen, 2005.
26	Bion, 1959.	60	Cilliers & Koortzen, 2005.
27	Bion, 1961.	61	Cilliers & Koortzen, 2005.

28	Lawrence, 1999.	62	Cilliers & Koortzen, 2005.
29	McDougall, 1985.	63	Cilliers & Koortzen, 2005.
30	Kets de Vries & Cheak, 2014.	64	Cilliers & Koortzen, 2005.
31	Koortzen & Cilliers, 2002.	65	Miller, 2013.
32	Bion, 1959.	66	Miller, 2013.
33	Koortze & Cilliers, 2002.	67	Cilliers & Koortzen, 2005.
34	Kets de Vries & Cheak, 2014.		

References

Armstrong, D. 2005. *Organization in the mind: Psychoanalysis, group relations, and organizational consultancy.* London: Karnac.

Beck, UC. 2012. *Psychodynamic coaching: Focus & depth.* London: Karnac.

Bion, W.R. (1959). Attacks on Linking. In E. Bott Spillius (ed.) *Melanie Klein Today: Developments in theory and practice. Volume 1: Mainly Theory.* 1988. London: Routledge.

Bion, WR. 1961. *Experiences in groups.* London: Tavistock.

Bion, WR. 1962. *Learning from experience.* London: Heinemann.

Cilliers, F & Koortzen, P. 2005. Working with conflict in teams – the CIBART model. *HR Future,* 51–52, October.

Cilliers, F. 2005. 'Executive coaching experiences. A systems psychodynamic perspective'. *South African Journal of Industrial Psychology,* 31(3):23–30.

Czander, WM. 1993. *The psychodynamics of work and organizations.* New York, NY: Guilford Press.

DeBoard, R. 1978. *The psychoanalysis of organisations.* London: Routledge.

Gharajedaghi, J. 1985. *Toward a systems theory of organization.* Seaside, CA: Intersystems Publications.

Hirchhorn, L. 1993. *The workplace within: Psychodynamics of organizational life.* Cambridge, MA: MIT.

Kets de Vries, MFR & Cheak, A. 2014. 'Psychodynamic approach'. In PG Northouse (ed). *Leadership: Theory and practice.* Los Angeles: Sage. 295–328.

Koortzen, P & Cilliers, F. 2002. 'The psychoanalytic approach to team development'. In R Lowman (ed). *The California School of Organizational Studies handbook of organizational consulting psychology.* Newark, NJ: Wiley & Sons. 220–235.

Krantz, J. 2005. 'Einige Gedanken über Reflexion in Organisationen'. *Freie Assoziation Zeitschrift für das Unbewusste in Organisation und Kultur,* 8(2).

Lawrence, WG. 1999. *Exploring individual and organizational boundaries: A Tavistock open systems approach.* London: Karnac.

McDougall, J. 1985. *Theaters of the Mind.* New York, NY: Basic Books.

Miller, EJ. 1993. *From dependency to autonomy: Studies in organisation and change.* London, UK: Free Association.

Miller, S. 2013. *5 top tips to systems psychodynamic coaching.* Tavistock Consulting Executive Coaching Programme. [Online]. Available: http://www.hrgrapevine.com/markets/hr/article/2014-08-07-5-top-tips-to-systems-psychodynamic-coaching [Accessed 15 June 2016].

Neumann, JE. 1999. 'Systems psychodynamics in the service of political organizational change'. In R French & R Vince (eds). *Group relations, management, and organization.* Oxford, UK: Oxford University Press. 54–69.

Newton, J, Long, S, & Sievers, B. 2006. *Coaching in depth: The organizational role analysis approach.* London, UK: Karnac Books.

Rice, AK. 1965. *Learning for leadership: Interpersonal and intergroup relations.* London, UK: Tavistock Publications.

Turquet, PM. 1974. 'Leadership: The individual and the group'. In GS Gibbard, JJ Hartman and RD Mann (eds). *Analysis of groups.* San Francisco, CA: Jossey-Bass. 337–371.

Von Bertalanffy, L. 1950. 'An outline of general system theory'. *The British Journal for the Philosophy of Science,* 1(2):134–165.

Wells, L. 1980. 'The group-as-a-whole. A systemic socio-analytical perspective on interpersonal and group relations'. In CP Alderfer & CL Cooper (eds). *Advances in Experiential Social Processes,* 2:165–198.

Chapter 10

RE-AUTHORING LEADERSHIP NARRATIVES

Chené Swart

Once upon a Time...

... there was an organisation that was doing very important work at a very important time in our world. Some may say that this work was done in some of the harshest conditions imaginable. Over the years of their short existence, a narrative had started to emerge and after having been told and re-told was called Failure and Invisibility. This narrative constantly chanted that the work they were doing did not really make a difference, was not even done well, and that nobody really knew about this work. So did it really have an impact?[i]

Come and join us on an adventure in discovering and exploring the re-authoring lens with its accompanying ideas, practices, knowledges[ii] and skills of living that came together with these leaders in the forever-evolving and "ongoing conversation"[1] called the organisation.

I have been journeying with organisations and leaders in re-authoring work for the past 11 years. As I share these insights and practices, I stand on the shoulders of all the leaders and work-communities[iii] who have seen me, taught me about their worlds, and dared to walk in the diversity of their "exotic" and "extraordinary lives."[2] These insights and actions have transported me and "I have become other than who I was" at the outset of these journeys in the way I think, and in the way I have been confronted to "reconsider established understandings" as my "settled certainties have been shaken up."[3] I see these leaders and work-communities as "fellow travellers" who have "transported" me to witness "powerful expressions of insider experiences" because they have taken me into "territories of knowledge that I could not have known."[4] All of these journeys have enabled me to have an appreciation of the relevance of the re-authoring lens and skills for leadership practices in organisations.

The purpose of this chapter is to lay out the land of the context, philosophical understanding, maps, and enabling practices that re-author leadership narratives with and within organisations.

We will explore the following questions:

- How can the re-authoring lens and practices invite the subordinate storylines of leadership to come out of the shadows and inform alternative ways of co-constructing and co-authoring organisations?
- How can leaders co-author organisational narratives with the community of workers?

---

i   Throughout the chapter this organisational narrative will be our teacher in explaining the re-authoring lens and practices. This is a narrative of one of my clients with whom I recently had the privilege to journey. They have given me permission to use parts of their narrative for the purpose of this article. This organisational and leadership narrative will be our guide in explaining the re-authoring lens and practices throughout the article.

ii The word 'knowledges' refers to the multiplicity of knowledges that an individual, community or organisation has in the art and skill of living their lives in this world.

iii Pierre Blanc-Sahnoun introduced me to the idea of speaking about the workforce as work-communities, which opens up much richer descriptions and possibilities. I use the terms 'work-communities' and 'community of workers' interchangeably.

This chapter will explore the context of a world for which the re-authoring approach becomes a lens to see and a pen to write. We will also unpack the philosophical ground that informs the re-authoring lens as well as explore what this approach means for leadership and organisations. In addition, this chapter will provide maps that can guide leaders and organisations in re-authoring and co-authoring their individual, communal and organisational narratives. Lastly, the chapter will describe the enabling conditions for the re-authoring lens and name some of the gifts that this approach can bring.

What is Water?

There are these two young fish swimming along and they happen to meet an older fish swimming the other way, who nods at them and says, "Morning, boys. How's the water?" And the two young fish swim on for a bit, and then eventually one of them looks over at the other and goes: "What the hell is water?" [5]

What is the water that organisations and leaders are finding themselves in? How can we see the water or know it? Why does it matter? What the hell is water?

The way in which we speak, think and act does not fall from the sky. Leaders and organisations are shaped by the "communities and histories they come from, and the cities, nations, and economic systems that have formed them, as well as the ideas of the global world that they form part of through access to technology."[6] We grow up in these communities and societies and we take for granted that our way of being and doing is the way things are as it becomes normal, to the point where we do not even realise that we are swimming in water. These taken-for-granted ideas and beliefs are carried by language and embodied in all of us.

We become part of, join in with, are "thrown" into a way of talking and being that precedes us. One is already embedded in a tradition of being. We inherit a vocabulary that is a way of being, so that our language speaks us rather than us speaking our language. Contrary to the conduit theory of language, ideas do not exist in the mind prior to being formed into speech. The language we inherit is the context that allows concepts to become taken-for-granted.[7]

Why don't we know that we are swimming in water? Over the years our ways of thinking and doing have become divorced from the history, culture and worlds they have grown from as they attained some form of truth status presenting itself as "the way things are" or as "normal." These taken-for-granted beliefs and ideas hide their history and also hide how they are informed by people in our societies who are perceived to have knowledge and stand in positions of authority.

How can we see the water we are swimming in so that it is no longer hidden? The following questions can be asked to start unpacking the taken-for-granted beliefs and ideas: Where do these ideas come from? Whose voices are privileged by these ideas, and what do these beliefs have in mind for the organisation and its leaders? How are these ideas influencing the organisation and its leaders?

When we start to see the taken-for-granted beliefs and ideas for what they are, we can unpack and deconstruct the truths, practices and the vocabularies of the water so that they can be "more explicitly known."[8]

This water is not innocent because it has huge implications for what is called for in a particular time when it comes to leadership and organisational work. Therefore the meanings we make about our own identities, work, leadership and organisations are informed by taken-for-granted ideas and beliefs of the water we swim in. Let's start unpacking some of the important taken-for-granted beliefs and ideas that have an impact on organisations and leaders.

Scarcity[9] is one of the dominant taken-for-granted beliefs and ideas which daily hum that there is not enough for everyone in our business and organisational world. There are not enough resources, time, profit, products, compliance, talent, market share, growth, alignment, skills, and innovation, which in some organisations sometimes lead to an inhumane pace, anxiety, competitiveness and fatigue.[10]

Secondly, the taken-for-granted beliefs and ideas that dominate in organisations are still largely influenced by the thinking, practices and structures of a world that is seen as static, certain and predictable, and therefore in need of "command and control" leadership.[11] Within such a world, organisations and leaders are often called upon and interested in "discovering best practices, benchmarking against world-class organizations, collecting the 'right data', and continual searches for the singular cause and expertise. Because this orientation tends to search for the 'right answer', 'best solution', and so on, there is also an implicit tendency to seek out experts who can supply tested solutions."[12] These taken-for-granted beliefs come at a price because by the time evidence is collected to create best practices, the conditions have changed enough to make them likely to have become obsolete. Within this understanding, leaders are sometimes headhunted from other organisations in order to apply the best practice and turnaround strategy that was successful in their previous organisation sometimes "as is" in the next context.

Another taken-for-granted belief and idea that influences the organisational world is the notion of the individual self (especially in leadership) that requires leaders to trade him-/herself as a commodity or property to be owned, and whose personal resources and strengths can and should be used and developed to full capacity.[13] We therefore have numerous leadership styles and many forms of assessment to categorise and place leaders on a "range of continuums, tables and scales" in which they are "induced to work to close the gap"[14] between these locations and the understanding of what is currently considered normal, and the human nature of a good leader.[15] When we can measure leaders according to "tables of performance",[16] we can also design the appropriate development path for them. If leaders do not shape or fall in line with the standard norm of a particular organisation, "problematization"[17] sets in, and the individual leader sometimes becomes the sole focus and object of blame for problems in the organisation. These messages of deficiency draw a static line in the sand for the leader and remove the responsibility for thinking and deeper conversation about the "water" that is influencing and impacting in this situation.[18]

These are just some of the taken-for-granted beliefs and ideas that have an impact on organisations and leaders in what we have started unpacking as the water. Some of the other dominant beliefs and ideas that also have an impact on organisations and leaders are patriarchy, the belief in never-ending growth, and the fascination of the success of businesses in first-world countries, to name a few. What are the beliefs and ideas in your organisation that constitute the water?

What is the re-authoring lens, and how can it bring practices to understand, challenge and make sense of the taken-for-granted beliefs and ideas of the water we swim in?

The Re-authoring Lens

What can the re-authoring lens offer to the organisational narrative of Failure and Invisibility? The power of the narrative of Failure and Invisibility is that it is hidden. Until we unpacked the context (water) in which this organisation was serving, leaders in the organisation saw themselves as the problem; they were invisible failures making no real impact. Understanding the context enabled the organisation to name the context, which they called the Soup and the Mess. The narrative of Invisibility and Failure did not fall from the sky but was birthed from and supported by the context of the Mess and Chaos. For the first time organisational leaders could see how they have internalised the stories that the context was telling them and could again choose what kind of relationship they would like to have with Failure, Invisibility in the Chaos and the Mess. At the same time as they were unpacking the Chaos and the Mess and its influence on their lives and work, they also saw narratives that were different from these dominant taken-for-granted beliefs and ideas. These different narratives had been dampened by the Chaos and the Mess, so much so, that their worth seemed insignificant. As the organisational members were standing in a new relationship to the context of the Mess and the Chaos, they could see, for the first time, that they were not totally taken over by the context; but their daily practices told a different story of work, relationships, hope and action towards an alternative future of Peace. As meaning-makers and story-makers they were writing a different narrative, even in the face of the Chaos and the Mess. The re-authoring lens gave back the pen in the writing and co-writing of the preferred organisational narrative called "Real People doing Real Work towards Ending the Conflict", a narrative for which there was a storehouse of evidence, practices and skills of living and serving.

The re-authoring lens provides the practices to take back the pen in the authoring of our individual narratives and the co-authoring of our collective narratives. In this approach, narratives are seen as the basic unit of experience. Human beings weave moments and events together in a coherent storyline across history and time and as they make meaning of these narratives in a particular context, they draw conclusions about who they are, what they can become, how they should relate, and what reality is all about.

From the viewpoint of re-authoring, human beings and the organisations they represent are seen through practices that have grown out of a deep understanding and acknowledgement of the influence and effects of the context (water) as mentioned in the section above. This lens provides ways to unpack, challenge and expose the context, as well as navigate and co-author ways of being in the context (water) that speak of the shifting of conversations and narratives. Furthermore, the re-authoring lens provides a counter-narrative, an alternative response and way of being to the dominant ideas of scarcity, individualism and the so-called certainty and predictability of this world.[19]

The melting pot of the wisdom and "insider knowledges"[20] of organisations and leaders I have journeyed with, the VUCA[21] world, and the ideas of poststructuralism,[22] social constructionism,[23] community building work,[24] interpersonal neurobiology,[25] Narrative therapy,[26] Dialogic Organisation Development[27] and Paulo Freire's critical pedagogy work[28] all come together in co-constructing the re-authoring lens for leadership and organisational work within the context (water) of organisations.

Firstly, the re-authoring lens sees human beings as active participants in the construction of their lives and their worlds although they might be unaware that they are participating in the shaping of their lives.[29] While our lives are informed by the water of the taken-for-granted beliefs and ideas, life is not seen as a "direct reproduction of the knowledges and practices of culture" because it "renders invisible the specific achievement of meaning-making"[30] and story-making.[31] Because human beings are meaning-makers and story-makers, organisations and leaders live and act in ways that do not only reproduce these taken-for-granted beliefs and ideas but resist and challenge the water by making meaning through language, behaviours, and embodied emotions.[32] Human beings then live through their bodies[33] and convey meaning in "both doing and nondoing"[34] that shape their actions[35] and have consequences for their lives, relationships and what we would call reality.[36]

However, contrary to the ideas of individualism, the meaning we make is not an individual act, but happens in the interaction between individuals, communities and organisations. A very important understanding in this melting pot of approaches is the notion that human beings are relationally connected and socially constructed[37] through history, culture and taken-for-granted beliefs and ideas. In this regard, Narrative Therapy[38] ideas challenge the notion of the individual self and propose a multiplicity of selves, intentions and "authenticities"[39] that are constructed and negotiated as we make meaning of our identities in various relationships.

In addition, meaning does not pre-exist the interpretation of experience, and all meanings are linguistic and social achievements as people construct meaning by trafficking in narratives and by taking experiences of life into "narrative frames."[40] Human beings are therefore seen as "multi-storied" and "narratively resourced"[41] as they construct meaning from their rich histories and memories. These re-authoring ideas challenge the single and thin accounts that scarcity often supports in its descriptions of leaders and organisations, which sound like: "You are a bad leader"; or "You are a visionless organisation."

The re-authoring lens provides practices that create the conditions where human beings as narratively resourced beings are invited to unpack narratives that get them stuck and do not take them forward (for example, Failure and Invisibility), and enrich and thicken alternative preferred narratives[42] (for example, Real People doing Real Work) that speak of ways of living and being that take individuals, leaders and organisations forward.

One of the growing ways in which the world is having an impact on organisations is described today in the acronym VUCA,[43] which speaks of *v*olatility, *u*ncertainty, *c*omplexity and *a*mbiguity. This world sees evolving and changing markets and realities that challenge the detailed long-term strategies engineered for a certain and predictable world that no longer exist. Stacey[44] emphasises this point when he explains that uncertainty and unpredictability are fundamental, irremovable aspects of organisational reality which mean that no one knows with any confidence what will happen; all we can rely on is the fact that we will be surprised. The rapid success of businesses such as Uber, Airbnb and Alibaba (to name only a few) are examples of the surprises of this uncertain and unpredictable world.

In this VUCA world, we need the Dialogic Organisational Development (OD) Mindset[45] as a very important ingredient in the melting pot of re-authoring wisdom because it sees organisations as:

- An ongoing conversation that is built on emergence, generativity and narrative.
- A "means to ends that are constantly in a flow of creation and re-creation and are not viewed as a 'thing'." [46]
- "Meaning-making systems in which the reality/truth is continuously created and re-created through social interactions and agreements [and] open to many possible interpretations."[47]
- "Self-organizing, socially constructed realities that are continuously created, sustained, and changed through narratives, stories, images, symbols, and conversations."[48]

When an organisation is seen as an ongoing conversation according to the Dialogic OD Mindset, shifting the nature of the relationships with one another and therefore the conversation that flows from these relationships leads to shifting the narratives of work-communities. These work-communities are invited to experiment with the possibility of an alternative future amid the taken-for-granted beliefs and ideas (water) from which organisational narratives grow and are informed. This shift can occur by changing "who is in the conversation with whom, how these conversations take place, increasing conversational skills, what is being talked about, and by asking what is being created from the content and process of current conversations. Talk is action."[49] When talk is action, the "words, writings and symbolic forms of expressions do more than convey meaning; they create meaning"[50] and shape how we think, what we perceive, and "what makes sense to us and others."[51]

As a result, narratives and the hosting of different kinds of conversation are the most important discursive phenomena for understanding how people in organisations make meaning.[52] The emphasis on narrative modes of story-making occurs because "such accounts reveal meaning, without making the error of defining it."[53]

These kinds of conversations invite emergence, narrative and "generative metaphors",[54] that enrich the future stories of the organisation with "evidence and actions from the past and present. [T]he future is not without evidence of the possibility and potential of the preferred story an organization is living into."[55] When this alternative meaning is named through meaning-making together, transformation can happen when our "language changes" in what is named and as we "redescribe" our organisation.[56]

To create the environment for work-communities to participate in collectively co-constructing narratives, we have to invite the multiplicity of narratives of an organisation to be spoken "as is" through deep human connection built on invitation, welcome and gifts.[57] In this deep human connection, work-communities are invited to learn *with* one another and not *for* one another[58] as informants and co-constructors of the communal narrative. "The moment the word 'community' is introduced, it invites notions of care, collective wisdom and knowledges, gifts, and neighbourliness to enter a world that is so often rooted in assumptions of competition, success, hoarding knowledge, and doing it my way as the only way."[59]

Re-authoring Leadership with and within Organisations

In the Chaos and Mess one of the leader's narratives felt trapped and stuck. It was a narrative of the Shadow of doubt and of victimhood that came to visit when the voice of Chaos and the Mess became too overwhelming. The Shadow was also a leadership narrative that did not have all the say, or the last say. There were counter-narratives of freedom and love that challenged beliefs and ideas as well as narratives of hopes and dreams for real peace to reign. Not only were there alternative beliefs and ideas as counter evidence to the narrative of the Shadow, there were also relationships in which the leader stood that spoke of different ways of being and doing as the narrative of Light started to appear. The leader's relationship with her gracious and loving father, even as he faced severe violence, was only one relationship that offered different conclusions and counter-evidence to the narrative of the Shadow. As the leader understood the impact of the Chaos and the Mess on her leadership narrative, actions and options in the art of living and leading became available beyond what is the right and good way to lead according to dominant understandings. There was a crack in the Shadow where the Light could begin to shine through more clearly.

This section will unpack the meaning of the word and world of leadership as it grows from the previous section's philosophical understandings and the context within which organisations are seen. We will explore questions such as: What does this viewpoint on re-authoring mean for leadership? What are the necessary leadership skills and practices to navigate in the context of the water? What is the impact on leadership in organisations when the organisation is seen as an ongoing conversation?

Leadership and the ideas around leadership did not fall from the sky; they were crafted and made meaning of over many centuries in various cultures and contexts. What was and is local and specific cultural understandings of leadership have in some cases become privileged understandings that are communicated across the globe through technology, literature as well as leadership- and business schools. All these claims of knowing the right and good way to be a leader in this time sponsor "identity conclusions"[60] that grow from cutting edge ideas and thought leadership on offer from leadership schools, literature and cultural consumer stores of our global world. These dominant taken-for-granted beliefs and ideas about leadership are then sold as universal practices, true for all times and in all contexts, in what we have come to know and call 'best practices'.

These so-called universal practices lead to the marginalisation of local and specific understandings around leadership and marginalised cultural understandings are sometimes taken and 'sold' on the market, divorced from the contexts that can sustain them. We are therefore left with the following questions: Who is allowed to speak about leadership, and in what way? Who do we consider to be experts in this field? Whose voices are not included, and why?

The re-authoring lens offers a "counter-narrative that reconstructs the current notions of leadership. It is not a new model, with new, distinct characteristics and qualities. It proposes a lens, a way of being, seeing, engaging and participating in this world, that invites a different relationship for the leader"[61] to their organisations, themselves, and the context in which the organisation works.

Firstly, the viewpoint of re-authoring invites leaders to draw on their own unique local and specific narratives of leadership that are often "domesticated"[62] and called nothing special or important in the face of these dominant understandings of good leadership. Therefore, leaders are seen as primary authors who hold the "storytelling rights"[63] to their own narratives, not as biographies, but as autobiographies. As leaders draw from this treasure chest of hidden understandings and knowledges through culture, memory, embodiment and narrative, it opens up possibilities for the "kind of leadership story that leaders prefer, and enables them to define the task of leadership for themselves."[64]

Secondly, the re-authoring lens invites leaders to understand that they are relationally connected to their communities, cultures and contexts from the place where their identities are formed. These leadership identities are socially constructed through history, societal and business beliefs and ideas, organisational structures, their own stories of work, and are co-constructed by the organisations of which the leaders are a part. Within this understanding there is a multiplicity of narratives, relationships, moments, meanings and events that inform leadership and therefore "leadership becomes a reflective and dialogical project, co-created in interaction"[65] with the organisation. As a result, leaders are constructed by the organisation and the organisation co-constructs what leadership means in this particular context at this particular time.

Thirdly, re-authoring practices enable leaders to co-create conversations and narratives that shape, constitute and maintain relationships, identities and organisational realities in preferred ways. From the viewpoint of the re-authoring lens, leaders are seen as the convenors of conversations where all are invited to work from their preferred narratives and where conversations, meetings and initiatives are guided by an awareness of the co-authoring capacity of all in the organisation to shift and celebrate the narratives and metaphors that move the organisation forward, in what Snowden[66] would call "more stories like these."

When an organisation is seen as an ongoing conversation, leaders have the privilege of convening gatherings and meetings (both formal and informal) wherein the ongoing conversation by its mere existence and practice creates and co-creates an alternative narrative together. The leader's ability to handle dialogue then becomes an "essential qualification parameter."[67] In these gatherings, attention is given to how we speak, what we speak about, generating metaphors and vocabulary of the conversation, and images that resonate with the ongoing unfolding of the narrative and its accompanying practices and skills. Since words creates worlds,[68] "new vocabularies are invitations to new possibilities", which suggests that leaders "pay attention to new voices, new action possibilities at the margins that can suggest new worlds of meaning."[69]

The re-authoring understanding also enables leaders to identify, unpack, question and challenge societal beliefs and ideas (water) that influence organisational culture by harnessing and inviting the unique knowledges or "insider know-how"[70] and skills of the work-communities beyond "the way things are" or "this is normal." In the Dialogic OD Mindset, this challenging practice is referred to as the creation of the "disruption in the status quo."[71]

Leaders can therefore be seen as "entrepreneurs of meaning"[72] because they listen to, unpack and challenge societal beliefs and ideas and stuck narratives. They also create conditions where meaning is constructed and co-constructed so that narratives can be 're-meaned', re-authored, and co-authored. As entrepreneurs of meaning, leaders are attentive to the "appearing of what appears",[73] as they are in constant conversation with the emergence of all the layers of narratives and meaning in the organisation, with its "variety of different narratives about the same thing, and sometimes even competing narratives about the same things."[74]

In conclusion, the leaders' role in the organisation as an ongoing conversation is to understand their own narratives and how they influence their practices, to convene conversation where meaning could be collectively named, to challenge and unpack taken-for-granted beliefs and ideas, and to invite the co-authoring of the emergence of the alternative narrative.

The next section will provide maps, scaffolds, and practices for the journey.

The Re-authoring Maps and Practices for the Journey

> As the leader understood the Chaos and the Mess and the competing individual leadership narratives of the Shadow and the Light, the ability to see the organisational narrative and their own participation in it became more visible. The leader was now able to host conversations where the problem was the problem and not the person, where the unique leadership quality of each individual narrative of leaders was valued and seen to contribute to the diverse gifts that show the way forward. Leadership now became the hosting of the re-authoring journey of the collective organisational narrative as environments of deep human connection were created that invited and welcomed the alternative narratives to be named and lived into. As an entrepreneur of meaning and the weaver of conversations, the leader becomes an active participant co-leading and co-authoring the forever emergent culture and preferred future of the organisation.

Re-authoring work is emerging work, work that is co-constructed in the moment, with these possible maps always serving in the background, much like a scaffold,[75] and definitely not a strict process to follow slavishly.

Co-constructing an environment that invites narratives

Leaders play a very important role in co-creating the environment that can invite and trigger the meaning-making and story-making skills of people. In this environment leaders:

- Invite everyone in the room to have a voice
- Ask unsettling and generative questions

- Respect participants as the authors and agents of their own narratives and co-authors of the organisational narrative, and
- Acknowledge the words and the emotions generating these words, the meaning and the experience of the meaning, as they focus on what is being said and what is experienced.[76]

Co-creating this inspiring environment with a community of workers invites deep connections to open up multiple subordinate storylines that enable rich narratives to be told, new meaning to be made, and preferred futures to be named. "The work-community speaks about and to the idea that not only do people come to work, produce, serve and ensure profit, but they are also a community of human beings, working together to earn a living and co-create a working environment that is in line with their values, hopes and dreams for the future. On all levels the community of workers is seen as key informants and contributors to what is known and can be known in the future (i.e., the vision) of the organisation."[77]

Because "knowledge is a communal production" and "not the product of accurate diagnosis or representations" all that is "deemed 'real' and true emerges in the context of relational exchanges and communities."[78] Knowledge and what can be known are not the sole responsibility of the leader, because work-communities bring their own knowledges and giftedness to an organisation, and this collaborative knowing becomes a collective act. As an outcome of the creation of this environment, the invitation to participate in the "co-creation of knowledge invites practices of responsibility and accountability as [the leaders] co-construct knowledge together. Leading then becomes something leaders do with groups/teams/communities and not a responsibility that is taken up on behalf of, for, and over others."[79] Leadership becomes a way of being (or an ethics) that guides how we engage with others in community rather than an identity or a position that we take up.[80]

But how do we create the initial welcome, how do we greet?

Saying "Hello" from the African ground

> *"[A]s Westerners [we] want to brush over things, so dominated by what we have constructed as 'time'. It is as if we want to fast-track to intimacy and connectedness, without giving anything meaningful from our lives as a gift to the other – not even our time."*[81]

Re-authoring work creates the environment that enables us to pause and live into the rhythm of the telling of narratives that cannot be rushed and pushed. It is a rhythm that challenges ideas around speed and so-called effectiveness, "as it joins hands with African culture in redeeming time as a gift to see, be touched by and connect with one another as human beings."[82] This human connectedness means that we pause long enough to "see the news in the eyes of the other"[83] and care enough to ask generative questions that touch on issues that are personally meaningful and that people care about deeply.[84]

What we "experience" in these environments is an "affective reaction to which we give meaning"[85] and therefore the way we gather and the connections created enhances the experience which then also adds another layer of meaning. Zimmerman[86] further says that "bodily based emotional (chemical) reactions have as much to do with social behaviour as socially specified ways of acting does, it's not just discourse." Therefore, as we create the environment for human connectedness, we also create the possibility for affect and meaning that can flow over into our social behaviour as communities within organisations.

We have used the following questions to construct the greeting and the welcome to invite our human connectedness to enter as the ground level from where new ways of acting and doing can grow:

- On whose shoulders are you standing as you enter this room today?
- If you had to design a T-shirt that would help us understand who you are, what would it say or what would it look like?[87]
- What fires your curiosity as you come to this meeting?

In the next section we will unpack the practices that create the environment for these kinds of conversations and experiences.

Practices that open up the conversation

Once we have created the environment for connectedness and community as human beings, we now look towards the practices that would hold the conversation so that emergence, narrative and meaning would be invited and honoured.

Leaders are "vehicles of power" who are always in the "position of simultaneously undergoing and exercising this power"; [88] therefore they have the platform to deconstruct their power so that the multiplicity and diversity of all the narratives can come together and be spoken. In the way in which they welcome, invite, listen and ask questions, leaders can deconstruct their power through careful curiosity and generative questions.

These practices are much like the brain surgery or the keys for opening up new neuro-pathways,[89] because they help people to access narratives that may be hidden or long forgotten, or have overgrown through the years. As these preferred moments, enactments, affect, relationships and narratives are unlocked and uncovered, these pathways open up new possibilities that provide the stepping stones for entering and thickening these pathways, meanings and eventually the narratives we tell.

Table 10.1 provides a list of humanising practices that can help leaders generate the keys for unlocking their individual, team, communal or organisational narratives in new and exciting ways by creating the conditions for the meaning-making skills to be accessed and the words and worlds to be "re-meaned."

Table 10.1: Humanising practices for re-authoring conversations

Avoid	*You are invited to*
Judging and evaluating	Be carefully curious
Assuming	Ask questions that you do not know the answer to by using the vocabulary of the narrator(s)
Fixing, solving problems and intervening	Elevate the narrator to primary authorship
Giving advice and reframing	Listen generously [90] and be open to being surprised
Giving applause and affirmations	Share gifts and reflections
Practices that come from a place of knowing about people and things they do not know about themselves	Practices that come from a place of not knowing about others as we have a deep appreciation for their uniqueness[91]

These practices invite new ways of having conversations which create new experiences and can also change meaning.[92]

The re-authoring lens enables conversations that become an opportunity to author, re-author and co-author narratives that matter to us deeply through the amazing story-making, meaning-making capacity.

The organisation as ongoing conversation focuses on "how conversations unfold, what narratives currently define the way things are, and the ways that might lead to new interactions and processes among different actors that will create new narratives that in turn enable new ways of thinking and acting to emerge."[93]

By participating in the practices of creating the welcome, leaders can "make and remake the world by introducing new ways of talking."[94] "The shift in one conversation by the way we are talking and being will have a ripple effect into all of the others because the interconnectedness of the web of narratives moves the organizational socially constructed narrative."[95]

Leaders as conversation weavers

As a result, the leader becomes a "'conversation weaver' as he/she takes strands developed in one conversation into the other."[96] As conversation weavers, leaders have an amazing opportunity to host conversations and meetings where the multiplicity of narratives are honoured and challenged, and the ones that move us forward can be thickened and committed to. In creating this environment, leaders invite the multiplicity of diverse narratives and identities as an important ingredient "for real dialogue, emergence, and new possibilities to take place."[97]

Leaders as conversation weavers talk and act differently in what we can call a "type of praxis: a way of acting into the everyday forms of relating that create our social world."[98] This praxis implies that leaders strive to stop speaking 'to' people and start speaking 'with' people, and invite "respect for the knowledges of the lived experiences of people."[99] As leaders start to speak with people, their role as entrepreneur of meaning is to "become a sense maker who notices emergent dynamics and redirects the flow of interactions and conversations."[100]

Leaders as conversation weavers and entrepreneurs of meaning convene conversations that honour the multiplicity of narratives, ask generative questions, and challenge taken-for-granted beliefs and ideas as they know talk is action and their praxis matters in shifting the narratives of the organisation.

The next section will provide the unpacking of the landscape of re-authoring practices that leaders can use in their organisations.

Unpacking the Re-authoring Lens

This is a map and explanation that both organisational consultants and leaders can use to explain how the re-authoring lens can be used in organisational conversations.

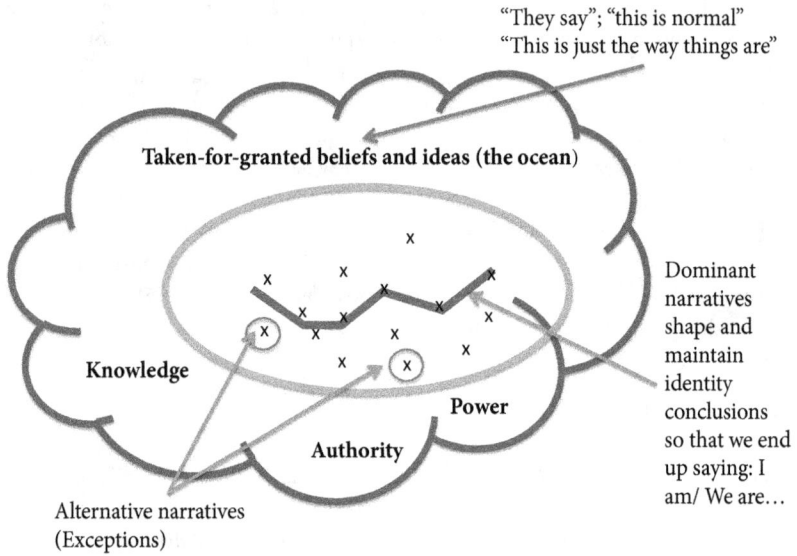

Figure 10.1: Map illustrating the use of the re-authoring lens in organisational conversations

Human beings are 'storying' beings that have two very important skills with which they navigate their lives, namely story-making and meaning-making skills. As human beings we connect the dots of our lives through our meaning-making capacity, and those threads of meaning then become the narrative we tell about who we are (identity), what our relationships are like (community), and how we see the world (reality).

As we tell and re-tell these narratives over many years, we gather more and more evidence to support the meaning we have made, and dominant narratives are constructed because we are no longer open to evidence to the contrary. Although the dominant narratives are well known, they can become thin or single stories, the ones of which we say, "I am or we are always...."

We weave significant moments as well as new moments into conclusions about our identities, our relationships and realities. Narratives are therefore very powerful as they shape and maintain who we are and who we can become as individuals and communities.

But these narratives do not fall mysteriously from the sky. They are crafted in a particular cultural and societal context (water) governed by taken-for-granted beliefs and ideas that inform the narratives we tell about ourselves, teams, communities and organisations. An example of a recent belief and idea that has been quite successful in recruiting participants is the idea that a human being can be a failure or a loser. "Never before has the sense of being a failure to be an adequate person been so freely available to people, and never before has it been so willingly and routinely dispensed."[101] We are therefore hearing people echoing these ideas and beliefs as we judge others and ourselves in the pursuit of not being the one who does not make it, who loses it, or who fails.

We grow accustomed to and also come alongside these beliefs and ideas to the point that we do not even realise that we are still swimming in this water (context).

At this point we can unpack the beliefs and ideas of any story we are curious about. For example, if we put leadership in the middle of a circle on a page, we can ask the following questions:

- What do "they" say about leadership (or the name of the organisation/any curiosity that matters) in our organisation?
- What is considered normal in our organisation when it comes to leadership?
- When do they say "this is just the way things are" when it comes to leadership?

After we have explained the re-authoring lens, we can start unpacking any narrative about which we are curious.

Unpacking narratives

> *"The unpacking of narratives is not focused on diagnosing or solving any problem or fixing any deficiency or finding a solution."*[102]

In the practice of unpacking narratives, there are no narratives that are right, correct, or best. All narratives have a history, a beginning, an end, and something in-between. Enquiring about the history of narratives as well as when these narratives were the strongest and the weakest opens up the landscape of discovery for narratives that might have been forgotten or meaning that can be made in new and profound ways.

Narratives also influence us as they have an effect on our bodies, work, leadership, our families, and all the other aspects of our lives. Therefore it is very important that we unpack these influences so that we are able to choose which of these narratives take us forward and which of the narratives gets us stuck.

The re-authoring lens walks away from "blame and walks towards a communal understanding of problems and the re-writing thereof. Leaders within this approach understand and speak about problems in a different way that positions problems as a problem story with which we stand in a relationship and which we can collectively re-write if we choose to do so. This practice has no need to solve the problem but invites a new relationship with the problem and as a result lives into the possibility of an alternative counter-narrative."[103]

In the pursuit of handing back the pen in the hands of leaders and organisations, the biggest invitation is to name the narrative and/or create or name a metaphor or image that will help authors in their decision to participate in these narratives. We can always choose the kind of relationship we want to have with narratives, and therefore the re-authoring lens opens options for people to redefine or revise their relationship with narratives. At the point of choice regarding the relationship with narratives, it could be useful to co-create a ritual as an embodiment of the choice.

Enriching or thickening narratives

> *The alternative exception moments*[104] *are sometimes left out in the weaving of our narratives, and rightly so, as they show the competing and ambiguous nature of our lives. We live and make meaning from a multiplicity of moments and therefore we live in the paradox and complexity of these lived experiences.*

It is very important to note that alternative or preferred narratives are not imagining a future for both the leader and the organisation of which there is no evidence or that does not already exist in some form. Alternative narratives are built upon competing moments, relationships and practices that tell a different narrative to the dominant problem narratives in organisations.[105] The rich "story development"[106] of these alternative narratives mean that leaders or organisations would like to see more of these different/alternative/preferred narratives. They can be thickened through:

- Naming the narrative in words, metaphors or images
- Exploring the values, commitments, gifts, purposes and skills that inform this narrative
- Unpacking the history of the narrative while also considering when this narrative was the strongest and when it was the weakest
- Imagining how this narrative will influence various aspects of leadership and organisational culture, and
- Co-creating a ritual that will welcome this narrative more fully.

Narratives are created through language; therefore language is the medium for looking again at the narrative to rewrite it. When the narrative is named in the vocabulary of the leader or the organisation, generative questions focus on assisting it to be retold, "so that it becomes more richly described and open to re-authoring."[107] Because narratives are created through language and meaning-making, they can shift or transform whenever new or alternative evidence, language, knowledge, relationships or ideas and beliefs emerge from the conversation.

As the new and alternative ideas and images emerge, "options for action that have not occurred before and new ways to change become available as [leaders and organisations] make personal voluntary commitments to new behaviors and projects."[108]

Now that we have named the alternative narrative, what do we do next?

Telling the story

The telling of both the leaders' and organisational narratives provides a more compelling way to communicate a vision or strategy than the usual PowerPoint slides. Epston[109] comments on PowerPoint slides as the death of the mind, an insult to a story and an impoverished form of argument. Human beings are 'storying' beings who story their lives, and sharing the stories of leadership, cultural change and initiatives in this re-authoring lens helps the listeners to relate and also make meaning again from their own understanding and narratives.

Enabling Re-authoring Journeys

Critical success factors in this re-authoring work are the invitation into the understanding of the approach and lens and also human beings' capacity to story and make meaning. Without sufficient experience of the power of narrative within the understanding of this approach and lens as well as the broader understanding of the VUCA world, people in organisations get stuck in blame and never see how they are participating authors in the organisational narrative. They are left with thin[110] stories and conclusions about all that goes wrong and who is to blame, or they reach for quick fixes that take the organisation back to familiar responses, leaving nothing to the imagination.

Leaders and organisations engaging in re-authoring practices need to understand that these practices will disturb the way things are and that there will be a lot of questions and curiosities about organisational life as everybody has known it. The diversity of understandings must be invited, acknowledged and engaged with so that the organisation can collectively move forward. As we host conversations that honour the multiplicity of narratives, we honour the need to draw on the multiplicity of the stories/potentials/views of people inside the organisation in order to deal more effectively with the complexity of the VUCA world outside the organisation.[111]

In true emergent fashion, the organisational narrative is never finished, as each conversation becomes a springboard for future ones. Because of the continuous movement, an organisation and leader are always on the way to making sense as they participate in re-authoring organisational narratives. This is contrary to the taken-for-granted beliefs and ideas around change as a process that can be engineered, summoned and designed with outcomes we are told are predictable and certain.

In the Dialogic OD Mindset "transformational change always involves disruption to the ongoing patterns of self-organizing"[112] in which leadership can play a very important role. Transformation in an organisation is invited through the acknowledgement that culture is the sum total of the diverse narratives we tell and the meaning employees on all levels have made of the significant events, enactments, practices, leadership and moments over time. Organisational culture is further informed by the taken-for-granted ideas of the context in which an organisation functions and these beliefs and ideas add another layer of meaning and complexity that influences the organisational narrative.

When leaders practise this approach and lens they are facilitating movements in organisational conversations away from and towards movements in re-authoring as given in Table 10.2.

Table 10.2: Movements in re-authoring conversations

Moving away from	Moving towards
Content first	**Connection first** [113]
Are we jumping into an agenda without acknowledging our humanity?	*Have I created the space where my team members experience connection to one another as human beings?*
Blame	**Ownership** [114]
Are we just looking for who is to blame?	*Are we asking how are we contributing to this narrative? Are we co-authors of this narrative in some way?*
The person is the problem	**The problem is the problem** [115]
Are we making the problem personal?	*Are we taking ownership as a team and naming the problem and our relationship to it?*
Thin stories	**Rich descriptions/stories**[116]
Are we satisfied with easy answers and solutions for complex challenges?	*Are we allowing all the views to be spoken by creating an environment for all the team members to speak so that the complexity and diversity of everyone's views can be honoured?*
Isolation	**Community** [117]
Are we trying to figure out things alone?	*Are we inviting people we trust – even if they think differently – as well as our team members to think with us and support us?*
Telling	**Asking questions**[118]
Are we telling our team what to do?	*Are we asking questions that enable team members to come to their own conclusions and decisions or to go and look for answers?*

Re-authoring Gifts for Leadership and Organisations

The re-authoring lens can bring various gifts to both leadership and organisations and because of the emergent nature of this work, these gifts will be beyond anything which can be named and imagined at this moment.

Re-authoring gifts for leaders

Leaders can participate in the processes of generativity, especially as they invite the unique vocabularies and narratives of the community of workers to influence the ongoing construction and reconstruction of the social reality of the organisation.

In addition, leaders can now better perceive, seek to understand, ask generative questions, and act on events and conversations because they are participants in the co-creation of emergence, generativity, and organisational meaning-making as it happens.

As the authorship of leaders' own narratives and co-authorship of the organisational narrative bring collective ownership beyond blame, leaders see and recognise their own participation in the shaping, creation, and conveying of the organisational reality.

Re-authoring gifts for the community of workers

When the community of workers engage in new ways of talking and thinking, their agreements to talk and act differently bring about not only authorship of their own narratives but also co-authorship of the organisational narrative. This co-authorship enables the organisational narrative to be re-written, as the community of workers are actors and participants in this organisational drama.[119]

Another gift that the re-authoring lens brings is the possibility of "buy-in of the work-community in terms of commitment and ownership of any organisational strategy, vision or initiative that flows from their knowledges and expertise."[120] When their voices, knowledges and narratives have been included in moving the organisation forward, they have already been invited to take ownership and take part in this process.

In addition, this approach enables a different and sometimes new perspective on the work-community's lives, history, identities and the organisation that brings renewed energy and possibility.

Not only new eyes and perspective are given through this approach, but also new practices that enable the community of workers to link their stories about the purpose of their work with the "collective objectives"[121] of the organisation.

Re-authoring gifts for the organisation

When leaders and the community of workers are invited to be co-authors of the organisational narrative, it "generates knowledges and narratives that are home-grown and owned in ways that can take the organisation forward."[122]

The re-authoring lens helps organisations to re-engage with neglected aspects of their history and narratives in ways that do not seek to blame, problematise or judge, but rather open up possibilities and enable organisations to move forward. It invites organisations to make new meanings of experiences not previously understood or unpacked as it initiates steps never otherwise considered.

These practices and skills also enrich the language, "offer generative images, and enable people to respond to the societal reality that emerges from having different conversations with participants holding a diversity of ideas and points of view."[123]

Because this lens invites new ways of talking and being, it enables organisations and leaders to have everyday conversations that help narratives to become unstuck.[124]

The most important gift to both leaders and organisations is that it enables thinking that goes beyond what leaders and the community of workers routinely think. The experience of a generative change process "produces new images and ideas that provide people with new eyes to see old things, resulting in new options for decisions and actions that they find appealing."[125]

All of these practices can present the gift of disruption that may lead to the emergence of new possibilities and realities in a significant way.

Re-authoring work invites leaders and organisations to participate as they stand in the "midst of a complex flow, in which a multiplicity of beginnings, middles, and ends are in play simultaneously",[126] a complex flow that is forever on the move as the weaving of various individual stories creates and evolves into the cultural water of the organisation, moving leaders and organisations forward as they become authors and co-authors of collective narratives.

Endnotes

1   Bushe & Marshak, 2015a.
2   White, 2004.
3   White, 2004, p. 45.
4   White, 2004, p. 47.
5   Wallace, 2008.
6   Swart, 2015, p. 349.
7   Barrett, 2015, p. 65.
8   White, 2004, p. 105.
9   Saunders, 2013.
10   Swart, 2013, pp. 103–104.
11   Mellon, 2015, p. 57.
12   Bushe & Marshak, 2015b, p. 13.
13   White, 2004, pp. 128–137 & Swart, 2013, pp. 119–120.
14   White, 2004, p. 169.
15   Swart, 2013, p. 121.
16   White, 2004, p. 88.
17   Madigan, 2014.
18   Sandison, 2015.
19   Tonninger, 2015.
20   Hancock & Epston, 2008.
21   See endnote 11.
22   Foucault, 1977, 1980.
23   Burr, 1995 & Gergen, 1991, 1994, 2003.
24   Block, 2008.
25   Zimmerman, 2015a, 2015b.
26   White & Epston, 1990 & Swart, 2013, 2015.
27   See endnote 1.
28   Freire, 1993, 1994.
29   White, 2007.
30   White, 2004, p. 104.
31   See endnote 29.
32   Zimmerman, 2015a.
33   Zimmerman, 2015b.
34   Bushe & Marshak, 2015c, p. 37.
35   White, 2004, pp. 70–71.
36   White, 2004, p. 86.
37   See endnote 23.
38   See endnote 26.
39   White, 2004, p. 85.
40   White, 2004, p. 75.
41   White, 2004, p. 90.
42   White & Epston, 1990, Morgan, 2000 & Swart, 2013, 2015.
43   See endnote 11.
44   Stacey, 2015, p. 153.
45   See endnote 1.
46   Storch, 2015, p. 197.
47   Bushe & Marshak, 2015b, p. 17.
48   Bushe & Marshak, 2015b, p. 25.
49   Bushe & Marshak, 2015b, p. 18.
50   See endnote 47.
51   Bushe & Marshak, 2015b, p. 22.
52   Ibid.
53   Goppelt, Ray & Shaw, 2015, p. 396.
54   Marshak, Grant & Floris, 2015.
55   Barge, 2015, p. 189.
56   Bushe & Storch, 2015, p. 113.
57   See endnote 24.
58   Freire, 1993, p. 56.
59   Swart, 2013, p. 141.
60   White, 2004, pp. 119-147.
61   Swart, 2013, p. 122.
62   See endnote 2.
63   Madigan, 2011, p. 16.
64   Swart, 2013, p. 123.
65   Stelter, 2014, p. 113.
66   Snowden, 2015.
67   Stelter, 2014, p. 36.
68   White, 1991.

69	Barrett, 2015, p. 71.	98	Goppelt, Ray & Shaw, 2015, p. 372.
70	White, 2004, p. 99.	99	Freire, 1994, p. 26, 1993, p. 30.
71	Bushe & Marshak, 2015b, p. 29.	100	Barrett, 2015, p. 73.
72	Hamel, 2009, p. 93.	101	White, 2004, p. vi.
73	Goppelt, Ray, & Shaw, 2015, p. 397.	102	Swart, 2015, p. 362.
74	Swart, 2015, p. 364.	103	Swart, 2013, p. 125.
75	See endnote 66.	104	See endnote 33.
76	See endnote 33.	105	Swart, 2015, p. 355.
77	Swart, 2013, p. 135.	106	White, 2004, p. 21.
78	Barrett, 2015, p. 69.	107	See endnote 102.
79	See endnote 67.	108	See endnote 101.
80	Carlson, 2015.	109	Epston, 2015.
81	Swart, 2013, p. 147.	110	Geertz, 1973.
82	Ibid.	111	See endnote 19.
83	Mpahlele, 2015.	112	Bushe & Marshak, 2015b, p. 21.
84	Bushe & Storch, 2015, p. 118.	113	See endnote 24.
85	See endnote 33.	114	Ibid.
86	Ibid.	115	Morgan, 2000.
87	Blanc-Sahnoun, 2013.	116	Geertz, 1973 & White, 2004.
88	Foucault, 1980, p. 98.	117	See endnote 24.
89	Lasersohn, 2015.	118	See endnote 28.
90	Stelter, 2014.	119	Swart, 2013, p. 148.
91	See endnote 80.	120	Ibid.
92	See endnote 33.	121	See endnote 47.
93	Marshak, Grant & Floris, 2015, p. 83.	122	See endnote 119.
94	Barrett, 2015, p. 75.	123	Storch, 2015, p. 198.
95	Swart, 2015, p. 367.	124	Ibid.
96	Goppelt, Ray & Shaw, 2015, p. 376.	125	See endnote 84.
97	Bushe & Marshak, 2015c, p. 46.	126	Goppelt, Ray & Shaw, 2015, p. 391.

References

Barge, JK. 2015. 'Consulting as collaborative co-inquiry'. In GR Bushe & RJ Marshak (eds). *Dialogic organization development: The theory and practice of transformational change.* San Francisco, CA: Berrett-Koehler Publishers.

Barret, FJ. 2015. 'Social constructionist challenge to representational knowledge: Implications for understanding organization change'. In GR Bushe & RJ Marshak (eds). *Dialogic organization development: The theory and practice of transformational change.* San Francisco, CA: Berrett-Koehler Publishers.

Blanc-Sahnoun, P. 2013. Conversations in Bordeaux. France, October.

Block, P. 2008. *Community: The structure of belonging.* San Francisco, CA: Berrett-Koehler Publishers.

Burr, V. 1995. *An introduction to social constructionism.* London: Routledge.

Bushe, GR & Marshak, RJ (eds). 2015a. *Dialogic organization development: The theory and practice of transformational change.* San Francisco, CA: Berrett-Koehler Publishers.

Bushe, GR & Marshak RJ (eds). 2015b. Introduction to the dialogic organization development mindset. In GR Bushe & RJ Marshak (eds). *Dialogic organization development: The theory and practice of transformational change.* San Francisco, CA: Berrett-Koehler Publishers.

Bushe, GR & Marshak RJ (eds). 2015c. Introduction to the Practices of Dialogic OD. In GR Bushe & RJ Marshak (eds). *Dialogic organization development: The theory and practice of transformational change.* San Francisco, CA: Berrett-Koehler Publishers.

Bushe, GR & Storch 2015. 'Generative image: Sourcing novelty'. In GR Bushe & RJ Marshak (eds). *Dialogic organization development: The theory and practice of transformational change.* San Francisco, CA: Berrett-Koehler Publishers.

Carlson, T. 2015. (Personal communication: Notes on draft chapter, in an email received on 11 November).

Epston, D. 2015. Workshop notes. Kenwood Therapy Centre in Minneapolis. 5 May.

Foucault, M. 1977. *Discipline and punish.* London: Penguin.

Foucault, M (ed C Gordon). 1980. *Power/knowledge: Selected interviews and other writings, 1972–1977.* Translated by C Gordon, L Marshal, J Mepham, K Sober. New York, NY & Toronto: Pantheon Books, a division of Random Inc).

Freire, P. 1993. *Pedagogy of the oppressed.* New revised 20th anniversary ed. (MB Ramos, Trans). New York, NY: Continuum.

Freire, P. 1994. *Pedagogy of hope: Reliving 'pedagogy of the oppressed'.* (RR Barr, Trans). New York, NY: Continuum.

Geertz, C. 1973. 'Thick description: Toward an interpretive theory of culture'. In C Geertz (ed). *The interpretation of cultures.* New York, NY: Basic Books.

Gergen, KJ. 1991. *The saturated self: Dilemmas of identity in contemporary life.* New York, NY: Basic Books.

Gergen, KJ. 1994. *Realities and relationships: Soundings in social construction.* Cambridge, MA: Harvard University Press.

Gergen, M & Gergen, KJ (eds). 2003. *Social construction: A reader.* London, UK: Sage.

Goppelt, J, Ray, KW & Shaw, P. 2015. 'Dialogic process consultation: Working live'. In GR Bushe & RJ Marshak (eds). *Dialogic organization development: The theory and practice of transformational change.* San Francisco, CA: Berrett-Koehler Publishers. 371–399.

Hamel, G. 2009. 'Moon shots for management'. *Harvard Business Review,* 87(2):91–98, February.

Hancock, F & Epston, D. 2008. 'The craft and art of narrative inquiry in organisations'. In D Barry & H Hansen (eds). *The Sage handbook of new approaches to organisation studies.* London: Sage Publications Ltd. pp. 485–502.

Lasersohn, B. 2015. Notes on conversation in Johannesburg, 4 August.

Madigan, S. 2011. Narrative therapy. Washington DC: American Psychological Association.

Madigan, S. 2014. Presentation at a workshop. Pretoria, ZA, 5–6 September.

Marshak, RJ, Grant, DS & Floris. M. 2015. 'Discourse and dialogic organization development'. In GR Bushe & RJ Marshak (eds). *Dialogic organization development: The theory and practice of transformational change.* San Francisco, CA: Berrett-Koehler Publishers. 77–99.

Mellon, L. 2015. 'Applying brain science to business' *Dialogue,* June/August.

Morgan, A. 2000. *What is narrative therapy? An easy-to-read introduction.* Adelaide, AU: Dulwich Centre.

Mpahlele, L. 2015. Conversation at the National School for Government, Pretoria, ZA. 3 September.

Sandison, K. 2015. (Personal communication: Notes on draft chapter, in an email received on 7 November 2015.

Saunders, O. 2013. 'Shifting the economics'. In C Swart (ed). *Re-authoring the world: The narrative lens and practices for organisations, communities and individuals.* Randburg, ZA: Knowres Publishing. 100–102.

Snowden, D. 2015. Workshop notes Flourish Conference. Intundla, ZA. 24 August.

Stacey, R 2015. 'Understanding organizations as complex responsive processes of relating'. In GR Bushe & RJ Marshak (eds). *Dialogic organization development: The theory and practice of transformational change.* San Francisco, CA: Berrett-Koehler Publishers.

Stelter, R. 2014. *A guide to third generation coaching: Narrative-collaborative theory and practice.* Dordrecht, NL: Springer.

Storch, J. 2015. 'Enabling change: The skills of dialogic OD'. In GR Bushe & RJ Marshak (eds). *Dialogic organization development: The theory and practice of transformational change.* San Francisco, CA: Berrett-Koehler Publishers.

Swart, C. 2013. *Re-authoring the world: The narrative lens and practices for organisations, communities and individuals.* Randburg, ZA: Knowres Publishing

Swart, C. 2015. 'Coaching from a dialogic OD paradigm'. In GR Bushe & RJ Marshak (eds). *Dialogic organization development: The theory and practice of transformational change.* San Francisco, CA: Berrett-Koehler Publishers. 349–370.

Tonninger, W. Personal communication: Notes on draft chapter, in an email received on 9 November 2015.

Wallace, DF. 2008. 'In his own words'. *The Economist,* 19 September. [Online]. Available: http://moreintelligentlife.com/story/david-foster-wallace-in-his-own-words. [Accessed 16 June 2016.]

White, M. 1991. 'Deconstruction and therapy'. *Dulwich Centre Newsletter,* 3:21–40.

White, M. 2004. *Narrative practice and exotic lives: Resurrecting diversity in everyday life.* Adelaide, AU: Dulwich Centre Publications.

White, M. 2007. *Trauma and narrative therapy. Part 1.* New York, NY. 1 April. [Online]. Available: https://vimeo.com/34671797. [Accessed 16 June 2016].

White, M & Epston, D. 1990. *Narrative means to therapeutic ends.* New York, NY: WW Norton.

Zimmerman, J. 2015a. Workshop notes. Narrative Therapy Conference. Somerset West, ZA. 19–20 August.

Zimmerman, J. 2015b. 'New-ro narrative therapy: Brain science, narrative therapy, poststructuralism, and preferred identity in couple relationships'. *Family Process* (forthcoming).

Chapter 11

ACTION LEARNING

Rose Pillay and Gerrit Walters

Reference has been made to the nuances of a postmodern outlook in organisational studies due to the "chaotic, paradoxical and transient nature of order and disorder". Similarly, it has also been highlighted that the present pandemonium in our society is attributed to varying complexities which require leaders to "operate from the highest possible future, rather than being stuck in the patterns of our old experiences".[1]

The connotation in these views advocates a radical stance towards learning, in order to confront organisational turbulence and dilemmas. Organisations are becoming conscious of this reality. Hence, new ways of transforming the leadership development landscape are perhaps a worthwhile quest. In this domain, it is apparent that novel learning interventions are necessary in order to change mind-sets and behaviours, and the myopic regimens of past learning programmes must be discarded.

Action learning has been recognised as a valuable methodology in achieving this shift, with the prospect of palpable impact on business results. Action learning, and in particular business driven action learning, is a leadership development solution which responds to the complexity residing within the leadership development landscape across organisations globally. Although some authors propose that action learning is "new and revolutionary", it dates back to over 60 years ago. Perhaps the suggestion is that organisations are only currently recognising the intrinsic value of action learning and incorporating the methodology in their leadership development solutions. An alternative view would be that organisations are deviating from complex leadership development interventions and contesting for uncomplicatedness – "… few concepts have been so simple and so powerful"[2] – they are going back to basics. This may be the paradox that leaders strive for – simplicity amidst the complexity.

A myriad training and development media have gained negative ripostes from audiences on the basis that they exhibit zero worth beyond the confinements of the classroom. Research indicates that in the USA an estimate of 30 billion dollars per annum is allocated to training and development initiatives. If this learning is not translated into action in the workplace, then it may be viewed as a futile investment.[3] This dogmatic approach to learning depletes organisations' resources without producing a sufficient return. Action learning fervently endorses value in the business, on varying levels, as a crucial component in the architecture which entails a resolution of an identified problem.

Furthermore, considering the present constraints on resources (nationally and in global economies), traditional learning in the existing climate is quite challenging. Hence, more financially feasible learning ventures should be sourced to mitigate the financial vulnerability of many industries.[4] However, there is also a notion suggesting that it is not sufficient to propagate cost-efficient learning mechanisms. In order to manage the austerity of the current situation, generative learning is required to address organisational problems.[5] Thus, for organisations to serve their markets adequately while operating as viable going concerns, the existing challenges have to be addressed and sustainable growth sanctioned. Action learning possesses elements that uphold these tenets and promote systemic learning. It creates a platform for innovation and business advancement which equates with the precepts of a learning organisation. It is fast becoming the learning medium for enhancing business results, and assists organisations to respond more appropriately to the constantly changing operational environment.[6]

Against this organisational backdrop and context, Action Learning will be discussed in this chapter, covering its origins and main proponents and its key theoretical concepts and claims, with a view to positioning a main expression, business driven action learning, and its link to leadership. The significance of action learning in today's organisational leadership context will be demonstrated by exploring the collaborative nature of action learning, the integration of action learning principles in relation to the core elements of leadership, and the generation of a practical roadmap for application.[7]

Origins of Action Learning

The genesis of Kurt Lewin's action research gave birth to two phenomena, namely, action learning and action science. While both action learning and action science encourage building on intra- and interpersonal relationships, some authors suggest that action science goes deeper in focusing on the intrapersonal, cognitive responses of individuals.[8] Action learning practitioners may contest this assertion as the potential of shifting individuals on an intellectual and psychological level through the action learning process is attainable. Subsequently, sentiments have largely moved to recognition that the world of business is increasingly geared towards collaboration as opposed to autonomous practices. Action learning is seen as an ideal premise to inspire collective leadership engagement.[9]

Reginald Revans, a British astrophysicist, is regarded as the father of action learning owing to the introduction of the concept in the mid-twentieth century. Revans's first implementation of action learning was in the British National Coal Board in 1952, shortly after the Second World War, where he was confronted with the disconnect that existed between formal education and the demands from industry.

Revans believed that action learning is a fluid, unstructured phenomenon that serves multiple causes and audiences.[10] Hence he was deliberate in not prescribing a definition for action learning in order to eliminate any limitations that it might rouse. Action learning also poses no recommendations on implementation, but rather principles to guide processes. This feature defines the innate worth of action learning as an avenue to prompt learning, advance performance, and assist organisations to cope in compound, precarious markets.

Observing the current state of leadership effectiveness that is marred by a growing divide between leaders and followers; widespread deficit of trust in leaders in society at large; and scepticism regarding the purpose and sustainable value add of leadership development interventions,[11] one may argue that action learning is as relevant today as it was in the time of Revans's first intervention.

Definition of Action Learning

While Revans was deliberate in not defining the concept of action learning, the inherent purpose is clear. It is primarily used as a learning methodology for problem-solving. He stressed the importance of the self-directed nature of the small group (consisting of 5 to 6 individuals), which he called a "Set". The Set sought to solve "wicked" problems through learning from and with each other.[12] These problems have been described as strategic and tangible business challenges that present a dilemma for the organisation. In other words, they are nonlinear in nature and require a systemic mind-set to arrive at holistic solutions.

Many writers have attempted to define the term. The following are a few examples showing that action learning:

- Entails deriving learning from tangible experiences and reflective practices through group engagements, testing, researching and leverage, building relationships for gaining new insights. Here, there is a large emphasis on team synergy to generate the learning[13]
- Is a socially transformative process where agents in the system, through collaboration and reflection, experience individual and social transformation. Again, learning is dependent on interactions within the group and it moves to a higher level of social change[14]
- Involves a small group grappling with a real challenge, in an active learning mode, that inspires learning for the individual, the group and the organisation.[15] In this pedagogical process to problem-solving, it implies that action learning is the dominant method to reinforce leadership development.[16] Here, the significance lies in the communal learning of the group in the pursuit of finding solutions to business dilemmas
- Is a method of collaboration and inquiry into real problems that requires reflection and learning from previous experiences to create concrete results[17]
- Necessitates reflecting on experiences, which is the basis for learning through action, and extends beyond "learning by doing",[18] but incorporates facilitated reflection, deriving new knowledge, and bringing intelligence to perceived experiences.[19]

Aligned with the elements of action learning is the concept of lifelong learning. The formula for lifelong learning is a move from orthodox discontinuous theoretical learning to continuous practical application through work activities. Sustainability of learning is the envisaged outcome of this approach.[20]

The review of the many definitions of action learning confirms that there are some variations to the definition but no considerable contrasts. The three elements that appear most predominantly are:

- *Praxis of action through reflection on experience*

  The notion is that action learning theory necessitates reflecting on experiences, which is the basis for learning through action.

- *Collaborative team engagements*

  The significance lies in the communal learning of the Set in the pursuit of finding solutions to business dilemmas. This further implies that through the interaction of the Set, individual leadership challenges are explored.

- *Objective of resolving a problem in a specific organisational context*

  Action learning has a clear purpose which entails the recommendations for or resolutions to a tangible business challenge for a defined business situation.

A most recent definition contribution captures the essence of the above themes and emphasises the systemic nature required for sustainable learning:

"Action learning is a systemic learning journey, aimed at resolving business and leadership challenges, which manifest through deep questioning, team collaboration and reflective practices in order to create sustainable learning organisations."[21]

Business Driven Action Learning

As with the definition of action learning that lends itself to different interpretations, varying practices have surfaced over the years. In 1996, a group of practitioners met in southern France to share experiences and what they had learnt from engagement with action learning in organisations. The observation was that some organisations (particularly in Europe) were employing action learning for predominantly self-development. Others affiliated with the 'Americanised' version, and concentrated more on resolving business problems.[22] Considering both extremes, a space of balance (between the business challenge and the personal challenge) was proposed. This gave birth to the business driven action learning (BDAL) approach which was founded by Yury Boshyk. It is positioned closest to Revans's methodology, which alludes to the likelihood BDAL is the dominant approach and embodies the essence of the classical action learning style.[23]

Business driven action learning, as the name implies, focuses on solving business problems while enhancing the leadership capabilities of individuals and teams in order to encourage sustainable change in the organisation.[24] It is a more holistic approach to action learning as the purpose lies in creating solutions for the leader (= personally) and the organisation (= collectively). Therefore, the following content of this chapter will focus on this form of action learning in order to elucidate the practical application of action learning as a leadership development solution.

Benefits of BDAL

There are many illustrations regarding the significance of action learning in response to the current context of business. However, it would be naïve to assume that it is the panacea for problem-solving and leadership development. What can be advocated is that the flexible nature of action learning allows for its implementation as a standalone product or as part of other learning solutions. Figure 11.1 provides a demonstration of the various layers of potential benefits.

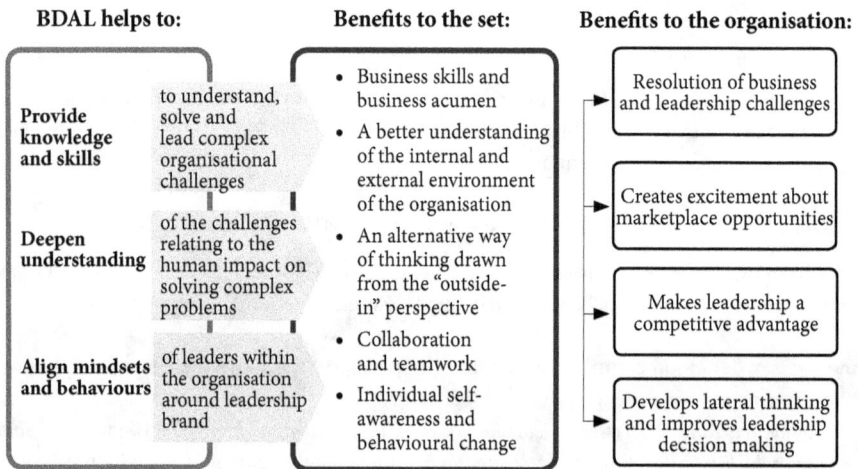

BDAL helps to:	Benefits to the set:	Benefits to the organisation:
Provide knowledge and skills to understand, solve and lead complex organisational challenges	• Business skills and business acumen	Resolution of business and leadership challenges
Deepen understanding of the challenges relating to the human impact on solving complex problems	• A better understanding of the internal and external environment of the organisation	Creates excitement about marketplace opportunities
Align mindsets and behaviours of leaders within the organisation around leadership brand	• An alternative way of thinking drawn from the "outside-in" perspective	Makes leadership a competitive advantage
	• Collaboration and teamwork	Develops lateral thinking and improves leadership decision making
	• Individual self-awareness and behavioural change	

Figure 11.1: Benefits of Business Driven Action Learning

To ensure successful delivery, Boshyk (2002) has identified key building blocks, which are explored in the next section.

Key building blocks of BDAL

It has already been stated that action learning has a variety of shapes, and the manner in which it is implemented is subject to the specific developmental requirements of the organisation. BDAL serves as a practical process map to guide organisations in the design and delivery of action learning programmes for leadership development. The nature of a BDAL programme fosters seven components (as depicted in Figure 11.2). Boshyk alludes to BDAL's being an all-inclusive programme with "moving parts".[25] In this regard, the configuration of unstructured, flexible components without prescribed execution techniques is portrayed.

Figure 11.2 gives a representation of the seven component parts that form the generic process map for business driven action learning. These components are essential in creating a robust action learning programme architecture.

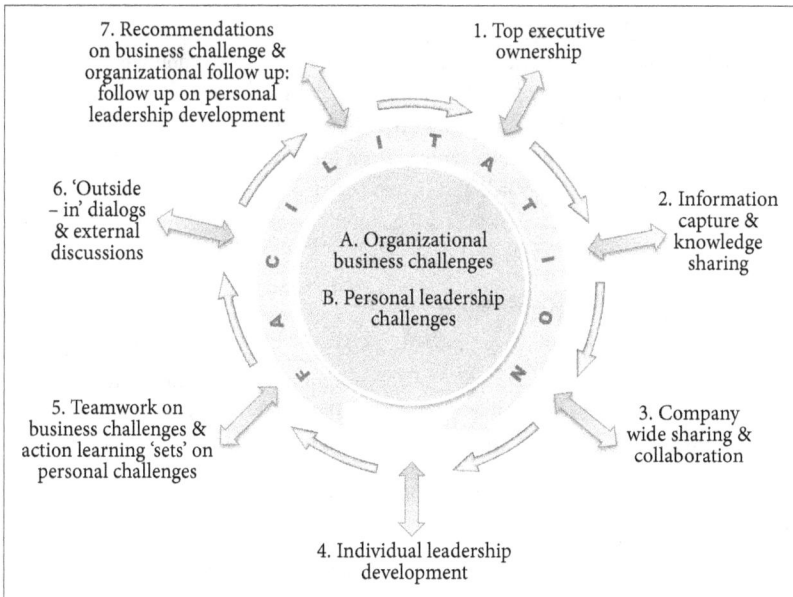

Figure 11.2: The process map of Business Driven Action Learning[26]

1. Top executive ownership (that is, sponsor involvement and ownership)

Senior management sponsorship and visibility are vital for the success of the programme as the sponsor contrives the business challenge. In tandem with responsibility, the expectation is that the sponsor plays a leadership role that motivates participants, guides their progress, and shows observable support for the overall journey.

2. Information capture and knowledge sharing

Information gathered should be housed centrally and communicated to the business. As participants work on the business challenge, a large amount of data will surface through the research and analysis phase. In a parallel process, participants will progress with their personal learning. This information needs to be captured and made easily accessible as a means of managing the knowledge of the group. The captured information is beneficial for personal, general and post-programme reference.

3.   Company-wide sharing and collaboration

Involving a larger audience spurs wider collaboration and supports the internal research stream. Hence, a communication strategy to transfer and receive information from the organisation is useful.

4.   Individual leadership development

While the group works on the challenges of an action learning Set, the input of a Personal Development Advisor (PDA) is beneficial in order to clarify issues around personal challenges and assist with understanding the results from the assessments (for example, 360° psychometric measurement, or a learning style questionnaire). This, however, does not involve an intrusive role as the Set still functions independently.

5.   Team work on business challenges and action learning "Sets" on personal challenges

It is in "the dynamics of learning Sets"[27] that the activities of the group and the interaction of team members instigate specific emotions. This implies that there is a great amount of intensity within the Set which incites deep learning from the context and from each other. Creating an awareness of this and a safe space to confront the issues offers insights into organisational behaviour. It is the ideal setting for personal and team learning. Team learning is favourable from a perspective of innovation as knowledge is generated and shared through the diversity of the members. Thus, the value derived from the Set has far-reaching implications other than solving the business challenge.

6.   Outside-in dialogues and external discussions

A meaningful segment of the process embroils an external perspective of business through "outside-in" exposure. The outside-in piece of the programme has to be skilfully designed to optimise the contribution towards the business challenge and personal learning. It allows participants to view the challenge from a different perspective in order to gain new insights.

7.   Recommendations on business challenge and organisational follow up on personal leadership development

Recommendations to the business challenge are presented to the senior leadership team for instant feedback on acceptance/non acceptance of the solution. Alternatively, the panel of adjudicators may accept the solution only partially, which will require further work, even beyond the Set. Although the Set disbands after the presentation of the recommendations, the intention is that the members will carry the learning forward and still come together (formally or informally) as a way of continuing to improve on their personal challenges. In many instances, companies do not follow through with this aspect, but where they do, there is an appreciation of the ease with which BDAL can be implemented in the daily operational tasks.[28]

The action learning toolkit

In tandem with the implementation of the seven component parts of the business driven action learning, introducing the action learning toolkit is fundamental to the process and the application of learning outside of the programme. Boshyk[29] created a toolkit that aids facilitators to present learning exercises at opportune times. The design of the toolkit also enables participants to use it as a standalone learning mechanism to create a problem-solving culture within the organisation. Some examples of the key tools are represented in Figure 11.3.

According to Figure 11.3 there are three classifications of tools:

- The **business challenge tools** assist with acquiring a deeper understanding of the processes involved in exploring and solving the business challenge.
- The **leadership challenge tools** are an aid to individuals in the Set to enhance relationships and solve their personal leadership dilemmas.
- The **reflection tools** are a guide to instilling reflective practices for the individual and the Set as a collective.

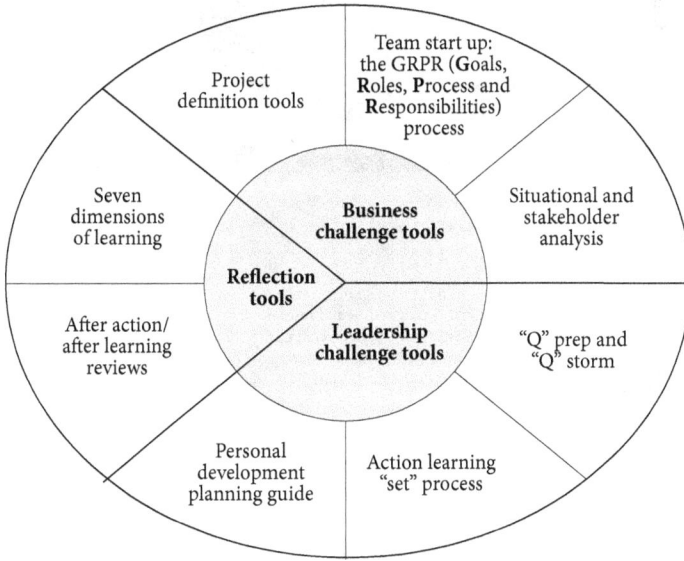

Figure 11.3 : Action learning toolkit
Source: Adapted from Boshyk (2013)[30]

Doing it well – critical success factors for a generic action learning programme

Along with incorporating the process map and a toolkit, there are specific factors that contribute to the successful delivery of BDAL programmes. The model in Figure 11.4 highlights five areas that programme designers must be mindful of when creating the architecture.

Mind-set and role of programme designers

- Awareness of integration points for a holistic design
- Assist with crafting the business challenge, properly position the sponsor and endorse lateral thinking
- Skilled caretakers who hold the pieces and stakeholders together

Prerequisite features

- Strong sponsor involvement throughout, with leadership support
- Tangible, relevant and strategic business challenge
- BDAL is practically dealing with real work issues in a learning environment created by the learning set
- Strategy directs programme design
- Selecting the right team for better results and encourage mixed teams

Learning application features

- As part of the programme, arrange regrouping of participants to help with application

Mind-set and role of programme designers

Prerequisite features | Content features | Application of learning features

Support features

Content features

- Reflection
- Critical thinking
- Rapid learning
- Competitiveness
- Discovery through curiosity and questioning
- Challenging the status quo
- identification of change areas
- Problem-solving
- Adopting a toolkit
- Outside-in experiences

Support features

- Supportive organisational culture
- Communication and marketing
- Time and resource availability
- Stakeholder engagement
- Role of the facilitators

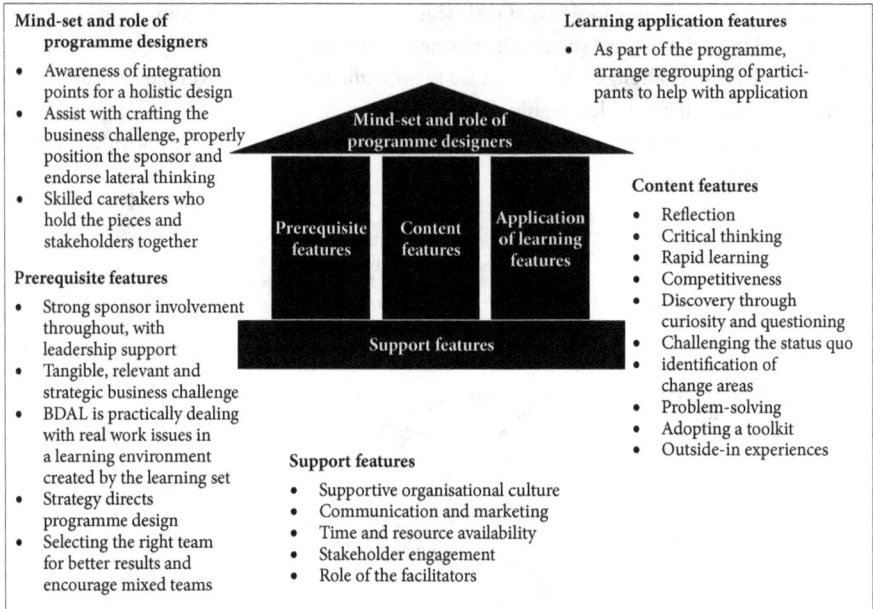

Figure 11.4: The process map of Business Driven Action Learning[31]

- ### *Mind-set and role of programme designers*

Programme designers are significant to the overall outcome of the process. Therefore, there is merit in ensuring that they adopt a systemic and integrated mindset. As the architecture contains many parts, the completeness of the process lies in the integration of the various pieces. For example, connecting leadership competencies to the business challenge requires a level of dexterity from designers as it must be experienced by participants as an obvious fusion.

- ### *Prerequisite features*

Specific criteria must be in place before commencement of the programme. These factors (for example, senior sponsorship) are an indicator of the organisation's stance and commitment towards implementing the recommendations to the business challenge.

- ### *Content features*

As part of the formal content pieces, topics that will enhance problem solving around the business challenge and spur leadership growth is beneficial. The business challenge and individual leadership challenges (or the collective leadership challenge) will guide the content to be covered.

- ### *Support features*

The Set operates within the organisational system. Hence, the requirement is for the organisation supports the process before, during and after the programme. A key support feature within the Set is the action learning facilitator who prompts thinking (through deep questioning) and offers relevant tools when required by the Set.

- *Application of learning features*

Since BDAL is intertwined with real work and the Set is designed to allow for the practice of new behaviours, application of learning can be easily achieved. However, as a formal support function, regrouping after the completion of the programme would be a valuable addition to the process.

The uptake of action learning – when should it be implemented?

A key requirement for implementation *is organisational readiness*. The rudiments of action learning embrace the idea that professionals themselves, within the organisation, can resolve problems, as opposed to invoking the knowledge of external consultants. Hence, organisations that accept the principles of action learning are inclined to trust their employees' capabilities and are not reliant on consultants to solve their problems.

When there is *evidence* of a complex business challenge, a supportive sponsor, the right 'mix' of participants, the allocation of time and resources, an emphasis on leadership development, and a desire to implement solutions, action learning is an advisable choice.

The traditional, dogmatic approach to learning depletes organisations' resources without producing a sufficient return on the investment of time and money. If organisations are serious about making learning practical with the prospect of injecting value back into the organisation, action learning provides this opportunity.

Application of BDAL globally

Business driven action learning is being employed more frequently in organisations as it addresses changes in the businesses such as intense competitiveness, globalisation and increasing shareholder value.[32]

General Electric has been showcased as a good example of how to implement action learning in projects successfully. They understand the importance of sustainability and securing their investment in people in order to reap benefits into the future. To this end, a robust follow-up strategy is in place which includes yearly class reunions.[33]

Business driven action learning was also introduced among some of the high-potential leaders in the Walt-Disney Company in Asia Pacific. The result of this initiative allowed a change of business practice which reaped a potential of $50 million in revenue for the organisation.[34]

At Du Pont, BDAL was introduced to accelerate revenue growth. Three important criteria were recognised as success factors in the action learning Sets. These included senior management involvement (sponsorship), a defined selection process, and project development support.[35]

These examples indicate that the uptake of BDAL is addressing key business issues.

Leadership through an Action Learning Lens

From a leadership perspective, leaders are being equipped to contend with the mounting complexity by learning how to reconcile dilemmas, collaborate more effectively and broaden their business perspectives. Hence, this section provides more insight on the link between BDAL action learning principles and leadership development.

One can argue that a traditional view on leadership and leadership theory, in its most elementary form, is represented by the tripod of leader(s), followers, and the acting on shared goals.[36] It is through this tripodal relational lens that deeper insight into the philosophy, principles and practices of action learning can be obtained. Figure 11.5 illustrates the tripod and the relationship with action learning.

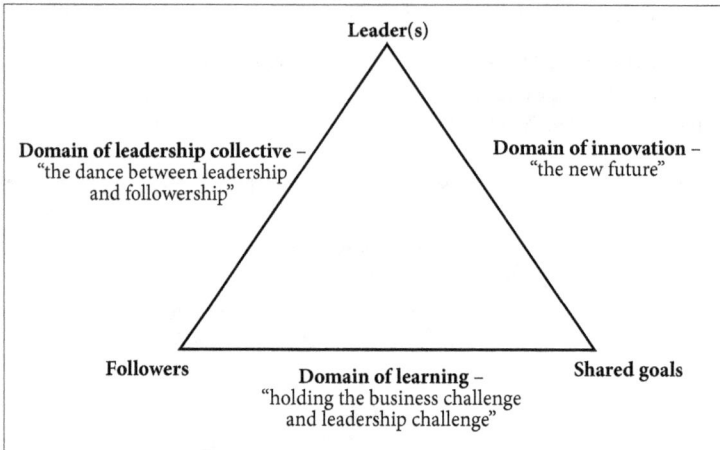

Figure 11.5 – Action Learning through the leadership lens

- **Domain of leadership**

The nature of the action learning Set allows for the collaborative interaction between leader and followers, where individuals step into the act of leadership, as and when the context so requires. Action learning advocates that the Set is a self-managed entity, which implies that the leadership role is applicable to each Set member. Revans emphasised a participant-led approach that speaks to the interchangeable positioning between leader and follower.[37]

- **Domain of learning**

Action learning, and specifically business driven action learning, promotes the healthy tension inherent in holding a business challenge and a personal leadership challenge, as the optimal leadership development context. It is in the space between **followers** (Set members) **and shared goals** that the key characteristics of BDAL manifest themselves. The shared goal in this context is in reference to the defined business challenge. There is also the expectation that participants share their personal leadership challenge with Set members as an opportunity to receive feedback as they grow into their leadership roles.

- **Domain of innovation**

It is in the relational space between **leader** (collective leadership) **and goals** that sustainable solutions emerge (innovation).

Business driven action learning promotes sustainability in three main fields. These are:

- The resolution of the business challenge contributes to improved business results which directly aid the sustainability of the organisation's existence.
- Leadership challenges hover over personal learning and accountability, which promotes sustainable behavioural change.
- The application of learning within the Set to make learning itself a sustainable feature is another area that embodies sustainability.
- Therefore, Set members (in other words, the leadership collective) have the opportunity to attain goals through solving organisations' "wicked" problems, enhancing leadership capabilities and re-positioning learning – an integrated process towards the "emerging future".

Action learning and emerging leadership theory

Action learning can further be positioned through the alternative lenses of emerging leadership theory, such as shared and distributed leadership; applications of complexity science; and relational approaches. In this context, the argument is that the tripod is too narrow. It is proposed that the leadership elements of Direction, Alignment and Commitment (DAC) are essential leadership outcomes, with the understanding that it is the presence of DAC that marks the occurrence of leadership.[38] To this end, the principles within BDAL correspond with this lens of leadership.

With regard to *direction,* the business strategy is the compass. The business challenge stems from the organisation's strategic imperatives, and directs the design of the action learning programme. *Alignment* is represented by the engagement of Set members. In this instance, there must be alignment on the scope of the business challenge, the project plan, and overall recommendations. Thus, alignment is congruent to collaboration. *Commitment* is first required from the sponsor and senior leadership who hold the business challenge. Participants are equally accountable in committing their expertise, skills and time to the process and other Set members. It necessitates participants to "trust the process and trust the people".

Practical implementation on a BDAL leadership development programme

The above theoretical account provides an overview of the key building blocks to consider in the design of any action learning programme. We will now position the theoretical building blocks in a practical example. These building blocks have been designed into a leadership development programme, requisite for top talent, which incorporates action learning as the underlying methodology.

Programme architecture

Figure 11.6 shows the high-level architecture of a BDAL programme with specific emphasis on direct and indirect action learning elements.

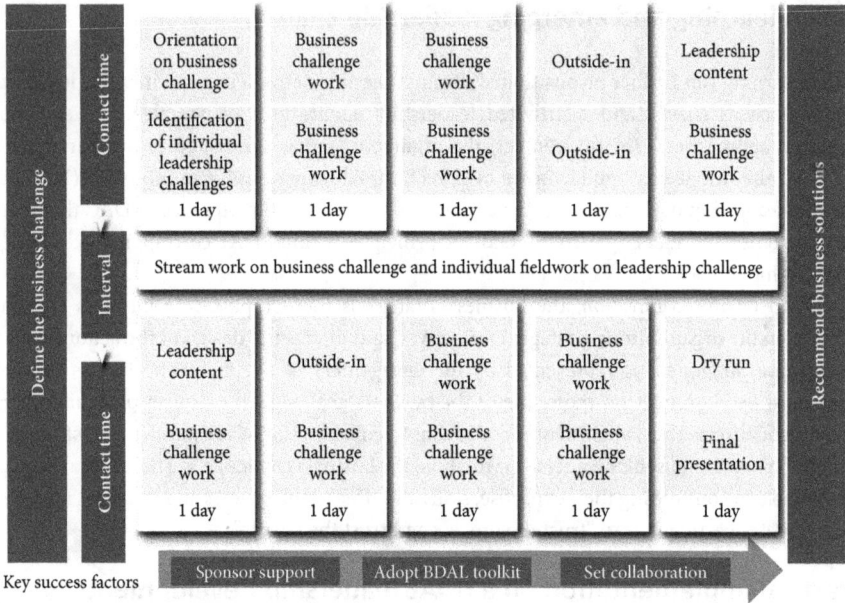

Figure 11.6 – BDAL programme architecture[39]

Critical success factors for the BDAL leadership development programme architecture

With reference to the elements that support the successful design and delivery of action learning programmes, the points below give a summary of the key considerations with respect to the architecture:

- *Mind-set of programme designers*: Designers are conscious of different pieces of the architecture and strategically build a seamless flow between content, action learning facilitation, experiential learning, coaching, and measurement.
- *Strong sponsor involvement throughout, with leadership support*: The leadership role that the sponsor plays in the programme will add substance not only to the business challenge, but also to the engagement of participants.
- *Tangible, relevant and strategic business challenge*: The sponsor, in consultation with other key leaders, will give input into the business challenges on the programme as they need to align with the strategic imperatives of the organisation.
- *Participant selection is based on top talent and cross functional teams*: The programme is aimed at sourcing the top talent from the talent pool, who will be able to lead the organisation into the future.
- *Role of the facilitator*: Both action learning and content facilitators on the programme are positioned to challenge the mental models of participants and facilitate processes for them to find the viable solutions.
- *Outside-in experience*: The programme has clear segments in the architecture that allow for different outside-in experiences. This includes exposure to experts on specific content (in line with the business challenge), immersions, and virtually simulated laboratories.

Conclusion

The purpose of this chapter was to give an account of action learning theory, in particular business driven action learning, its link to leadership development, and the practical application of the tools and principles. In the current organisational context, where complexity is so prevalent, action learning presents an opportunity to respond to this complexity through the resolution of business dilemmas. Furthermore, the learning environment of the Set allows for participants to expand their personal leadership capacity. The richness lies in the simplicity of the learning process and the uptake of an integrated toolkit. These act together to serve the outcome of a systemic learning journey that produces sustainable results for the organisation and its participants.

Endnotes

1	Morgan, 1997.	21	Burns, 2002.
2	Scharmer, 2007.	22	Pillay, 2015.
3	Weisbord, 2004.	23	Boshyk, 2011.
4	Egan, 2008.	24	Nithya, 2011.
5	Colley, 2012.	25	Boshyk, 2002.
6	Warhurst, 2012.	26	Mercer, 2000.
7	Dilworth, 1998.	27	Horan, 2007.
8	Lewin, 1946.	28	LeGros & Topolosky, 2000.
9	Raelin, 1997.	29	Boshyk, 2013.
10	Revans, 1978.	30	Ibid.
11	Raelin, 2006.	31	Rigg & Trehan, 2004.
12	Petriglieri & Petriglieri, 2015.	32	Boshyk, 2011.
13	Pedler & Abbott, 2013.	33	Mercer, 2000.
14	Zuber-Skerritt, 2002.	34	Horan, 2007.
15	Passfield, 1996.	35	LeGros & Topolosky, PS 2000.
16	Marquardt, 2007.	36	Drath et al., 2008.
17	Marquardt, 2000.	37	Pedler & Abbott, 2013.
18	Martineau & Hannum, 2004.	38	Drath et al., 2008.
19	Gregory, 1994.	39	Boshyk, 2011.
20	Gibb, 2009.		

References

Boshyk, Y. 2002. 'Why business driven action learning?' In Y Boshyk (ed). *Action learning worldwide: Experiences of leadership and organisational development*. Basingstoke, U.K. and New York: Palgrave Macmillan, Hampshire.

Boshyk, Y. 2011. 'Accelerating global growth, innovation and leader development through business driven action learning: What is it and how is it being used today in global companies?' *Global Executive Learning and the Annual Global Forum on Executive Development*. Singapore. pp. 1–24.

Boshyk, Y 2013, 'Course notes for masterclass on Business Driven Action Learning', presented in April 2013 at Eskom College, Midrand, Johannesburg, South Africa.

Burns, R. 2002. *The adult learner at work: The challenges of lifelong education in the new millennium*. Crows Nest, N.S.W., Australia: Allen and Unwin.

Colley, H. 2012. 'Not learning in the workplace: Austerity and the shattering of illusion in public service work'. *Journal of Workplace Learning*, 24(1):1–19.

Dilworth, RL. 1998. 'Action learning in a nutshell'. *Performance Improvement Quarterly*, 11(1):28–43.

Drath, WH, McCauley, C, Palus, CJ, Van Velsor, E, O'Conner, PMG & McGuire, JB. 2008. 'Direction, alignment, commitment: Towards a more integrative ontology of leadership'. *Leadership Quarterly*, 19:635–653.

Egan, TM. 2008. 'The relevance of organizational subculture for motivation to transfer learning'. *Human Resource Development Quarterly*, 19(4):299–322.

Gibb, A. 2009. 'Meeting the development needs of owner-managed small enterprise: A discussion of the centrality of action learning'. *Action Learning: Research and Practice*, 6(3):209–227.

Gregory, M. 1994. 'Accrediting work-based learning: action learning – a model for empowerment'. *Journal of Management Development*, 13(4):41–52.

Horan, J. 2007. 'Business driven action learning: A powerful tool for building world-class entrepreneurial business leaders'. *Organisation Development Journal*, 25(3):75–80.

LeGros, VM & Topolosky, PS. 2000. 'DuPont: Business driven action learning to shift company direction'. In Y Boshyk (ed). *Business driven action learning: Global best practices*. Hampshire and London, UK: Macmillan Press Ltd.

Lewin, K. 1946. Action research and minority problems. *Journal of Social Issues*, 2(4):34–46.

Marquardt, MJ. 2000. 'Action learning and leadership'. *The Learning Organisation*, 7(5):233–40.

Marquardt, MJ. 2007. 'Action learning: Resolving real problems in real time'. In M Silberman (ed). *The handbook of experiential learnin*. San Francisco, CA: Pfeiffer.

Martineau, J & Hannum, K. 2004. *Evaluating the Impact of leadership development: A professional guide.* Greensboro, NC; Center for Creative Leadership.

Mercer, S. 2000. 'General Electric's executive action learning programmes'. In Y Boshyk (ed). *Business driven action learning: Global best practices*. London, Macmillan Press Ltd.

Morgan, G. 1997. *New mindsets for seeing, organizing and managing*. Newbury Park and San Francisco, CA: Sage Publications.

Nithya, R. 2011. *Intentions and interpretations of action learning*. MA dissertation, University of London.

Passfield, R. 1996. 'Action learning for professional and organisational development: An action research case study in higher education'. Unpublished PhD thesis, Griffith University. Queensland, Australia.

Pedler, M., & Abbott, C. 2013. *Facilitating action learning: A practitioner's guide. Maidenhead: Open University Press.*

Petriglieri, G & Petriglieri, J. 2015. Can business schools humanize leadership? (23 February 2015). *Academy of Management Learning & Education.* INSEAD Working Paper No. 2015/18/OBH. [Online]. Available at SSRN: http://ssrn.com/abstract=2568625 [Accessed 7 June 2016].

Pillay, R. 2015. *Business driven action learning: A systemic model for learning within a state owned business.* PhD Thesis, University of KwaZulu Natal.

Raelin, JA. 1997. 'A model of work-based learning'. *Organisation Science*, 8(6):563–578.

Raelin, JA. 2006. 'Does action learning promote collaborative leadership?' *Academy of Management Learning & Education*, 5(2):152–168.

Revans, RW. 1978. *The ABC of action learning. Altrincham, Manchester (UK): RW Revans.*

Rigg, C & Trehan, K. 2004. 'Reflections on working with critical action learning'. *Action Learning: Research and Practice*, 1(2):151–167.

Scharmer, CO. 2007. *Theory U: Leading from the future as it emerges*. Cambridge, MA, USA: Society for Organizational Learning.

Warhurst RP. 2012, 'Learning in an age of cuts: Managers as enablers of workplace learning'. *Journal of Workplace Learning*, 25(1):37–57.

Weisbord, M. 2004. Productive workplaces revisited. San Francisco, CA: Jossey-Bass.

Zuber-Skerritt, O. 2002. 'The concept of action learning'. *The Learning Organisation*, 9(3):114–124.

SECTION 5

LEADERSHIP STORIES

Chapter 12

LEADERSHIP STORIES

Introduction

In its very essence, the organisation is a dialogical network of interpersonal interconnections based on conversations, expressed in the form of stories. Stories are naturally-occurring phenomena in organisations through which information, shared experiences, expectations, culture, and identity are passed on. Stories are the very fabric of organisational life. They add a psychological dimension to organisational life through its feeling and experiencing dimension in the form of sense-making, meaning-giving, as well as emotional attachment and involvement which rational, empirical information and lack of knowledge cannot provide.

Storytelling infuses the whole Strategic Leadership Value Chain. It is persuasive leadership-in-action. A story as a form of conversation is capable of representing and transferring complex, multidimensional organisational realities to listeners in a simple and effortless way in order to make sense of, and give meaning and purpose to, organisational reality.

At its most basic level, storytelling as a conversation (or dialogue) refers to what is being said and listened to between people. The word 'dialogue' stems from two Greek roots, "*dia*" and "*logos*", jointly suggesting the sense of "meaning flowing through". Stories help organisational members to make sense of who they are, where they come from and fit in, and what they want to be. They help reduce organisational uncertainty, complexity and ambiguity by quickly and coherently disseminating information; they frame organisational events through their value-laden features; and they promote organisational culture and identification by establishing a context for organisational members.

Using stories is one of the best ways to:

- make abstract concepts meaningful;
- help connect people and ideas;
- inspire imagination and motivate action;
- give "breathing space" in the frenetic and merciless task-driven nature of the organisation;
- allow different perspectives to emerge;
- create sense, coherence, and meaning;
- develop value-centric descriptions of situations, allowing knowledge to be applied and solutions to be found;
- convey organisational values and culture;
- communicate complex messages simply;
- connect people into a shared frame of reference; and
- inspire change.

In the *first instance* leaders are, and have to be, storytellers about themselves: from where they have come; who they are; what they stand for; what they believe in; what they want to achieve and how; and what they want to leave behind as a legacy. The character, competence, connectedness, caring and commitment of leaders are manifested *inter alia* in how well they understand, and are able and willing to share, their personal journeys as leaders: from the past, through the present, into the future. It is a most powerful way in which to connect with others.

In the *second instance*, leaders have to be able to tell the story of the organisation they are currently involved in: the identity and ideology of the organisation; where the organisation has come from; its desired future destination and legacy; the journey travelled to date by the organisation; the journey still to be travelled; and how things are done and not done in the organisation.

This Section provides examples of the first kind of leadership stories: leaders' stories about themselves as leaders.

The accompanying box gives a list of the leaders whose stories follow – with their respective core themes – are included in this Section.

LEADER'S STORY	THEME OF STORY
Bridgette Gasa	*Good leaders unite people*
Johan van Zyl	*Get to know yourself early on in your career*
Dave Macready	*Leadership built on vision, belief and passion*
Gill Marcus	*What matters is the greater good*
Monhla Hlahla	*Moving effectively through the stages of leadership impact*
GT Ferreira, Laurie Dippenaar & Paul Harris	*Leader excellence asks for a distinct, shared leadership philosophy*

References

Boje, D. 2008. *Storytelling organizations.* Thousand Oaks, CA: Sage.

Boyce, M.E. 1996. 'Organisational story and storytelling: A critical review' *Journal of Organisational Change Management,* 9(5):5-26.

Christie, P. 2009. *Every leader a story teller – storytelling skills for personal leadership.* Johannesburg, ZA: Knowres.

Denning, S. 2011. *The leader's guide to storytelling,* San Francisco, CA: Jossey-Bass

Gabriel, Y. 2000). *Storytelling in organisations: Facts, fictions and fantasies.* New York, NY: Oxford University Press.

Ibarra, H & Lineback, K. 2005. 'What's your story?' *Harvard Business Review,* 1–7, January.

Veldsman, D & May, M. S. 2012. 'The stories that leaders tell during organisational change: The search for meaning during organisational transformation'. Unpublished Masters thesis, University of South Africa, Pretoria, South Africa.

Good leaders unite people

Bridgette Gasa

Article published in Sake Beeld on 24 September 2015.
Translated from Afrikaans. Used with permission

It is becoming increasingly difficult in South Africa's economic and political climate to structure consensus on how best to define leadership that is required in all of society. Across dinner tables and in social settings there is a discussion around the lack of leadership and the accompanying anecdotes are around an increasing depletion of leaders of exemplary and unquestionable character and disposition. This discourse is usually accompanied by an incomplete analysis of the state of collapse in public entities, and the questionable behaviour of those in leadership in private entities/society at large and, of course, in the political sphere.

How we define leadership has in itself transformed from a phase of one to two or more distinct stages or a whole new meaning in and of itself. One would ask: are we fast becoming a country whose leadership and moral compass is consistently being rigorously reviewed? There are all sorts of arbiters who use a litmus test – known only to themselves – to weigh in on this leadership discourse. I have often found myself battling to understand what it is that we should know and appreciate today regarding leadership. In this quest I reflected back on inspirational leaders who have inspired me – living or dead – to gauge what it is that was or is commendable that we could learn from them. I also reflected on the definition of leadership itself.

To respond to the first point of reflection: I have been greatly inspired by people who are not only visionaries but have consistently been resolute in the execution of their vision. I have drawn inspiration from people who were bold enough to take decisions that may not necessarily have made them popular but were imbued with the requisite emotional intelligence to be able to carry through those tough decisions. I have learnt from individuals who were not only self-aware of their strengths and weaknesses, but were also astute self-masters.

To respond to the latter point of reflection: Leadership in my view is, firstly, about possessing an innate ability to rally stakeholders around a set of common objectives. Secondly, it involves efforts beyond the rallying, which often require one to take full accountability in ensuring that the followers of that common vision are active participants in the functional application of all aspects necessary for the attainment of that vision. Thirdly, leadership is about arriving at an end and having the requisite humility to accept the outcomes. If the end has yielded desired outcomes, one celebrates with the collective. If the end has an adverse outcome, inspirational leaders draw key learnings and refine the approach for yet another attempt.

If the above definition in three parts finds resonance with most readers, the questions to ask ourselves about leadership therefore are: Does this innate ability to rally exist in South Africa in healthy doses across all sectors of society? Does its existence further the aims of a positive set of outcomes? Are our leaders accountable and present right throughout whatever process they may have initiated?

It is true however that identifying individuals with the 'right stuff' to be leaders is more art than science. After all, the personal styles of superb leaders vary and, just as important, different situations call for different types of leadership.

One of the greatest leadership mistakes I personally have made in the past was to be too trusting of results that get tabled before me. As a result I ended up having someone within our organisation who caused us a tremendous amount of reputational damage. Had I enquired thoroughly enough, had I 'peeled' to yet another layer, the facts about the person's character flaws would have been starkly before me – preventing me from making that appointment.

I learnt through that experience that empathy is sometime misconstrued or abused by those whose aim is to take you for granted in the first place. One may argue that during certain pressured times I had lost that enquiring edge whilst trying to balance too many responsibilities at the same time. I am not suggesting that leaders ought to now acquire paranoia and dig in unnecessary trenches. However, taking things and people at face value, and as they present themselves to one, can prove quite costly at times.

Looking at the demands that lie ahead, our country will require leaders who are able to self-govern; leaders with that innate ability to rally others around a set of common objectives; leaders who are not absent in the application process of those set of objectives and are accountable throughout the process. These leaders must emerge from all sectors of society if our country is to realise the imagined future well-articulated in the national vision.

Bridgette Gasa holds a PhD in Construction Management. She is the Founder and Managing Director of The Elilox Group, a consulting firm active in infrastructure development and agricultural enterprises. Prior to that she was Executive Head of the Khukhulela Consortium, an infrastructure Group. She was a member of the National Planning Commission. In 2008 she received the Department of Science and Technology's award for the leading woman scientist in industry. In 2013 she was crowned as Africa's most influential businesswoman in the category: basic industries.

Get To Know Yourself as a Leader Early On in Your Career

Johan van Zyl

Article published in Sake Beeld on 18 June 2015.
Translated from Afrikaans. Used with permission

In life many opportunities present themselves, but very few of us grasp them enthusiastically and meaningfully, with both hands. In my view this is the first important step towards true leadership: the ability to identify and act on opportunities. Arguably, one of the main indicators of weak leadership is an inability to identify actual strategic issues, which then culminates in missed opportunities. An organisation which lets an important window of opportunity close, is already on a slippery slope towards obsolescence.

Clearly, to be successful within a given context, you need to focus on those aspects which will strengthen your unique leadership style. Personally, I cannot but overemphasise the importance of focus. Slacking off is never an option – and in my view, a healthy dose of impatience is a prerequisite. My advice is to determine where you can make a difference, and then to focus on measurable outcomes, because measurables influence behaviour. A leader not only needs to recognise and reward achievement, but also to penalise underachievement.

I advocate an eclectic management style – a mixed bag, if you will. Many would categorise themselves as a specific type of leader. In my view a specific situation calls for a specific type of leadership. In some cases it is best to take control and say: 'This is how we're going to do it.' In other instances it is better to take a step back. Easier said than done, especially when things are not going according to plan.

South Africa faces a number of core challenges: widespread poverty, relatively high unemployment, an oversupply of lowly or unschooled labour. All these factors conspire to limit our economic growth to a snail's pace. Leaders in the private sector in this country cannot solely prioritise business. It is imperative for organisations to make social and socio-economic issues part of their strategic plan, along with a corporate social responsibility programme as part of their daily business dealings. I do not advocate that heads of companies dabble in politics. Rather, they should investigate how a changing socio-economic landscape will impact business confidence in their specific industry or sector.

Business people face two other important challenges: workplace diversity and black economic empowerment. Despite being seen as challenges, these issues provide wonderful business opportunities. A more diverse workforce – especially at senior levels – implies that more diverse ideas will be forthcoming, which will make the company more resilient within an already complex business environment. A diversity of ideas is the life blood of successful innovation.

One aspect of leadership which benefits from more inclusive discourse is values. If leadership revolves around taking responsibility for the bigger picture, rather than being all about power, we create space for conversations around common values. Companies should follow a top-down approach. This means that the leader sets the pace and the personnel follow his/her example.

As a leader, where does personal development fit into the equation? I argue that this is vital in the early stages of an individual's career, and something for which each of us must accept personal responsibility. It is imperative not only to know yourself, but to be honest with yourself: about both your strengths and your weaknesses.

In conclusion, I believe true leadership reflects the power and success of a team, rather than the abilities of a single individual.

From 2003 to June 2015, Dr Johan van Zyl served as Executive Group Head of Sanlam. He is the former head of Santam, and served as Vice Chancellor of the University of Pretoria and as a consultant for the World Bank. He holds two PhDs, one of which is a DSc in agriculture. He currently serves on the board of numerous companies and is a member of the Royal Society of South Africa.

Leadership Built on Vision, Belief and Passion

Dave Macready

Article published in Sake Beeld on 20 August 2015.
Translated from Afrikaans. Used with permission

When I am asked about leadership, I immediately think of the great leaders I have known who have exuded vision, belief and passion. Our own Madiba embodied all three of these qualities, shining a light in the dark for all of us to follow and creating a passionate, contagious belief in a better, more sustainable future for all South Africans. He demonstrated that by inspiring the inner core of those he led, a great leader can define a new reality and make possible what was previously impossible or unimaginable.

Leaders with vision often come to the fore in a time of crisis, when their ability to see the bigger picture is most needed. Leaders need to see around corners and look beyond current realities to envisage a new future. They must be able to change mindsets and create belief – faith without evidence – in a better future that doesn't exist yet. All boats rise with a tide. Leadership is only really challenged when the tide goes out. It is in this empty space – a void etched with dark spaces where everyone looks around at everyone else and there are no obvious answers, only questions – that great leaders emerge.

As important as vision is belief. Belief in self, belief in those being led and belief in a better tomorrow. Rudy Giuliani, the mayor of New York at the time of the 9/11 attacks, immediately understood this. Instinctively he knew that what a city reeling with shock needed more than anything was a unifying force: a strong, resolute, resourceful leader confident about finding solutions. He swung into immediate action to address basic needs, both physical and emotional, steering New Yorkers away from fear, grief and despair to a shared belief in their ability to overcome the crisis.

Reinforcing every great leader's vision and belief is passion. Passion is everything. It stems from a feeling, a feeling of being part of something, something you believe in, something bigger than yourself. Years ago I watched a movie called *Any Given Sunday* in which Al Pacino played a coach who had only a few minutes in which to motivate his exhausted team to persevere and succeed. Few things I have watched have been as simply passionate or powerful as the 'Inch by Inch' speech he delivered. With deep commitment and raw honesty, he reignited his team's belief in their winning skills and got them to summon all their strength, passion and fire to achieve their goal, literally in this case.

That scene struck a chord with me because of the basic truth it captures. Great leaders must connect and identify with those they lead to unleash the full power of passion, tenacity and perseverance. That connection needs to be built on reciprocal trust: every leader must engender the absolute conviction that he or she has the team's best interests at heart, and at the same time convey the belief that the team has what it takes to deliver excellence.

Of course, vision, belief and passion alone do not guarantee moral, ethical or servant leadership, as despots and tyrants from Hitler to Pol Pot have proved. Fine leadership, leadership that is for the greater good, requires the essential qualities of integrity, courage, humility and humanity. I think Madiba again. I think Mahatma Gandhi. I think Thuli Madonsela.

Fine leaders do the right thing even when nobody is watching. They have the courage to make hard, but necessary decisions; the courage to abandon the past; the willingness to learn, unlearn and relearn; as well as the courage to be the change they want to see against all odds. Part of fine leadership may be inherent, but part is acquired through life's brutal lessons in wisdom. It cannot be taught in a classroom or lecture hall.

Abraham Lincoln, one of the wisest Presidents of the United States, achieved great things by creating an exceptional culture of learning, thinking and debating. Those he surrounded himself with were the best and brightest he could find, even if their opinions diverged from his own. Importantly, he had the courage to challenge the conventions of previous generations, and to abandon them where they fell short of the principles he stood for.

South Africa is under enormous political and economic pressures and faces significant challenges at this critical juncture in our history. We are a country calling out for inspiring and effective leadership in business, in labour, in government. We are a country desperate for leaders to have the courage to engage, shift perspectives and abandon our well-entrenched vested positions. Leaders who are prepared to invest in a new trust equation that brings business, labour and political leadership together to better serve the interests of a more sustainable, more inclusive South Africa. Leaders who selflessly put *all* South Africans' interests at the centre of the agenda.

Dave Macready is the recently appointed CEO of Old Mutual South Africa. He is a chartered accountant and a former partner at Deloitte in Cape Town and London. After choosing to return to South Africa in 1999, he held senior executive leadership positions in Syfrets, Nedcor Investment Bank and the Nedbank Group Executive before joining Old Mutual in May.

What Matters is the Greater Good

Gill Marcus

Interview conducted during March 2013 by Adriaan Groenewald of the Leadership Platform at the time Gill was the Governor of the SA Reserve Bank. Used with permission

Gill never had leadership ambitions. If someone addressed her as a leader she would probably look behind her. She says: "I don't see myself in that role. I never saw myself with an ambition to be a leader. I don't see that now." She simply sees leadership as "an honour bestowed on someone because people want to hear what you have to say, because you reflect, for them what's important".

For Gill it has also been a quest of "what matters to me?" What has been important to her is what kind of society we live in; what kind of values we have; who we are. She believes it is also a challenge of "to be or to have". For her personally 'to be' is more important. To have includes material wealth, your position and all your authority and for her this "has never been a part of what I see as important".

Marcus has never applied for a job in her life. In her teenage years she joined the ANC. From there on life was about what she could do to match her desire to make South Africa a better place. With whatever came her way she did her best and was asked to do more and more. In essence it has been like a symbiotic relationship of adding value by shaping situations and responsibilities, while these very situations shaped her views in return.

Remaining true to her values and purpose was always a given, but on her journey more started to matter. She explains that "when you are exercising your role or responsibility you have to take more into account". This 'more' to her is 'the greater good'. So, as a leader it is not only about what is right for you but what is right for the greater good. Marcus explains: "It (the role) can't be against your values, but it's not about yourself and when you are exercising judgment, it is about the greater good."

According to Marcus this mindset lifts the leader onto another level where, "it is not about how I feel today; this is secondary. I could be feeling totally lousy today but if this is what I have to do then this is what must be done". It seems that it is therefore about understanding yourself, the greater good and then the 'office' or position that is thrust upon you. She says: "The question is to draw the distinction between what is the authority of the office and what is your personal authority, because office has huge authority." Marcus believes the leader's personal conduct can add to the office or detract from it, and "your best combination is when you can combine your personal leadership and authority with the authority of the office, because then you can use that combination to effectively achieve what needs to be done".

Every day is a great adventure for Marcus and she loves waking up to a new day, needing only four hours' sleep. With the world being in its current state it can however be a challenge to sleep well, never mind waking up. She and her team try and understand the current global turmoil, by asking questions like: What are we seeing? How are we seeing it? What are the implications? What is our responsibility to do, "so that we can minimise the impact of an imploding world, because that's what's happening"?

While the Reserve Bank is an independent organisation of roughly 2 200 employees with seven branches across SA, it functions like an integrated stakeholder of society that is part and parcel of it. The independence according to Marcus stretches as far as "exercising our constitutional responsibility without fear or favour". Marcus highlights "we are in many instances the only African country that is a participant in our own right in many of the international forums, like the G20, G24, BIS. We have a voice internationally and try to influence decisions about the world we believe we need to live in". Marcus herself may be unique in that she has been in parliament, government and the private sector, which includes chairing the ABSA Board.

All of the above, and more, enhance confidence in decision making. When Marcus is comfortable that she has sufficient information and views she takes a decision. As a consultative leader she views consultation as a process where, whenever possible, the different parties should be in the same room so that they can bounce their views off one another. In this way it is not only consultation between the leader and individual parties but everyone's views will be aired and influenced one way or the other. This approach improves the chances of arriving at a collective agreement. Of course this necessitates quality, mature individuals that are knowledgeable yet willing to listen and even shift from their original positions, for the greater good.

Marcus expands regarding decision making: "I think there are different levels of decision making. There are decisions about organisational day-to-day issues that must be decided on, and then there is decision making around for example the monetary policy stance." In the case of the latter they do not simply make the decision when they meet as a committee every two months. They build up to that decision every day. So, when the time comes they pull all the preparation together, evaluate and decide. Marcus comments: "I would say it is the quality of the information and the quality of the people around and then the rigour with which you all examine the data and discuss what needs to be done. You want people with strong and thoughtful views, and I believe we have them here."

Marcus comes across as passionate, intelligent, purpose-driven, humble, human, engaging, approachable, fearless, a big picture thinker and authentic. Her weakness may be that she does not necessarily enjoy being a public figure. Then again, this could very well be her strength.

Gill served as Deputy Minister of Finance in the Government of Nelson Mandela from 1996 to 1999. In 1999 she became Deputy Governor of the Reserve Bank. After leaving in 2004, she held the Professorship of Leadership and Gender Studies at the Gordon Institute of Business Science, before going into business. In July 2009 she became Governor of the Reserve Bank. She stepped down at the end of her five-year term in November 2014.

Moving Effectively Through the Stages of Leadership Impact

Monhla Hlahla

Interviewed during 2011 by Adriaan Groenewald of Leadership Platform. Used with permission

In 2005 I met Monhla Hlahla MD Airports Company South Africa (ACSA) for the first time, as the newly crowned Businesswoman of the Year. I can tell you emphatically that the person I interviewed during 2011 and the one I interviewed in 2005 are two entirely different individuals. She carried herself very differently, with more quiet confidence, a certain calmness.

What happened? She allowed herself the time to move through what can be described as the 'four stages of leadership impact' and so gained invaluable experience.

The interview with Hlahla helped me refine this model.

- **Stage one: Understanding and acceptance.** The purpose of this stage is to understand (e.g. the organisation, people, environment, the drivers of organisation) and gain a level of acceptance from all stakeholders which one cannot claim but has to earn over time.
- **Stage two: Credible management/leadership.** The purpose of this stage is to leverage off the understanding and acceptance and lead for maximum impact. However, during this stage the leader may still be mostly focused on the self, e.g. how she leads; how she can become a better leader for the organisation and people.
- **Stage three: Leadership multiplication for legacy.** This is a powerful stage as the leader now mostly starts focusing on others, his/her leadership: how he/she can achieve through them by assisting them to be better leaders and how someone can in fact take over from him/her.
- **Stage four: Successful handover.** This is the exit stage. If the leader has moved through the above three stages, then this stage will mostly be a natural consequence. There will be a successor that is ready to take over, and the leader will feel ready for another challenge in his/her life.

Some leaders get stuck in one of the first three stages and hesitate or even refuse to exit, which could be detrimental to the organisation or country, depending on who the leader is. There are several reasons for this, some being rather obvious, but will not be expanded on here. It takes great maturity to positively and consciously set one's sights on stage four.

Hlahla's views correlate with this 'leadership impact' model as she believes that during her first few years she managed more than what she led. It was during this management period that she acquired more of an understanding of the overall business, and in time attained acceptance. As this happened it became easier for her to lead effectively – positively impacting on individuals, clients, suppliers, and ultimately the organisation.

Her concern is that there are too many leaders who move on to another job before they have had the opportunity to really lead effectively. Perhaps this happens because stage one can be so difficult. So, some leaders may be tempted to give up and move on, especially when a more attractive or lucrative offer comes along. But, just know that if one leaves for the wrong reasons it will be before you have truly added value to the people, the organisation and in fact oneself. There is no short cut to making any meaningful contribution. Hlahla believes very strongly in this principle.

She has now been the leader of ACSA for just on eight years and this is not an easy company to run. To me it seemed she is probably in stage three where she is making a difference with confidence, while focusing on her leadership under her.

Her stage one had serious challenges. The first one was a very difficult Chairman who did not trust her. There were media reports about their unhealthy relationship. Hlahla received lots of advice and counsel from family, friends and colleagues. The pressure to fight the issues through the media beckoned, but she declined and pushed on, even though at times she quietly sat in her office crying. Then she fired her Chief of Security, which of course made headlines on a regular basis. It also dragged several important ACSA stakeholders into the process, e.g. the government, police service.

Hlahla had difficulty with changes in Board members, heists at the airport; and an incredible amount of expansion that involves building operations. But, despite all these she seems to have navigated her way through the maze of challenges and eventually moved into stages two and three where she has now been leading for some time. She too had her opportunities to give up and leave, but did not.

During her leadership career at this very challenging State Owned Enterprise, she has learned some valuable principles that can assist every leader to move effectively through the leadership impact stages:

1.   Keep focusing on the core purpose of the organisation and its goal. When the difficult times arrive and counsel comes from all angles, one can listen sincerely and then make a decision that is good for the organisation and its purpose.
2.   The ability and humility to hear all views.
3.   Decisiveness is critical. Sometimes a situation needs someone to just make a call rather than someone to necessarily make the right call. What becomes more important then is one's ability to manage unintended consequences.
4.   Guts or courage.

Monhla served as the Managing Director and Chief Executive Officer of Airports Company South Africa SOC Limited from 2001 to September 2011. Prior to that, she was with the Development Bank of Southern Africa (DBSA), having joined in 1994 and successfully managed several large infrastructure projects. In 2005, she received the Business Women Association's (BWA) Business Woman of the Year award and the *Black Business Quarterly* (BBQ) Magazine's Woman of the Year award.

Leader Excellence Asks for a Distinct, Shared Leadership Philosophy

GT Ferreira, Laurie Dippenaar and Paul Harris

Christel Fourie, based on her doctorate on the leadership philosophies
of GT Ferreira, Laurie Dippenaar and Paul Harris

GT Ferreira, Laurie Dippenaar and Paul Harris were the founders of the FirstRand Group. They had a remarkable partnership that endured for more than 30 years whilst providing executive co-leadership to the Group they founded. A partnership like the FirstRand founders' one is not born. It develops. At times they battled together, but the end game was always more important than who got the credit. The cohesion was stronger than the conflict. It did not fragment on the back of personalities.

The founders' leadership philosophy is intricately linked to their business philosophy. The essence of their shared leadership philosophy pivoted on ten distinct axes.

Be who you are

As a leader, be who you are. It has to be how you are naturally. The founders applied a leadership style that was natural to them. A lot came about intuitively; from a real honest place. They did not copy from textbooks. They are quick to point out that there are different strategies that can bring about success. The important thing is to know which team you are playing on.

Love what you do and have fun

Do something you love and have fun along the way. A shared perspective is that if you enjoy what you do, it takes you further. Financial results are important. But of greater importance is whether people want to come to work. It links to what keeps exceptional leaders engaged. When they enjoy what they do, when they grow in their roles, when you let them get on with things and pay them well, that is when they stay. What is hard to achieve, is made to sound simple.

The right partners

Handpick partners: like-minded people and future leaders who are similar, but also different. How GT handpicked his business partners initially, set the scene. Look for someone you trust, who is honest and works hard. All three were inherently entrepreneurs; were equally hungry and keen; and, importantly, did not take themselves too seriously.

The three partners are also very different. In a nutshell, GT is a strategist, a diplomat, a world-class negotiator and a people's person. Laurie is the numbers man, embodies strong values, is a big thinker and excels at follow-through. Paul is a risk taker, a creative thinker, brings passion, a dealmaker at heart, and new ideas make his antennae go up. The biggest success factor of their partnership was that they complemented one another. GT thinks they were very lucky that their skills and temperaments complemented each other so much so that it landed them in the fast stream.

The founders made it known that they look for a certain kind of person. Like-minded does not mean sameness. What matters greatly is attitude and performance. Essentially, it has to do with

'Do you fit in?' They surrounded themselves with the strongest people and were not intimidated by this. FirstRand's leaders are typically picked young, picked on merit and do not 'run' for short stretches (= stable leadership). GT, Laurie and Paul were able to spot talent a mile away.

Being an architect

A leader is an architect. The founders brought a specific approach to business, rooted in empowerment and innovation that turned out to be highly effective in starting new businesses. A crucial mindset is that you do not have to be dishonest to be competitive. Outsmart competitors with ingenuity. Also, work harder than your competition. No matter what you do, you will not achieve the pinnacle of success if you work from 8 to 5.

Furthermore, if you want to cultivate innovation, be prepared to tolerate mistakes. The founders were disruptors, and disrupted long before it had earned a 'name'. Then they actively encouraged others to disrupt. Making bankers and professional managers think like owners formed part of their considerable legacy. They lived the owner-manager philosophy one hundred per cent. It was rooted in the belief that if you treat the business as your own, you care more. It asks for high competence and maturity in leaders.

Model the organisational culture

A leader cannot fake culture. The values of an organisation stem from the way that senior leaders behave. It sends a message to others as to how they should react in certain situations. Values, or in FirstRand's language 'the things your mother taught you', are lived and practised. It comes through prominently in RMB's slogan that has not changed in 30 years: *Traditional values. Innovative ideas.* The founders maintained that if the organisation continued to choose its leaders in the same way, the Group's entrepreneurial culture will prevail. The word 'trust' permeated the founders' story and leadership. If you have trust in an organisation, it leads automatically to a good reputation.

It is about the 'We' not the 'I'

The role of a leader is not to make all the decisions, but to facilitate good decision-making. Leadership is not solo work. There is no 'I' in leadership, only 'We'. The message, 'We did not do this on our own; we have been surrounded by brilliant people', was reiterated time and again. In business, the egos can be bigger than a building. A leader has to work with that. If you can get the team focused more on the importance of scoring and winning as a team, and less about who gets the credit, it creates a 'We' mindset.

Being a talent magnet

The founders epitomised an ethos and a culture that attracted talented individuals to working with them. What people sensed around these three was: 'Here you make your own future'. Paul framed it as: "You are your own Pty Ltd. You make your own destiny." Due to humble beginnings, the founders were not into the hierarchy side of things. They just wanted to get things done. They always worked with people rather than ordering them around. Essentially, they created an environment that they wanted to work in.

Grow people

Be generous and commit to growing people. The founders spent a considerable proportion of their time developing potential. They were generous in sharing their knowledge and experience. They were incredibly happy about others' successes. They listened; asked questions to challenge; raised the bar; sparked ideas; offered intellectual support; and gave people wings. They inspired others through their example. The potent combination of youth and grey hair was not lost on them. They created an atmosphere of success.

Seamless succession

The most important responsibility of a leader is that when you leave, there should not even be a ripple. Aim for a seamless handover. Leadership succession can be compared to running a perpetual relay. As a leader you take the baton and you run your best round and then you hand over to the next runner in the best possible way. Give those runners who need to take over the baton time to establish themselves, and then get out of their way. If you get the right people on board, succession is not really an issue. Laurie maintains that in a succession race, there are more candidates who can be ministers than presidents. A statesman is a leader who can take the right decisions not for own gain, but puts a business or country's interests above their own.

Be humble, confident, courageous and passionate

In the founders, we have a fine example of leaders who had a natural humility combined with being confident leaders. They conducted themselves with chutzpah and demonstrated courage and a work ethic hard to equal. They have always wanted to make South Africa a better place. They are leaders who are not just passionate about business. They are passionate about life.

In 1977 GT Ferreira, Laurie Dippenaar and Paul Harris founded Rand Consolidated Investments Ltd (RCI) from which FirstRand Group and its offshoots developed. At present the Group owns well-known banking brands such as First National Bank, WesBank, Rand Merchant Bank and Ashburton Investments. The founders have since retired from the Group but still hold various Board chairmanships and directorships. They all have post-graduate qualifications.

SECTION 6
THE FUTURE OF LEADERSHIP

Chapter 13

LOOKING AHEAD

The Future of Leadership

Andrew J Johnson and Theo H Veldsman

In closing our brief excursion into *Understanding Leadership* it is worthwhile repeating some key assertions we made in the opening chapter:

- leadership is under severe scrutiny, and;
- leadership is in the overheating crucible of a reframed/reframing world that is in the throes of fundamental and radical transformation, hence; and
- the search is on for better and different leadership, in the present and going into the future.

Going into the future, the need for organisations to have an ongoing, deliberate, comprehensive and in-depth conversation about leadership is an imperative if they want not merely to survive but also to thrive sustainably.

In this chapter we would like to gaze into the crystal ball by posing the question: If there is a need for better and different leadership going into the future, what would it look like with the conditions attached to such future-fit leadership?

To this end we explore the features of the growing crisis around leadership; the unfolding, future contextual leadership challenges; profiling the "context fit" leadership of the future; effective leadership engagement with the future context through Skilful Improvisation; and finally, the implications of Skilful Improvisation for growing and developing future-fit leadership.

Features of the Growing Leadership Crisis

Some of the important features of the growing leadership crisis that will have a significant impact on future leadership are:

- *Leadership no longer has any place to hide.* Leaders are in the public eye and under public scrutiny constantly because of the power of social media, and more stringent and expanding corporate governance requirements and demands.
- *Accelerating mistrust, anger towards, suspicion of, disillusionment in, and sense of alienation from, institutional leadership,* whether in business, the public sector, or in politics. There is a growing general public perception that "they are in it for themselves and their own enrichment. People and institutions are merely the means to satisfy their ego-centric needs, wants and purposes."
- *Greater and unrealistic expectations for "leadership on steroids".* There is little patience with new leaders taking time to settle into and acclimatise to their new roles. The pressure is for instant delivery from the word "go", often against unreasonable deliverables, goals and standards. In many instances, the leadership role expectations from stakeholders are unclear and ambiguous, resulting in decreasing leadership tenures, and higher frequencies of derailment and burnout.
- The *emergence of more spontaneous leadership* in more places, at more times and by more people, the growing trend of "leaderless revolutions". These revolutions are fuelled

by the multiplication and mobilisation power of social media in the hands of everyone, everywhere, anytime. The spontaneous revolutions are blossoming around issues regarding globalisation, climatic warming, technological innovation, religious "holy wars", and demographic displacements like the European refugee crisis. Recent examples of such "leaderless" movements include the #arabspring movements of the Middle East; the #occupy movements in North America and Europe; and #mustfall movements in the South African higher education sector.

- The **growing cancer of toxic leaders, followers and organisations** because of the fanatical worshipping of unfettered individualism and egocentricity to the detriment of the pursuit common good; the rampant growth in personal self-interest and self-love (in other words, narcissism); putting "Me Pty Ltd" at the centre; the weakening of the overarching authority of commonly accepted ethical values and norms, also because of value clashes resulting from increasing multicultural settings; and weak followers unable and unwilling to challenge toxic leadership courageously and fiercely.

Unfolding Future Leadership Contextual Challenges

Against the backdrop of the above features of the growing leadership crisis, what are the most apparent unfolding future contextual leadership challenges? We would like to explore these challenges in terms of the conceptual framework given in Figure 13.1, constructed around the relationships in which a leader is embedded.

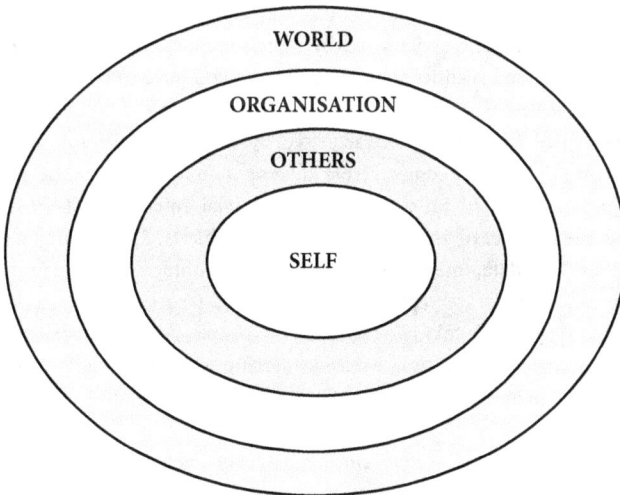

Figure 13.1 Leadership in relationship with the World, Organisation, Others and Self

According to the framework given in Figure 13.1, the leader's success resides in successfully connecting, nurturing and maintaining four interdependent, critical relationships – each with their unique interacting leadership challenges, demands and requirements – with the World; one's Organisation; Others; and Self. Each of the four relationship of leadership will be discussed in turn from a futuristic perspective. Though discussed separately and sequentially, the four relationships form an organic, systemic whole; are in constant reciprocal interaction; and form dynamic patterns, whether vicious or virtuous.

World

Much has been written and spoken about the VUCA World context of Volatility, Uncertainty, Complexity and Ambiguity, expanded here by ourselves to VICCAS: a World of increasing Variety, Interdependence (that is, connectivity), Complexity, Change, Ambiguity, Seamlessness and Sustainability. The counter, "dark" side of the above VICCAS features must also be considered: Over-standardisation, Over-dependency, Over-simplification, Over-formalisation, Over-control, Over-specialisation and Over-concentration. Going forward, the expectation is that the VICCAS Context will intensify.

The key challenges of the VICCAS Context are:

- Pressures arising from ***macro destructive and threatening global, socio-economic dynamics invading the global village***, such as wealth concentration in the hands of a few "Haves"; the significantly growing income gap; the relative impoverishment of the middle class; growing structural unemployment because of the Fourth Industrial Revolution (see below); and population displacement because of climatic change and value clashes (see below). The sensitive, interwoven fabric and tapestry of the World – the playing field of leadership – is being torn apart.

- Social media *fragmenting the world into "e-suburbs" of vast global (radicalised) interest groups* talking only to themselves in self-referential ways in self-created echo chambers; radical group recruitment via the Internet; the global tsunami waves of fads and fashions, uninformed opinions and views engulfing the world; the snowballing generation of vast amounts of unvalidated data, information and knowledge feeding and swaying public opinion; parochial, selective views fed by search engines, for example, Google's search engines defining siloed realities for people. Those who have to be led are "disappearing" and becoming faceless in cyberspace through virtualisation and digitisation.

- ***Vast technological innovation***, characterised by an exponential rate of change in and merging of multiple technologies across diverse domains such as the physical, digital, and biological manifested in, for example, Artificial Intelligence (AI), robotics, DNA sequencing, the Internet of Things (iot), driverless vehicles, 3D-printing, nanotechnology, biotechnology, big data, materials science, energy storage, and quantum computing. Digitisation and emails are replacing direct face-to-face leadership. It is believed that machines and systems are taking over, replacing people. Against the backdrop of keeping up with technological innovation, future leadership will have to align effectively in real-time technology, people, and working mode continuously relative to the strategic intent they are pursuing.

- Global fundamental ***value system clashes and tensions*** creating deep fault lines and schisms in communities, organisations and societies. Future leadership will need to build common, shared value spaces enabling diverse people to collaborate for the benefit and common good of all.

- The increasing ***untrammelled power of big global corporates*** – some bigger than states – leveraged from their control over vast resources globally, pressurising governments, institutions and stakeholders to "toe their line" in order to suit their parochial, narrow, corporate interests. The resources can be moved at the click of a mouse. The challenge to leadership is to move beyond narrow corporate self-interest and adopt a corporate social investment, common good, and a perspective infusing all of the corporate's thinking, decisions and actions.

- The growing ***mismatch of global institutions*** such as the United Nations (UN), World Bank, IMF, the International Court of Justice, International Criminal Court, and Interpol to oversee and deal in globally representative ways with the increasing contextual complexity of the World. Increasingly these institutions are becoming too simple for, and too unrepresentative of, the complexifying World. The leadership challenge is the re-creation of the existing, and the setting up of newly conceived, institutions matched to the requisite contextual complexity of the VICCAS Context.

Organisation

Against the features of the VICCAS Context, organisations (including institutions) to be led in the future will be facing at least the following challenges:

- The heightened *vulnerability of the organisation's reputation and brand* to social media used for mobilisation against organisations by lobby/interest/pressure groups. Future leadership will have to be a master of the social media, and dominate this communication in space-time.
- The *disruption of traditional business models* because of virtualisation and digitalisation, for example, Amazon, e-Bay, and the on-demand economy driven by the emergence of applications (apps)-based organisations, for example, Uber and airbnb. Future leadership will have to question their existing business model on a continuous basis from first principles.
- The *deconstruction of big corporates* into smaller, highly autonomous, network-based business units in order to instil corporates with nimbleness, agility, client centricity, and responsiveness. The leadership of the future will have to be a networker and alliance and partner builder. He/she will have to be outstanding at building deep and robust relationships.
- Increasing pressure for *demographic representivity* regarding race, gender and culture at all leadership levels from board-level down the organisation, reflective of the organisation's chosen operating arena. Diversity sensitivity will be essential for future leadership.
- Globalisation, enabled by digitisation and virtualisation, will force organisations and leadership to adopt a *global mindset* manifested in thinking globally but acting locally.
- Organisations and their leadership will need to be *future centric* by visiting the future in order to create previously unimaginable, desirable futures. They will then have to return to the present to realise that future. Merely extrapolating from the present into the future, and applying past success recipes, will be a cause of certain extinction for organisations.
- *Disruptive innovation* because of the Fourth Industrial Revolution will necessitate the ongoing re-invention of organisations in terms of client needs, products/services, markets, and modes of delivery. Organisations will be in a constant state of flux. Future leadership will have to be relentless innovators, entrepreneurs and risk takers.
- The increasing *"algorithmisation"* of professional knowledge, expertise and decision-making*, enabling para-professionals and users to take over work previously reserved for and claimed by professionals such as medical doctors, lawyers, chartered accounts, and psychologists.
- The *global demand for talent* appropriate to the VICCAS Context will lead to quicker promotion of leaders, resulting in less "intelligent" and mature leaders (see below) in senior and executive positions.
- The VICCAS Context will impose the imperative to shift from *the all-knowing, all-powerful single leader* to *shared (or distributive) leadership and the creation of leadership communities* in organisations, operating beyond hierarchy and function. This will enable the organisation to address more effectively the "wicked" challenges, problems and issues of the VICCAS Context.

Others

Some of the more important future challenges with respect to others are:

- The *range and diversity of stakeholders* of organisations and leaders will grow by leaps and bounds, also because of some of the above discussed trends and leadership challenges, such as the power of social media. Leadership will have to be knowledgeable about the diverse and conflicting needs of multiple stakeholders, including shareholders, the board, employees, suppliers, customers, regulators, competitors and the communities in which they operate, as well as the dynamics infusing each and among one another.
- In the VICCAS context there will be a *growing sense of disempowerment among stakeholders*, and consequently growing feelings among them of being helpless, threatened, anxious and angry. There will be a fervent, mounting, search for "the leader who can save us", creating the potential for followers to be vulnerable to leader exploitation and toxicity.
- The growing ambiguity with regard to *commonly accepted ethical values and norms*, also because of value clashes arising out of the growth in multicultural settings, giving rise to a greater need for value-based leadership, and to build on the "should" and "right". This leadership will need to focus not only on ethical leadership but also on creating a better society and world for present and future generations. Future leadership will have to be imbued by a moral consciousness, compass and courage leveraged from a transcendental leadership stance, namely "why?" leadership.
- The *growing power of public opinion*, solicited by ongoing surveys and referenda, and resulting in the *rise of opportunistic leadership* playing to the grandstand without a firm point of view, and acting without integrity. The need would be for future leadership acting with integrity from a clearly selected position.
- The employee base of organisations shifting to a *significant number of temporary/part time/contract workers* – many merely linked to the organisation through the Internet or an app – who have no real stake in and long-term commitment to the organisation. The challenge to future leadership would be how to engender high levels of engagement from these employees who in many cases have highly sought-after specialist skills.

Self

The challenges emerging from the above will require the future leader to dig much deeper into him-/herself, even though already being overstretched. Specific to the leader, at least the following major future challenges can be distinguished:

- The *constant onslaught on the leader's identity*: who and what am I?; what do I stand for?; what do I want to achieve?; to what end, and for whose benefit?
- The *rapid unlearning of a fixation on past success recipes*; being seduced by transient fads and fashions, and/or the fervent search for "silver bullets" propagated by snake-oil salespersons.
- More *frequent and widespread leadership transitions* requiring constant transitional adjustments by the leader. Leaders will have to be equipped with strong transition strategies and capabilities.
- A *tuned-in-ness to the vulnerability to succumb to toxic leadership*, arising out of the worshipping of individualism and giving rise to self-love; unclear, ambiguous, and conflicting values; the greying of ethics; and toxic friendly followers.
- Leaders running the risk of falling into the trap of *self-protective, "spin-doctoring" conduct* to protect themselves against relentless, merciless public exposure.

- A significantly greater likelihood and frequency of **burnout and organisational derailment** because of contextual pressures and unclear/unrealistic leadership expectations and demands by stakeholders. Leadership resilience will be a key future capability.

"Context Fit"-Leadership for the Future

A cursory scan of the contextual challenges discussed above, highlights the sizeable and seemingly overwhelming contextual demands on leaders going into the future. Leading in this unfolding new world is somewhat, in the words of Hixonia Nyasulu, Chairman of the women-controlled Ayavuna Women's Investments, "like playing tennis in the dark with unknown opponents, unexpected balls, unclear tennis court lines, and unpredictable weather". Equally, there are the possibly bewildering myriad leadership capabilities seemingly necessary to navigate and lead in the VICCAS Context, as elucidated above.

This situation could potentially leave an existing and/or aspiring leader deeply discouraged, with the natural, spontaneous response to withdraw, succumb or fight, instead of engaging positively. Going into the future, we submit that what is required is not a "silver bullet" set of specific capabilities, all needed at the same time in order to produce the "super" leader, able to be fully in charge at all times and under all circumstances; instead, the need will be rather to appreciate situation-specific leadership requirements and in this way identify, grow and develop context-fit leadership. Additionally, a community of leaders should be established, people who are able to lead effectively in a given/expected context through complementary, shared leadership, supplying collectively all of the necessary capabilities within and across situations.

Furthermore, in going into the future, a long-term, complex, and not short-term, mechanistic, vantage point to leadership should be adopted. Such a vantage point will enable us to re-imagine in a holistic, organic, integrated and dynamic way at a truly deep level a leader as a whole person embedded in his/her fourfold relationships with the World, Organisation, Others and Self, which will have to be dynamically and simultaneously aligned in real time.

Going Wide: Future-fit Leadership Capabilities Domains

Based on the above "design criteria", we would like to submit that contextual future-fit leadership will consist of five interdependent capability domains:

- *Able:* The hard and soft capabilities necessary to perform competently relative to contextual demands. The deployment of the required capabilities needs to be infused with the necessary qualities that will bring about hope, passion, caring, harmony, faith, confidence efficacy, courage and perseverance among followers, the psychosocial capital essential for followers to deal with the VICCAS Context effectively.
- *Intelligent:* Leadership who can observe, think, judge, act, learn and reflect with a growing understanding as they engage – conceptually and practically – with the VICCAS Context through converting experiences into information, information into knowledge, and knowledge into wisdom. The total "intelligence" (or meta-intelligence) of an excellent leader will consist of the five interdependent intelligence modes of Intra- and Interpersonal, Systemic, Ideation, Action, and Contextual Intelligence.
- *Mature:* Leadership able to engage consistently in relevant, productive, meaningful and constructive and uplifting ways with Self, Others, the Organisation, and the World.
- *Ethical:* Leaders and leadership who do the right thing for the right reasons in the right way in the right place and the right time with the right persons, that is, the "Should Do", the "Right thing".

- **Authentic:** Leaders and leadership which nurture and affirm the dignity, worth and efficacy of an individual(s), concurrently creating enabling, empowering, and meaningful work experiences.

Specific Future-fit Leadership Capabilities

Given the need for able, intelligent, mature, ethical and authentic leadership, required by the VICCAS Context, Figure 13.2 provides summarised clusters of suggested, more important capabilities ("Can Dos") for future-fit leadership, as per the leadership relationship dimensions discussed above – World, Organisation, Others, and Self. All of these capabilities are infused by the five capability domains of ability, intelligence, maturity, ethics and authenticity, as outlined above.

LEAD IN WORLD	LEAD ORGANISATION
• Agility • Responsiveness • Learning to learn • Systemic, integral thinking • Cross-cultural sensitivity • Purpose and meaning creation	• Political savvy • Risk taking • Disciplined execution • Collaboration and networking • Professional/technical expertise

Leadership who is able; intelligent; mature; ethical and authentic

• Authenticy • Integrity • Resilience • Inquisitive and curious • Deep thinking • Humility	• Caring • Diversity sensitivity • Stature • Active listening • Empathy • Personal visibility
LEAD SELF	**LEAD OTHERS**

Figure 13.2 Clusters of suggested, more important capabilities for future-fit leadership

Effective Leadership Engagement with the Future Context through Skilful Improvisation

It should be clear that even when one distils the future-fit capabilities required by leaders – as per Figure 13.2 – to respond effectively to the VICCAS challenges, the list is daunting and intimidating. Therefore, as suggested earlier, one should rather adopt a situational appreciation for the contextual, relevant application of particular capabilities. Such an approach may then lead one to think of effective leadership as an act of "Skilful Improvisation". Perhaps as the futurist, Alvin Toffler, points out, a "new" type of leader is called for, one who depends less on his/her intellectual and technical skills, and is instead one who is open to learning new things, unlearning old things that no longer serve, and relearning some things of value that have been forgotten. In this case, "effectiveness" can be defined as the extent to which a leader is able to achieve his/her intended consequences in a certain context. If leadership is action, it implies that such action can be effective or ineffective relative to the context concerned. Skilful Improvisation entails enabling and empowering leadership to re-invent him-/herself continuously in real time as contextual leadership challenges, demands and requirements shift, expectedly and unexpectedly.

Conceiving of leadership as Skilful Improvisation accepts certain future-fit capabilities will be required to lead effectively in the unfolding Context. In order to do so, leadership will have to develop – holistically and organically – deep capabilities with regard to all of the relationships he/she is embedded in across the five critical capability domains discussed above: ability, intelligence, maturity, ethics, and authenticity. The development of such deep capabilities will require fundamentally deep self-introspection and reflection because the barriers to true leadership effectiveness, organisational change, and excellence reside fundamentally inside the individual leader.

We contend that the VICCAS Context faced by leadership we have sketched in *Understanding Leadership* will only become worse. It is quite possible that by the time we have developed our leaders in what we consider the "necessary" capabilities, they will already have become outdated. Skilful Improvisation appears to be best suited to address the chaotic VICCAS Context adequately: the insight and will to be able to "read" the situation as a leader correctly; to exercise the right judgement; to choose from a set of capabilities such as those given in Figure 13.2 those that are situationally relevant skills as demanded by the task, people, organisational and contextual requirements; reflecting-in-action both on his/her own state of mind and the backtalk[1] of the situation, in order to perform effectively.

Impossible? Then perhaps leadership growth and development should be informed by the approach of artists. The above is precisely what jazz artists do so well.[2] Leaders know very well that life more often than not does not turn out in the way one has planned it. What if our thinking and doing are agile enough to bend with what we get served, analogous to the way in which jazz artists think and act. The jazz band may be playing a piece that they have rehearsed well, then unexpectedly someone makes a mistake. Now what if the thinking in that moment is: "There are no mistakes"; certainly not a "mistake" by someone else. Only the "mistake" of an inadequate in-the-moment response to the backtalk of the situation.[3]

Implications of Skilful Improvisation for Growing and Developing Future-fit Leadership

Skilful improvisation requires very deep personal development. Because leaders have little control over their external (chaotic) context, and quite likely become drained by its demands, it stands to reason that leaders will have to find resources internally in themselves. Such growth and development will include capacity growth and development in respect of the capability range indicated earlier (see Figure 13.2) but first and foremost in his/her relationship to him-/herself.

Going deep

This is essential because there is a blindness in all human beings through years of socialisation that necessitates that such growth and development drill deeper into the deepest layers of leaders' lived world if they are to be capacitated for the intensifying VICCAS Context. Figure 13.3 depicts the respective layers making up the leader's lived world, from "deep" to "shallow".

Visible, tangible

Action learning

Layer 6: Everyday Lived
Experiences and Actions

Layer 5: Capabilities

Layer 4: Style and Attitude

Layer 3: Decision Making
Framework

Layer 2: Value
Orientation

Layer 1: Worldview

Invisible, intangible
Double-loop learning, learning to learn

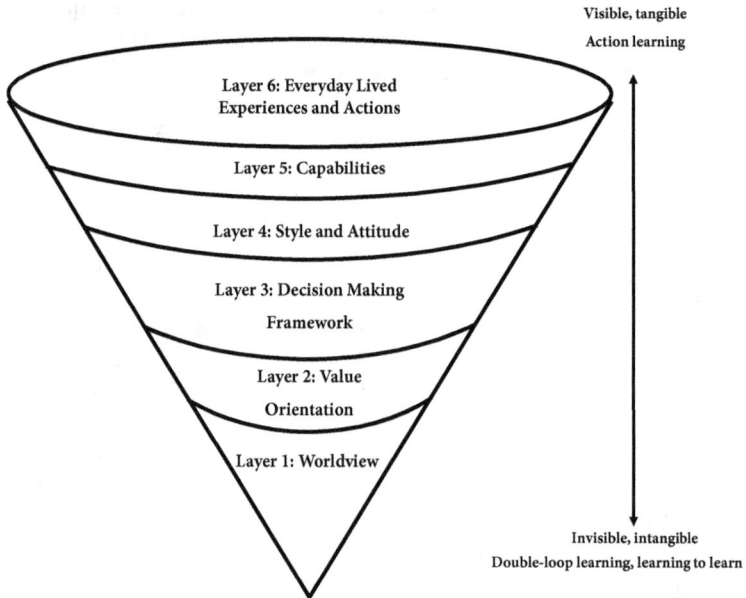

Figure 13.3 Layers making up the leader's lived world

Analogous to the building of a house, future-fit leadership growth and development have to commence with the deep Layer 1: Worldview (or Mental Model), and then proceed progressively to the more shallow layers in a "building onto" manner. Learning in this way will help the leader to bring his socially programmed blindness to conscious reflection, and develop new pathways towards effective leadership, including purposefulness: an authentic balanced disposition to the needs of others (= all stakeholders), the organisation, and the world. Learning approaches and methods will have to be employed by organisations that elicit valid information and knowledge about what individuals think and do at deep layers, because the default pattern of individuals is to employ defensive reasoning. We espouse leadership effectiveness, but as human beings we lack the ability to produce such holistic inside-out development. In addition, we are unaware of this serious, future-compromising limitation.

Bringing about deep learning

How do we effect this deep learning? As indicated earlier, one cannot simply focus on changing Layers 6: Everyday lived experiences and 5: Capabilities (see Figure 13.3). Layers 5 and 6 learning tend to break down when people experience stress because stress triggers default conduct. One has to change the underlying layers, in particular Layers 1 to 3, that drive the conduct, to Layer 6. Skilful improvisation requires drawing on deep, internal personal resources that this type of development endeavours to develop.

The knowledge organisations produce in our leadership growth and development programmes must be in the service of enabling leadership action with regard to Layer 6. Two expressions of such learning are (i) *double-loop learning*, aimed at getting to the mental models comprising underlying beliefs, values and attitudes (Layers 1 to 4) that perpetuate ineffective leadership action, in conjunction with (ii) *action learning*, focusing on conduct change through reflection on real stakeholder and organisational challenges (in other words, Layers 5 and 6) (see Figure 13.3). In the words of Argyris, Putnam, and McLain Smith,[4] methods will have to be employed "to make known what is known so well that we no longer know it, … so that it might be critiqued, … and to make known what is unknown, … the discovery of alternatives so that they too might be critiqued". Skilful improvisation contains such reflexive qualities.

Bridging the science-practice gap

Such leadership growth and development, based on sound scientific principles, will have the potential to respond adequately to bridging the perennial, ongoing science–practice gap. *Understanding Leadership* abounds with many such exemplars. In practice, this growth and development in organisations can be self-driven, technology-enabled, classroom- based, experiential and/or coaching, provided it conforms to its purposes: deep, inside-out growth and development from Layer 1 "upwards" towards Layer 6. Then and only then will organisations be preparing and delivering the right leadership in the right numbers at the right time and place, able, willing and empowered to perform effectively within the VICCAS Context.

Fundamental to this leadership growth and learning will be the need for academics and development practitioners to do less "esoteric", practice-estranged work that results in the growing gap between theory – the proverbial ivory tower – and practice. Within the VICCAS Context, real action research partnerships between academic institutions and business/non-governmental institutions/public sector are essential, focusing on leadership growth and development that is useful to leadership in the moment of action where it matters and will make a real difference. In other words, leadership growth and development that is characteristic of reflective practice, reflecting-in- and -on-action. Given financial pressures, organisations need to place a much greater emphasis on evidence-based, actionable knowledge to drive their change efforts. The speed of practice-referenced and -informed research delivery by academics will have to match the speed of change in the practical world. Otherwise, academics and academic institutions will rapidly become irrelevant to a VICCAS Context "running away" from them. They will become the extinct dinosaurs going into the future.

Conclusion

Having explored tomorrow's VICCAS Leadership Context with its features resulting in "wicked" leadership challenges, issues and problem, answering the remaining ultimate question posed in the Introduction is: "Is there a future for leadership?" Yes, there is a future for leadership, but it is conditional on:

- A *deep understanding of the unfolding VICCAS Context* going into the future in terms of leadership's fourfold relationships with the World, Organisation, Others and Self;
- *Adoption of a complexity vantage point* to leadership;
- From this complexity perspective, *re-imagine at a deep level leaders in a holistic, organic, integrated and dynamic way as a whole person*, in terms of their ability, intelligence, maturity, ethics and authenticity, as embedded in their fourfold relationships, all of which have to be dynamically aligned simultaneously in real time;
- Enabling and empowering leaders to engage with the Context through *Skilful Improvisation*;
- *Growing and developing leadership from the inside-out*, commencing with the deeper layers of leadership's lived world: Layer 1: Worldview through double-loop learning, progressing through action learning towards Layer 6: Everyday Lived Experiences and Actions; and
- *Forming vibrant two-way interactions between the academic and practice worlds*, producing just-in-time, evidence-based, actionable knowledge to drive change efforts to make leaders future-fit.

What a challenge lies ahead of all of us to make it happen in a world that is in desperate need of leadership excellence in order to ensure a sustainable, flourishing future for all.

Endnotes

1   "The situation talks back, the [leader] listens, and as he appreciates what he hears, he reframes the situation once again": *cf.* Schön, DA. 1983. *The reflective practitioner.* New York, NY: Basic Books.

2   *cf.* Also (a) Warren Bennis on jazz and leadership: "I used to think that running an organization was equivalent to conducting a symphony orchestra. But I don't think that's quite it; it's more like jazz. There is more improvisation"; (b) the leadership development training, styled on UK Channel 4s "Whose line is it anyway?", *Workplace IMPROV*, designed by stand-up comedian, Nadiem Solomon. The fundamental rule in this training is "pay attention".

3   Harris, S. 2011. *There are no mistakes on the bandstand.* TEDSalon NY2011.

4   Argyris, C, Putnam, R & McLain Smith, D. 1985. *Action science: concepts, methods, and skills for research and intervention.* San Francisco, CA: Jossey-Bass Inc. 237.

INDEX

www.ingramcontent.com/pod-product-compliance
Lightning Source LLC
Chambersburg PA
CBHW061733270326
41928CB00011B/2214